ALSO BY ADAM ZAGAJEWSKI

POETRY

Tremor: Selected Poems

Canvas

Mysticism for Beginners

Without End: New and Selected Poems

Eternal Enemies

Unseen Hand

ESSAYS

Solidarity, Solitude

Two Cities

Another Beauty

A Defense of Ardor

Slight Exaggeration

Slight Exaggeration

ADAM ZAGAJEWSKI

Translated from the Polish by Clare Cavanagh

Farrar, Straus and Giroux

New York

Farrar, Straus and Giroux
175 Varick Street, New York 10014

Copyright © 2011 by Adam Zagajewski
Translation copyright © 2017 by Clare Cavanagh
All rights reserved
Printed in the United States of America
Originally published in Polish in 2011 by Wydawnictwo a5, Poland,
as *Lekka przesada*
English translation published in the United States in 2017
by Farrar, Straus and Giroux
First American paperback edition, 2018

Owing to limitations of space, all acknowledgments for permission to reprint
previously published material appear on page 277.

The Library of Congress has cataloged the hardcover edition as follows:
Names: Zagajewski, Adam, 1945– author. I Cavanagh, Clare, translator.
Title: Slight exaggeration / Adam Zagajewski ; translated from the
    Polish by Clare Cavanagh.
Description: First American edition. I New York : Farrar, Straus
    and Giroux, 2017.
Identifiers: LCCN 2016033255 I ISBN 9780374265878 (hardback) I
    ISBN 9780374709631 (e-book)
Classification: LCC PG7185.A32 A2 2017 I DDC 891.8/5473—dc23
LC record available at https://lccn.loc.gov/2016033255

Paperback ISBN: 978-0-374-53751-7

Designed by Jonathan D. Lippincott

Our books may be purchased in bulk for promotional, educational,
or business use. Please contact your local bookseller or the Macmillan Corporate
and Premium Sales Department at 1-800-221-7945, extension 5442,
or by e-mail at MacmillanSpecialMarkets@macmillan.com.

www.fsgbooks.com
www.twitter.com/fsgbooks • www.facebook.com/fsgbooks

Slight Exaggeration

I won't tell all regardless. Since nothing much is happening anyway. I represent, moreover, the Eastern European school of discretion; we don't discuss divorces, we don't acknowledge depressions. Life proceeds peacefully around me, a gray and exceptionally warm December outside my window. A few concerts. A gifted young singer performed in the Lawyers' Club. Yesterday we went to a beautiful concert of Shostakovich's music (they also played the string quartet, *Au-delà d'une absence*, that his biographer Krzysztof Meyer composed and dedicated to him). I heard another piece for the first time, the Vocal-Instrumental Suite for Soprano, Violin, Cello, and Piano, op. 27, set to seven poems by Alexander Blok. Students from the Music Academy played: brimming with enthusiasm, technically marvelous. The final work, that suite, made a tremendous impression on M. and me. The concert marked the hundredth anniversary of Shostakovich's birth and so had a special charge, an extra jolt. The students lit candles on the stage and used just a few spotlights. They achieved an extraordinary kind of concentration. It's often like that when you hear young performers, still unspoiled by routine, by careers, young musicians playing joyfully, with their whole body, their whole soul.

•

The sense of joy nearly every time I find myself on Krakow's main square. In every season, at every time of day, I admire the space's majesty, the odd, cubistically arranged structures, symmetry and asymmetry conjoined, the airy Italian Cloth Hall set alongside the Marian Cathedral's Gothic gravity, like gigantic building blocks.

•

I'm reading about Gottfried Benn in *Poetry* magazine. Warsaw's *World Literature* just published a hefty selection of his poems, letters, and essays in a thick issue dedicated to Benn and Brecht. Both died in 1956, and the iron law of anniversaries unites them posthumously, fifty years after their deaths—two poets who have absolutely nothing else in common. Benn began to mock the application of Marxist theory to literature early on. His scornful attitude set him apart in leftist, literary Berlin, in the years before Hitler seized power: the unyielding aesthete amid the doctrinaire improvers of humanity . . . I go back to Benn's poems every so often, and they almost always electrify me ("Jena vor uns im lieblichen Tale . . ."); so do bits of his essays and virtually all his letters to Mr. Oelze, the businessman from Bremen. The letters are offhanded, a bit cynical at times, now and then a moment of pure poetry gleams. A petit bourgeois par excellence, Benn led the modest life of a craftsman (although, as we know, he was a doctor, a dermatologist, but he never earned much). In Oelze— whom he idealized, glorified, endowed with a higher social rank than he in fact possessed—he found an audience for his own ideas, observations, provocations, and projects.

•

I've been reading Karl Corino's thick biography of Robert Musil. Musil wrote a beautiful speech when Rilke died—he was among those who recognized the poet's greatness early on. I also found a description of the tragicomic talk Musil gave at the Congress for the Defense of Culture in Paris in June 1935. He had no idea that the Congress had been organized by the Communists, and thus only Hitler's system was open to criticism: the Soviet Union was off-limits. But Musil defended the artist's individualism and warned against the collectivism emerging in various European nations. He insisted, too, that there was no connection between culture and politics, that culture's very existence depends upon some delicate, capricious, unpredictable element, hence even a decent political system won't automatically produce great art. Some participants at that famous Congress even booed him; they'd been expecting propagandistic pronouncements, not considered, objective reflections. Corino also writes a great deal about Musil's poverty; he even considered suicide in the thirties, when he couldn't foresee any financial possibilities for him and his wife. Both the Nazis and the Communists attacked him— the very title of his great novel, *The Man Without Qualities*, must have angered them equally. After all, they labored to create a new man with sharply defined qualities. For both groups, he represented a "bourgeois epoch in decline." (But of course that bourgeois epoch didn't decline—or perhaps it declined and then recovered.) Musil spent the last years of his life in exile in Switzerland, where he lived even more modestly, in poverty and isolation. Thomas Mann was an important figure to him; he felt both love and hate, *Hassliebe*, as the Germans say, for the great writer. Everything turned out for Mann: even emigration wasn't a disaster. Those who knew Musil described the nervous trembling that overcame him whenever he heard the name Mann mentioned in conversation. Musil's perfect description of *The Magic Mountain*: the novel resembles a "shark's stomach." Mann's great novel contains, he meant, undigested fragments of existing European systems of thought, ideologies, and so on. Whereas *The Man Without Qualities* operates on an entirely

different principle; all the references to political and philosophical reality have an intermediate character, they're mystical, allu-
sive. Musil was captivated by *der Möglichkeitssinn*, the sense of
possibility, by whatever happens exclusively in the conditional.
The question remains: maybe, from this point of view, Mann
was right to toss thick chunks of actual ideas into *The Magic
Mountain*.

•

In Poland, Christmas is the most deeply, consistently familial of
holidays. Everyone celebrates at home. Christmas Eve is the piv-
otal moment. Houses and apartments become bastions of family
egotism, family love, if you will. Lone souls must suffer all kinds
of tortures if nobody from one family or another thinks to invite
them . . . You can't count on restaurants, they're closed. This year
Christmas Eve came on Sunday; by morning the streets were
silent. On Thursday and Friday I saw dozens of students heading off to the railroad station with their backpacks and bags;
Krakow empties out. By 7:00 p.m., the city is a ghost town. The
Main Square, which throngs with people every other day (and
even night), was dark, deserted, as in the war. M. and I went for
a walk, we strolled through the square, we couldn't get over the
eerie silence, darkness, emptiness. The countless restaurants
in every storefront of the square were—all!—shut, unlit. We
noticed only one spot on the square's expanse where some enter-
prising type had set up shop, suspecting that hungry, thirsty
people might still turn up. In an improvised wooden shed three
cooks fried sausages and chops and reheated cabbage and potatoes. This single warm and well-lit spot drew all the tourists, who
certainly couldn't understand why the normally welcoming restaurants had all closed shop. Why the churches were shut (and
would reopen their doors only after midnight mass). They didn't
know that priests, too, were sitting down to dinners including at
least twelve courses, that borscht steamed on the tabletops. Japa-

nese, Italian, French, and American tourists lined up for their humble sausages. We sat for a moment at one of the improvised tables, it wasn't too cold. The tourists alongside us inhaled the scent of cooked meat steaming up from plastic plates. Honey-colored drops of mustard on white trays. An oasis. It was a caricature of Bethlehem, that well-lit place beneath its wooden roof. I told M. I could imagine a play that might capture something of that moment. The silent city and tourists' hushed talk. So write it. But I can't.

•

I can't write poems in recent weeks either. It's not the first time it's happened. And it's not worth going on about either. There's not much to tell. Karol Berger found something Victor Hugo said on the subject—he told me about it as we were walking in Paris, in the 16ème. When someone asked him how hard it was to write poetry, he answered, "When you can write it, it's easy, when you can't, it's impossible."

•

The fall was long, warm, and mild, and I often passed little Boguslawski Street. St. Sebastian Street runs right beside it, a narrow passage transporting you from the Catholic city center to Jewish Kazimierz. At one point you walk along a wall concealing an enormous monastery garden. Then you cross Dietl Street, built where a branch of the Vistula once cut the city of Kazimierz off from Krakow like a moat—and you're in a different world. I usually pass the yellow-orange building where Czeslaw Milosz lived for some years. A tablet commemorates this. Before, the tablet wasn't there, but Czeslaw was. And Carol, his wife, who looked after the flowerbed in the courtyard. On the second floor, in an apartment that was first expanded, when they bought the place next door, and then, after his death, divided up again, as part of the estate. Boguslawski Street is empty now. An extraordinary

person, an exceptional mind once lived there, someone who defied the tendencies of his time (but who said we should yield to
the age's tendencies?), who tried to synthesize all the events and
ideas of his historical moment. He was the only serious intellectual I knew who studied even the Harry Potter series. What for?
To find out what children were reading, what draws them, and
what it says about a shifting world. He good-naturedly acknowledged *Harry Potter*; nothing bad in it, he said in his baritone. He
was more like Thomas Mann than Robert Musil: only what
really existed stirred him, not *Möglichkeitssinn*, not the sense of
possibilities. He didn't lack for mystical appetites, but his mysticism fed on the yeast of reality. In the long poems he was a
shark. And a shark in his reading, devouring theology and philosophy, poetry and history. I think of this when I meet young
poets on both sides of the Atlantic. Sometimes they seem to notice only the most recent issue of the trendiest poetry journal. As
if poetry weren't—among other things—a response to the state
of a world that shows itself in a thousand different forms, the
grief of the unemployed man sitting on a park bench on a lovely
April day alongside philosophical treatises and symphonies.

•

In November an evening dedicated to the poetry of Stanislaw
Baranczak in Manggha, Krakow's Japanese cultural center.
Swarms of people, mainly students, one of those events where
you have to get there a half hour early just to find a seat. It was
organized by the Publishing House a5; Ryszard Krynicki invited
a group of Krakow poets to read a poem each from Baranczak's
newly published *Selected Poems*. Wislawa Szymborska received
the privilege of reading one of Baranczak's loveliest poems, "She
Cried at Night." I read a poem from *Winter's Journey*, his extraordinary variations on the poems Franz Schubert used for his
Winterreise. A minor Romantic poet, Wilhelm Müller, wrote the
original German poems, which would most likely have vanished

if they hadn't been amplified by Schubert's marvelous music. In haste, impatient, the music hurries like fate. Its energetic, almost military rhythms contrast sharply with the deceleration winter brings to Northern Europe. Snow, frost, and mist slow life's tempo; fires crackle in chimneys, smoke rises slowly and uncertainly toward a cloudy sky. Baranczak's versions are both completely original and a perfect fit metrically for the music. Read separately, as individual poems, the impression they make may not be as great as "She Cried at Night," for example. Taken whole, though, in all their hallucinogenic melancholy, their thematic hints at modernity (an airplane, an urban street), a certain indefinable symbolism, they are unforgettable. Stanislaw, who suffers from a prolonged illness, couldn't travel from Boston, where he's lived for twenty-five years.

•

Today in the morning mail a present from Faber and Faber Limited, Ted Hughes's *Selected Translations*, edited by Daniel Weissbort. (Daniel Weissbort once drove me to the airport many years ago, early spring, in Iowa.) I begin the day by reading Yehuda Amichai in Hughes's translation. Amichai's poems burst with meaning; each line has something to tell us. Poetry involves two opposing kinds of textual "concentration": poetry as a fabric (where, as in the poetry of Saint-John Perse, the language stays consistently equidistant from a well-concealed center) and poetry as statement. Amichai is a royal representative of this second option, as is Herbert. Born in the same year, 1924, both these great poets have so much to say that they could never follow Saint-John Perse's lead in creating endless rhetorical epics. A certain resemblance links the two poets, whose imaginations fix on war and love (there's more love in Amichai) and are tempered by the classics in whom they placed their faith. Amichai read the Hebrew Bible, while Herbert had his Greeks. They must have sensed the kinship: they liked and admired each other. I met Amichai only once, at a festival in Rotterdam in, I think, 1983. He told me over breakfast at the hotel that he cared most about poets and artists born in 1924. I thought then that I'd been born too late. (I don't think so now.)

•

While sorting through my papers (something I should do more often), I came upon a clipping from a local paper, a review, by a young critic, of one of my books. The piece's title: "Old Wave." A typical example of disinterested and pointless malice. Since we all have to die someday, even young reviewers.

•

I'm reading Gerschom Scholem's essays, his polemics and intellectual portraits (the portrait of Rosenzweig, a polemic with Buber, and so on). As always when I read an intelligent author who writes with passion about the *sacrum*, I'm filled with religious yearnings.

•

Cioran takes Proust to task somewhere for the role music plays in his great novel. One of the book's central themes, it weaves and twines around the heroes' personal adventures. It prompts associations with concrete events from the past—but it doesn't open up onto something "altogether different." It's an intriguing observation. But who makes it? Cioran, who in most of his dazzling aphorisms strives to convince us that this "altogether different" doesn't exist. Only after hearing a Bach cantata or passion does he momentarily change his mind.

•

A poem is like a human face—it is an object that can be measured, described, cataloged, but it is also an appeal. You can heed

an appeal or ignore it, but you can't simply measure its meter.
You can't gauge a flame's height with a ruler.

·

My students and I read the poems of the Swedish writer Göran
Sonnevi in Rika Lesser's translation—in manuscript, since this
splendid volume couldn't find a publisher. In these truly wonderful poems—meditative, linking deeply personal elements with
observations derived from physics and biology—music nearly
becomes God. My friend in Berlin, the German writer Hartmut
Lange, says something similar about music, especially Mahler's
Song of the Earth. I argued with him about it, even though I listen
to music constantly and *Song of the Earth* is one of my favorite
works. I argued, since I can't see identifying music with God . . .
Poets who listen to pop music—their numbers are growing—
don't seem to have the same mystical leanings. The same is true
of jazz; I don't see it leading to idolatry.

·

I may be one of the few writers, not counting theologians, who
raises now and then the notion of the "spiritual life." In our time
we tend to speak, at best, of "imagination." It is a marvelous word
and encompasses a great deal, but not everything. Some people
look at me suspiciously because of this; they see me as a reactionary or at the very least a far-right-winger. I lay myself open to
ridicule. Progressive circles rebuke me or else look down their
noses. Conservatives don't understand it either. Poets a generation younger refuse to maintain relations with me. Only one
young Spanish poet told me in Barcelona that my essays may
signal that ironic postmodernism will someday be vanquished.
But what is the spirit, spiritual life? If only I were better at defining
things! Robert Musil says that the spirit is the synthesis of intellect
and emotion. It's a good working definition, a bit minimalist. It's

easier to say—as the theologists know—what the spirit isn't, in poetry, in literature. This approach isn't psychoanalytic, behavioral, sociological, or political. It's comprehensive; it reflects, like an astronaut's helmet, the earth, the stars, and the human face.

•

A few days in Paris at the beginning of January. The strangest sensation: I lived here for twenty years and left in 2002, but each time I come back, after half an hour everything seems absolutely familiar, obvious, as if I'd never left. We take the bus from Orly; before us rises a wall of ugly modern apartment buildings and the modest houses of the Parisian suburbs, just after that the Porte d'Orléans, some stadium, empty now, the avenue du Général Leclerc, then the avenue du Maine, then along the place de Barcelone, the work of Ricardo Bofill, a Spanish architect continuing, willy-nilly, the socialist realist tradition, and finally the place des Invalides. The bus stops right beside the Quai d'Orsay, that is to say, the Ministry of Foreign Affairs—passersby see only a vast building stretched along the Seine. In the thirties its general secretary was Alexis Leger, known to poetry readers as Saint-John Perse, the author of *Anabasis*. Few people realize that at that time Alexis Leger may have been the only poet on the globe to have a real say in bona fide political operations—since we won't count Mao Zedong, who was a monster, or, in a completely different key, Léopold Senghor, who became the president of Senegal decades later. There was admittedly no dearth of poets holding ambassadorial posts—the list would be lengthy—but ambassadors after all have no real power. But Leger was something else: he touched the instruments of power; he was the highest nonelective official in the French ministry. It might seem that the ancient dream of poets ruling the world had come true; one of our own finally wielded influence on the course of events. And what came of it? As it turns out, Leger (we must in this instance scrupulously separate his two names, political and poetic), who spent the war years in Washington as a political emigrant, is held in low esteem by historians of French diplomacy. They see him as an advocate of the soft line toward Hitler's Germany, one of those who promoted the cowardly Munich Agreement of 1939, that is, one of those who failed to recognize the real nature of the threat. So our emissary to the land of Reality seems to have been a disappointment . . . Should further efforts be made in this direction? Should future emissaries be sent? Perhaps not.

•

Still in Paris: a warm, damp January. In the subway cars, many passengers read thick novels, even at peak hours when the reader's head is encircled by the crowds of those who couldn't get seats. Paris is, after all, the capital of the novel. Writing and reading novels is a serious business in this city. Patrons of the subway and the vast suburban railroads require enormous quantities of reading matter monthly. As the publishing houses know full well: they churn out new volumes nonstop. The great bookstores, for example the famous Fnac chain, then erect little shrines devoted to specific novelists, shrines built around a photograph of a given author, which is then encased by stacks of books . . . As in Proust, who describes Parisian bookstores after Bergotte's death: he compares the fictional writer's books to angels with outstretched wings, keeping watch over their maker's soul. In Proust, though, this is a rare and marvelous moment—but in the Fnac chain it takes place daily, for exclusively commercial reasons. And these novels, written with an eye to subway riders and suburban commuters, are quickly forgotten. New books appear. They're rarely read twice. The bookstalls by the Seine overflow with thousands of yellowed novels from the last fifty or eighty years, novels that had their brief moment of fame, but must now soak and freeze beneath the naked sky—their fate isn't much better than that of the clochards. Books of poetry, not to mention the poets themselves, are a different matter in Paris. True, you do sometimes come upon the same posters with brief poems in the subway cars that you find in New York, but hardly anyone seems to notice; they're engrossed in their thick novels. (Once in Germany, when I presented my theory about easily forgotten novels, my neighbor at the dinner table hissed, "Das ist Kultur-pessimismus!").

•

We went to Paris chiefly for the fiftieth birthday of Miquel Barceló, a painter born right by the seaside in Mallorca. He was associated first with Barcelona, and then, after his first major successes, with Paris, but also with Africa, where he often spends time in Mali, painting, drawing, and sculpting. He returns from Mali laden with watercolors. Barceló is one of those artists who can't not work, although it's probably hard to separate his work from play, that constant shaping, cutting, drawing, modeling. Barceló's passion is representing the world—you see in him, in his paintings and watercolors, a childlike joy that shapes exist. He's an exceptionally sensuous artist. Some of his works, especially the simplest ones, those depicting animals or plants, or the rich submarine world of the Mediterranean (he's an experienced diver), emit a remarkable freshness, as if someone were seeing for the first time—with a lover's eyes—an acacia, a dog, a monkey, an octopus, a sea bream. Perhaps the zeitgeist (if it exists) is using Barceló—among others, of course—to put paid to the variety of abstract art whose hyperrationality has become unbearable. The chapel in the Palma de Mallorca Cathedral is one of his masterworks: a sumptuous, baroque complex of ceramics depicting the miracle of the loaves and fishes. It's an extraordinary festival of existence, a celebration of a life that has achieved the fullness of all its forms, or perhaps even exceeded it, since the fishes, the loaves, and the various creatures seem ready to burst, they've reached the line between ripeness and overripeness. Miquel is an avid reader of poetry; that's how we met, he'd read my poems in Maja Wodecka's French translations, and then we got to know each other through Rafael Jablonka, who owns a gallery in Cologne.

•

I'm reading Czeslaw Milosz's *Final Poems*, which were put out by Znak Publishers two years after his death. Even now, Milosz doesn't lack for opponents in this exceptionally polemical, and often petty, country; his fame and standing guarantee him, in any case, the distaste for greatness that accompanies democracy. His detractors insist that his poetic power declined in later years. But it takes only a few lines of his "Orpheus and Eurydice" to prove his critics wrong:

> He sang the brightness of mornings and green rivers
> He sang of smoking water in the rose-colored
>   daybreaks,
> Of colors: cinnabar, carmine, burnt sienna, blue,
> Of the delight of swimming in the sea under marble
>   cliffs
>
> (Second Space, *translated by Czeslaw Milosz and Robert Hass*)

Milosz's Polish opponents fall into several categories. Some simply aren't interested in poetry; they charge *The Captive Mind*'s author with treason, since he spent several years in the Communist diplomatic service. (He refused to praise nothingness, though; he didn't write a single poem suitable for inclusion in anthologies of Stalinist poetry.) And there are those who can't stomach the poet's aversion to Polish nationalism. An aversion that is, I must add, entirely justified. Charges arose shortly before Milosz's funeral that he wasn't a good Catholic, hence didn't deserve to rest in the crypt of distinguished Poles at the Paulinist Monastery in Krakow. Whereas those who do read poetry often

attack Milosz for his lofty, hymnlike tone. Flat, ironic writing is
the order of the day, while awaiting better times ahead.

When I read the line about "the delight of swimming in the
sea under marble cliffs," I recall a conversation I had with Milosz some years back; it was after a vacation M. and I had spent
with C. K. Williams near Lucca, in Tuscany. Now and then
we'd drive to the seashore at Bocca di Magra, a little town in
Liguria (from the autostrada you catch a glimpse of a sign adver-
tising the Hotel Shelley—the poet drowned there). The Magra is
a river that enters the sea at this point. When Milosz heard this,
he grew thoughtful, remembering times gone by. He'd spent
several vacations at Bocca di Magra—in the company of Mary
McCarthy, Nicola Chiaromonte, and other friends—he'd gone
swimming there, too, and always remembered the white marble
cliffs that looked at first like snow-covered mountains—in mid-
summer! But it's not snow, just marble, Carrara, a town famed
among sculptors, at the foot of white marble peaks. And the sea
there is deep blue, warm, salty, with little waves. Dashes and
irregular geometric figures appear and quickly vanish on the
water's velvety surface—these are the sea's papillary lines. Gulls
circle above the fishing ships. The coast is rocky here, as a Mediterranean seashore should be, since sandy, level beaches don't
suit the sea's character; they make it look like the pale, chilly
Baltic, it loses its deep cobalt hue.

Milosz died, thinking, working, writing poems almost to
the very end—as though he had sailed far out to sea, toward
Carrara, toward azure mists and white mountains.

Paul Claudel says somewhere, "Celui qui admire n'a jamais
tort" (He who admires is never wrong). I like thinking about
this sentence, so hopelessly out-of-date and so easily subject to
revision. In a fundamental way, though, it tells us that in a spiritual
sense, admiration and enthusiasm are far higher than criticism,
sarcasm, a purely ironic stance. In English they call it debunking;

we call it demystification, and it's the very air that newspapers
and most books breathe.

•

In April 2007, we visited Lvov with C. K. Williams and his wife,
Catherine, Georgia and Michael, and Agnès with her camera,
among others. We didn't stay long—just long enough to give me
that piercing shiver of mystery I'd experienced on earlier visits to
the city. And once again it was June—mild, long, slowly fading
evenings, evenings promising so much that no matter what you
do with them, you always receive the impression of defeat, of
wasted time. Nobody knows the best way to get through them.
March straight ahead or maybe sit at home before a wide-open
window so that the warm air, saturated in the sounds of summer, may permeate the room and mingle with books, ideas,
metaphors, with our breath. No, but that's not right either, it's
not possible. You can only mourn them, those unending evenings, mourn them when they pass, as the days grow shorter.
They can't be seized. Perhaps these long June evenings can only
be perceived by way of regret, remembrance, nostalgia. They
can't be plumbed: you'd need to head for the park, one foot in
front of the other, while sitting simultaneously on the terrace
and listening to the voices of the city fall still as the last blackbirds sing . . . But that won't do either. Birdsong has no form, no
adagio, no allegro. In a detailed study of music, a certain philosopher once observed that "nightingales don't listen to other
nightingales sing," only somewhat exalted people do. Hence you
can only tear yourself away when you get bored (let's be honest
here). Whereas a musical composition, subject to the discipline
of form, forestalls the moment of our boredom, unless it's one of
Wagner's operas from the Ring Cycle, marvelous, but a bit too
long. A sense of the secret: my family lived here. Here they
dreamed their dreams, planned, grieved, fell in love, built their

homes, died, visited graveyards. They thought the world was
Lvov, only Lvov. They returned here after every trip, which is
why this city, set on hills, was their geometric Rome. Here, worried or carefree, they rolled before them the great wheel of the
future, which spun throughout the seasons, through January's
brief days, sinking in the snow, and through June's endless
evenings, until at a certain moment it shattered, dissolved into
the air, died. And just when it died, I was born. At dusk, in June,
that distant life, which no longer exists—except perhaps on old
postcards, where it's diminished, turns into caricature, on postcards where we find, peering out at us, preposterous gentlemen
with overripe mustaches and ladies with frantic hats upon which
the gardens of Semiramis blossom, so that we can't see ourselves
in them at all. Only on these does it secretly appear anew. If only
we could listen more carefully, look more closely . . . Someday
something will happen, the inner reality will stand revealed. At
the same time I realize that this sense of mystery, of secrets
dwelling in these streets, in this park, is fleeting and hard to defend. If someone were to ask me ironically, "Mr. Zagajewski,
what actual mystery do you have in mind?," I'd be hard-pressed
to answer. I also know that there are people, some of them
highly intelligent, who can never be brought to acknowledge the
postulate of a mystery hidden in a city, or a park, or a quiet street
at dusk. No, they'd say, everything can be checked and measured, so and so many bird species make their home in the park,
including two subspecies of woodpeckers, along with twelve
squirrels, maybe two martens, and five bums. The policemen on
duty might easily survey the park and write up an unbiased re-
port conclusively proving that no secrets had been unearthed.

We stayed in the Hotel George, whose name is known by
every child in Poland, since it's become one of Lvov's symbols,
but it could use a little renovating now. As you walk down the
hallways, you feel the crumbling floor tiles beneath the carpet
that is meant to conceal them from the guests' eyes. It works

well enough, but it can't deceive the feet, whose sensitivity is well-known. Can symbols be renovated, though? I don't know.

•

Someone asked me not long ago why I don't write novels. Because I'm not a novelist. There are so many reasons that I wasn't able to formulate a clear, convincing answer at the time. But now, due to what the French so beautifully call *esprit d'escalier*, that is to say hindsight, one possible answer comes to mind: I'm not a novelist because, for unknown reasons, I belong to the tribe to whom no one confides petty social secrets. I keep noticing this: in the little world I've come to inhabit, in Krakow at the outset of the twenty-first century, there is no dearth of minor scandals, romances not entirely sanctioned by the legal and marital circumstances of those involved. At the same time, information, not always precise, is happily transmitted concerning the personal wealth of certain individuals perhaps located not so much within a given group as on its margins. In a word: gossip, more or less interesting. But no one tells me. For unknown reasons, I find out about such things last, if at all. For similarly unknown reasons all people fall into two camps: those to whom petty secrets are told, and those to whom they are not. Most information, or pseudo-information, of this kind likely never reaches me. So how could I be a novelist without having undergone even an elementary initiation into the life of my larger social circle? I don't know anything. Do I suffer because of this? Not in the slightest. But this alone suffices to keep me from writing novels, which feed on the secret knowledge of human weaknesses. Of course they are nourished by other talents and gifts as well. But even a writer of historical fiction projects backward a certain vision of the ordinary, everyday, and inalterable disruption of customs, which he comprehends courtesy of the kindly distributors of gossip. After due thought, though, I'm forced to conclude that the matter is in fact more complicated. Some of our greatest novelists, after all, clearly belonged to the ranks of those who are the last to know. To give one example: Thomas Mann kept an enormous distance from others; he reserved first names for only a handful of friends during his long life. Konrad Kellen, also known as Conny, served as Mann's research assistant for two years in Pacific Palisades; he recalls Mann speaking with his brother Heinrich in such a chilly, conventional, intellectual way that they might have been two professors just making each other's acquaintance. Certainly no one ever told their secrets to Thomas Mann, he kept himself under lock and key, and even if he hadn't, nobody would have dared to share some bit of trivial, if appetizing, gossip with that Olympian. But even Thomas Mann got by somehow: his novels and stories abound in major and minor scandals, suicides, bankruptcies, and betrayals. His own family didn't lack for such scandals, one generation after the next—so his family misfortunes came to his aid . . .

•

An odd moment in Lvov: At dinner on the first day, I suddenly accused my companions of completely misunderstanding the city. They were treating it, I complained, like any free city in Europe, like Liverpool or Bochum. They felt nothing, they scanned the streets and squares with indifferent eyes, as if they were no more than cameras, though this was no ordinary city, it held marvelous, hidden things . . . They're partly concealed beneath the coating of Soviet dust that still covers them, agreed, but it takes a certain imaginative effort to break through to them. This isn't self-evident Florence with its obvious, absolute beauty affirmed in a hundred different guidebooks; it's not Rome, whose loveliness any idiot can spot; no, this is something completely different, the city hides beneath a layer of vulgarity. It requires exploration, hence sensitive people should get to work and not simply sit back expecting miracles. This crippled city requires not only sight and hearing, but imagination. Imagination, it's true, bears only upon absent, distant places, as Proust says; we can't imagine the street on which we're actually walking, the room in which we're standing, the person with whom we're talking. But Proust lived in the classical era, before the disaster; he couldn't foresee that one day there would be half-abandoned, half-existing cities, cities covered with a tarp of ugliness, cities lost and half-recovered. He couldn't foresee that in such cities imagination becomes—must be—yet another sense, half imagination and half sensory apparatus, since here the everyday medically and empirically established senses don't suffice, they must be supplemented by a half-shut eye, intuition . . . He couldn't foresee our journey to Lvov, to a city that belongs to no one, not to those who left, nor to those who remain, and thus demands a new type of imagination. I didn't speak at such length, of course, I couldn't develop my argument, I was much more abrupt and emotional, clumsier, no doubt. Only now, as I sit in my room listening to music, can I write down what I really meant to say, conquering my eternal *esprit d'escalier*, I improve the imperfect reality of that evening when we sat in the cellar of that restaurant near Academic Street (the prewar name) in Lvov. Since after all I write this in order to revise my curtness, my clumsiness, to convert my scowls and half thoughts into longer, more convincing sentences.

They stared at me, not comprehending my outburst, but quickly concluded that they were dealing with a slightly abnormal person, a pilgrim to what was, for him at least, an extraordinary place. They understood, and the next day—as it seemed to me—they sensed something of the city's majesty, its radiance . . .

•

The young Mandelstam—like his fellow Acmeists, from whom he took several key convictions—rejected Symbolism, what he called Symbolist fogginess; he couldn't tolerate poking around in hazy, dimly lit otherworlds. He favored concreteness, the palpable reality inhabited by humans; he admired architecture as

the visual synthesis of inner and external worlds. He also insisted that the poet wasn't a priest, as some Symbolists claimed,
but simply a craftsman, an artist, the intelligent, free master of
a middle kingdom and not the emperor of the unseen. In point
of fact, though, Osip Mandelstam, like the other Acmeists, was
defending moderation, the middle ground, a halfway point
between Symbolism, with its passion for otherworldly expanses,
on the one hand, and militant Futurism, on the other. The Futurists, with their boundless faith in the glories of a dawning new
age, had succumbed to an illusion, as they would soon discover,
especially in Russia—but also throughout Europe, unless, like
Marinetti, they sided with the victors and took their place at the
very edge of the totalitarian wave. This was also an argument
about the nature of modernity: the Futurists were addicted to
novelty, to the new world, while the Symbolists loathed it, feared
it, repudiated it. Only the Acmeists succeeded in fusing precise—
sometimes even affectionate—attention to modernity with a
patient search for the spiritual vitamins that the new reality
lacked. Mandelstam's chosen perspective and place still retain
their value today.

•

After our return from Lvov we went to see Aunt Ania, my
father's sister, younger by four years, although also past ninety—
we showed her a map of Lvov and asked her where our various
family members had lived. She's the last person alive who might
know this. The last conscious person among all her siblings.
Whenever I see her, she says, complaining, No one needs me now.
And I answer, Of course we do, I need her, only she still remembers
that lost reality, all those prewar street names are dead philo-
logical terms for everyone but her. She smiles shyly, unconvinced,
but she never refuses to answer my questions. I can't talk with
my father anymore, alas, his memory has contracted to the size
of a coffee grain, it no longer exists. He doesn't get out of bed, he

no longer knows anything, he only eats and sleeps, he waits for the end without knowing that he's waiting, maybe long-gone things appear to him in dreams, we don't know. But his sister still remembers these old things. She remembers everything about Lvov perfectly. She told us about Franciscan Street, about the building of the school, apparently a trade school, where my grandfather, the director, lived with his family before they moved to 10 Piaskowa Street, to their own little house bought with what he'd saved through many years of frugality. We still have my grandfather's notebooks from the first part of the twentieth century, the account books where he kept track of expenditures—and one rather mysterious heading appeared fairly regularly: luxuries. There weren't many such luxuries, though; my grandfather seems to have been a thrifty, organized, practical person, and in the midtwenties, he used the money he'd put aside—and that hadn't been eaten up by luxuries—to purchase the little house at 10 Piaskowa. And Piaskowa is just past Franciscan Street and the trade school. Someone—I don't know who, it was an anonymous gift—sent me electronically a collective photograph of the students and teachers at the trade school, the standard, conventional group portrait. The instructors (the so-called teaching body) sit in front, including, of course, a priest on my grandfather's right. The pupils stand behind them in sailor suits. Sailor suits, in landlocked Lvov, with its one little river, the Poltva, confined to an underground tunnel! (Although it should be added that Lvov sits in the middle of a watershed; one stream feeds the Black Sea while the Poltva answers the call of the Baltic.) My grandfather, who must be fortysomething, doesn't particularly appeal to me in the photo, he seems completely defined by his social position. He doesn't look like someone I'd like; there's no trace of the kindly old gentleman I knew and loved after the war. And I kept asking for Lvov addresses. Aunt Busia and her husband, Uncle Joseph, a couple who had to fight for family recognition (since she was Jewish, cursed by her own family when she ran off with a goy, and he likewise defied his family to marry her) lived on Sykstuska Street. Whereas Aunt Berta, my godmother—short, hunched, stern, rather chilly, an old maid, a music teacher; I still remember her from her brief visits to Gliwice—lived on Grottger Street in Lvov (it links Franciscan Street with Lyczakowska). Aunt Berta was also among the deportees; of her modest possessions she kept only the piano, her sole means of support; she hung on to it even through her years of Krakow poverty. At one point—I remember this from my father's old stories—she lived at a Krakow officers' complex, in the kitchen of some friends or distant relations, and during the day they often told her to "go for a walk" so she wouldn't disrupt their domestic routines. She'd already reached retirement age, her hosts must have, too, otherwise they would have headed off to work and she could have stayed in the kitchen . . . Or, who knows, maybe they only drove her out on Sundays. It's hard to imagine such cruelty, but that's clearly how it was, maybe just for a little while, maybe that whole setup didn't last long, I don't know for sure and can never find out now. She left the piano to me, her godchild, since I was hurt that she'd never paid me much attention—but how could she fuss over me while pacing Krakow's streets and waiting to get back to her improvised home? After her death it became abundantly clear that I, her godchild, heir to her modest estate, had no perceptible musical talent whatsoever (nor did my sister), so my father sold the piano and used the profits to buy two bicycles, one for me, the other for my sister. I'll leave the sensitive reader to assess the symbolic value of this act. In any case, for me this marked the beginning of a passionate love for bicycling, for rides that often led in the direction of what had been a German highway. (Thus, from a Lvov piano to a post-German highway.) I still remember the scent of my first bicycle, the smell of the leather from which the seat was made, and the separate scent of the lacquered handlebars. My first bicycle came from East Germany, while the second, a sports model with gears that I had for many years, was from Czechoslovakia. Bicycles of the fraternal nations. But let's get back to Lvov addresses: my mother's family lived off Grodecka Street, Aunt Ania didn't remember the name of the side street. Grodecka is the long street that still links the suburbs with the once-imposing railroad station, which was built, like most of Lvov's most majestic structures, under the Hapsburgs, and designed for great, sentimental farewells and heartfelt welcomes. And the Namysl family, I asked, where did they live? That was the family of the husband of my father's older sister, Aunt Maria, who ran a garden shop after the war; she was a wise, courageous soul whose life was difficult and bitter. The Namysl family lived on Saint Wojciech Street. And finally Aunt Wisia, my grandmother's sister—who lived to almost one hundred, getting by on little things, small emotions, collecting silver pencils and scissors and postcards from Opatija, humming outdated melodies, heaving sighs in French, recalling balls from before the First World War—lived at 30 Zyblikiewicz Street, along with her mother and brother. Was it really 30? Aunt Ania wasn't sure. It's worth noting, though, that only here, with Aunt Wisia, to whom she was tied so closely by intimacies, shared tastes, and an inevitable dislike (they lived beneath the same roof for decades, two old maids; they regularly fought, made up, then fought and made up once more), did she remember the number—though it remained slightly in doubt. We certainly won't hold it against her.

•

How do we keep on living after the deaths of our close friends? But somehow we get by. Our substance must consist partly of indifference, of gray, unfeeling metal, since we manage, even fairly well, after our friends, our close, our closest friends have gone. We laugh, we go to good restaurants, we read the new books that they will never know. The first moment of grief, when we've just learned that someone close has died, is terrible.

It's not even grief, it's pain and protest in pure form; the word *grief* already contains an element of resignation, of making peace with what has taken place. But in that first moment there are no words, no acceptance, no resignation. It's as if a hole had been torn in existence. The earthquake reveals an abyss. A moment of tears and rage, and Logos can do nothing here. Logos steps aside discreetly. Then the rift gradually closes, and the drawn-out process of mourning begins, we slowly start crossing the footpath over the ravine, and with time the scar takes on the color of healthy skin. But there are the deaths you never accept. I never accepted, will never accept, the death of my nephew Marek. He was only ten, he didn't yet know who he was. And we didn't know who he'd become, what he'd turn into. He was a good-looking, charming boy. Poles are partial to euphemisms, we always say, They'll be reunited in the afterlife. Or, We'll meet again on the other side. Or, He's looking down on us from heaven. As if heaven were a grassy yard we could watch from the kitchen window, checking from the corner of our eye to see that the kids and the dog are playing safely, there's no danger. We treat the dead like children. An overly domesticated Catholicism lends itself to such carelessness, it resists mysteries exceeding the imagination. I often think of Joseph Brodsky, one of the most extraordinary people I ever met, about his different personae. Sometimes he was the brilliant, arrogant intellectual, whom strangers feared to approach; but at thoughtful, quiet moments, he could be the most considerate of friends. I remember our conversations: he'd launch into great monologues, proclaiming his mad metaphysical theories, while I played the skeptic, pointing out the inconsistencies and incongruities in his arguments. His monologues frequently arose from his work in progress; they were trial runs for the essays in which he elaborated his theories. He often returned to the topic of religion, which would, so he claimed, include more infinity after breaking with the great natural religions. The religions we'd received through family or social traditions held too little infinity, they'd struck bargains with the historical material that packaged them. I objected, I said that you couldn't build a religion the way that Dr. Zamenhof had constructed Esperanto, and that he, Joseph, was proposing just such an Esperanto when we really needed to sustain the infinity contained in existing religions, to nurture it, just in case, like the embers of a bonfire, stirring it, kindling it, in hopes of raising a greater flame. I think he liked our conversations, he even liked my skepticism, he needed it, he needed opposition, resistance. Once I called him from Houston, just after arriving from Europe, after parting from my family, from M.; the change of place grieved me, and I anticipated a warm, friendly conversation to cheer me in my small-scale melancholy. No such luck: Joseph wanted to find out what I thought of Horace. I suspected that he was writing an essay about the poet, and I was correct. So I had only Horace to console me.

•

So there were three children: my father was the middle child, Ania came later. The oldest was Maria, Aunt Maria. An old photograph still hangs in Aunt Ania's apartment, a genuine sepia photograph, not sepia-tinted, stylized. It shows the whole family out walking somewhere near Lvov, in the forest, on some gentle slope. My grandfather strikes a tour guide's pose—the family might be out in the woods, but they're not dark, ominous woods, you won't get lost. No, they're on the outskirts of town, and no one's frightened, least of all my grandfather, an experienced pedagogue, a fearless teacher, who could doubtless daunt even a wolf, if some terrifying, wild wolf was to turn up in that suburban forest. My grandfather would address the wolf so sternly that the beast would slouch groundward and slink back to its dark abode. I know from family legends that Grandfather gave his three children to understand that they were expected to master three subjects: swimming, stenography, and German. Swimming, stenography, and German: Is this really the ideal skill set? It hints at the spirit of enlightenment, the optimism that prevailed after the First World War, that horrific catastrophe after which they started dancing the Charleston. There will still be thoughts and ideas worth taking down, and any number of assemblies and organizations will require a competent stenographer; the ubiquitous tape recorder had not yet made its appearance. There may still be a few (but only a few) ferries or ships to go down, hence the necessity of swimming lessons. People still vividly recalled the *Titanic*, after all, which went to the bottom in the small hours of April 15, 1912; my father was born on December 16 that same year. But my grandfather's three commandments must have come later, in the postwar era, when Poland regained its independence. And thirdly, lastly, in this part of Europe, German would always come in handy. I don't say that my grandfather foresaw the next war and the German occupation. And German didn't prove particularly useful during the Nazi occupation in any case; only Nazi language helped, and the Poles weren't permitted to speak it. When my grandfather proposed (or imposed) these three skills, he wasn't anticipating Auschwitz or the Communists, labor camps or exile. He must have been, in the first part of his life, a man of iron will, bent on survival and even success. A man of the Enlightenment, committed to progress achieved step by step, through minor sacrifices and unflagging effort. I've already mentioned his careful calculation of family and personal expenses, the small sums he managed to put by until he was able to purchase a little house. He'd certainly never read Nietzsche; if he'd absorbed those teachings, he wouldn't have urged his children to learn German. Since if they'd used their German to study Nietzsche's writings, they would have discovered that nothing exists, that there is no foundation, no ground beneath our feet, that the surface on which we step has no more substance than the clouds floating above us on a summer day. In which case, neither stenography nor swimming serve much purpose. Floating in the clouds was beyond the siblings' strength. Only art might have brought some relief, but art didn't inspire them, with the exception of Aunt Ania, who played the piano, who knew and loved music. All three children survived the war and occupation, but my grandfather couldn't have predicted that any more than he could have known that a second war would follow the first, a far crueler war, and that during this war the German culture he revered, and to which he partly belonged, through his German mother and his studies, would be seized by madness. And if anything helped them, it wasn't stenography, swimming, and German, but just plain blind luck. Of the three, the oldest, my aunt Maria, stood out for her deep faith. She suffered great misfortunes: the death of her child and the death of her husband. Little Myszka was a charming, cheerful child; I remember her well, her kind laughter, never directed against others. She died of diphtheria. I've never stopped mourning her death, such a good-natured, sweet, pretty child; it still hurts my heart to think of her. I imagine what she, Maria, Myszka's mother, must have suffered after the death of her little girl, who died at the age of seven, what she must have suffered all those years, though she never said a word on the subject. Aunt Maria also lost her husband, Uncle Romek, a man of great charm, exceptionally careless, as is often the case with people of great charm. (Mirrors should be kept from such people so that they won't perceive their extraordinary appeal.) After his tragic death she had to fight to survive, to help the family—financially, too, since she had to pay all the debts her dead husband had accrued. She ran a small garden shop, which yielded some income, but required slave labor on her part; she rose at dawn, or even earlier, to light the fire in the greenhouse stove (we didn't yet have those wonderful stoves possessed of the electronic intelligence that permits them to start at a preordained time when commanded weeks or months in advance). She was always tanned, with the brown skin of those who work outdoors and never think of "going to get some sun" in the manner of office workers looking yearningly out the window on bright May days; her palms were dry, with skin worn from the endless handling of plants and flowers, of chrysanthemums on the eve of All Souls' Day—it was a paradox. Here she was, a woman who'd lost her beloved husband and daughter, making her best money of the year just before All Saints' Day, when she'd sell vast quantities of white and yellow chrysanthemums, especially since her nursery lay directly en route to the cemetery, along a usually quiet street that once a year, on November 1, drew thousands of people to the cemetery, all of them buying chrysanthemums. Fate was apparently so malicious, so refined, that it contrived to place this woman, whom it had punished so harshly, from whom it had taken her nearest and dearest, conveniently adjacent to the cemetery. I don't think she ever used hand creams; taking care of her worn palms never crossed her mind. In our family, our typical intelligentsia (but hardly *intellectual*) family, where everyone, including me, sat at desks, at tables, hurried to offices, to institutes, to schools, only she worked out of doors, only she had a farmer's skin. Everyone else aspired to life behind a desk; my grandfather's desk was enormous, adorned with dictionaries and encyclopedias; my father's was much smaller; while I never had a proper desk, I usually worked at a table, or, as now, in an armchair with a laptop on my knees. All of us, my sister and my mother, too, when she wrote letters, we all fell prey to the workings of some mysterious force that propelled us toward a desk or, at very least, a table. As if a desk were a stronghold, a fortress to shelter you from the wild world's onslaughts. Except for Aunt Maria. Unlike her father, my grandfather, she belonged not among the Enlightenment's disciples, but with the deeply religious, the deeply silent. I know she read serious works on theology, I would guess that she knew how to pray (an ability far rarer than it seems), but she was a quiet person, like all in my family—with the exception of my mother and also my grandfather, who talked nonstop, even through the Occupation, he never stopped talking, in the Lvov trams, which was extremely dangerous, and then under Communism, he kept on talking, loudly and emphatically. But everyone else in my father's family was quiet. Aunt Maria's silence, it seems to me, grew from her religion—I sensed her conviction that things linked to faith must be left unexpressed, that they're lost when spoken, they become banalities. I admired her for being different, for the deep devotion that she wouldn't, couldn't share with us—she was the opposite of those pious hypocrites who place their religious fervor on public display. She was an antipietist, a brave woman with a splendid sense of humor. I admired her so much, but I couldn't tell her, I didn't know how. How could I tell her, in my quiet family? I was part of that taciturn family. I wanted to learn to speak, but I knew it would take many years. Only now can I tell her that. Now I'm talking about her, thinking about her, not for the first time and certainly not for the last, about her suffering and her courage, about how hard she worked, how she battled to survive the deaths of those she loved most, how she kept silent. My father's silence was rather ethical in nature—he dismissed orators and rhetoric. But his sister Maria kept silent for different reasons. Perhaps those who pray truly and deeply inevitably watch their words around others.

•

When the Krakow tram skirts the Planty Gardens and unexpected blocks of churches, palaces, and ordinary buildings abruptly shoot from the close-up shots of trees, bushes, and streets, when, for example, a view of Stolarska Street and the Marian Cathedral's proud towers suddenly opens for a moment, I feel as though I'm viewing an old-fashioned stereopticon. Beneath my fingers I feel the swells of a living city that combines its medieval origins with the modest modernity of the early twenty-first century.

•

Uncle Romek had vast charm. More than this: he came to our puritanical family a bit like a visitor from another planet—from a family that played, that celebrated its gatherings with friendly games. In our—truly rather puritanical—family, such goings-on were unthinkable. Everything was modest, frugal. Mother would tell us, my sister and me, about the menu when her future in-laws invited her for dinner the first time. My father's parents stood ever so slightly higher in the social hierarchy than my mother's family, but their life was infinitely more spartan. Mother's far more carefree parents always lived, so I gather, a little beyond their means. But when she turned up for dinner, or perhaps lunch, with my father's parents, they served her ground schnitzel. Mother remembered this, laughing, to the end of her days. Ground schnitzel at the first dinner for their son's fiancée! It was scandalous, unheard-of. She laughed about it years later, but it must have hurt at the time. Ground schnitzel. My father always patiently explained, always, even decades after the event, that she must understand, certain principles were always observed in that household, the menu never varied simply because they were expecting guests. Since they had planned on ground schnitzel, ground schnitzel it would be. In no case was this to be taken as a show of hostility directed toward the new arrival, my father would explain time and again.

So my Uncle Romek came from an entirely different background, from a clan in which a son's fiancée would never, under any circumstances, be welcomed with ground schnitzel, even though our family was nowhere so well-off as his own. And in Gliwice, in Maria and Romek's large apartment, in their vast, so I thought, living room, where the entire family gathered for holidays and name days, Uncle Romek set the tone with his whims and inventiveness. He arranged games, competitions, and skits, largely for the young people. We had no one who could play

Chopin or Schubert for us on the piano. For all that, though—
I understood this much later, through the memoirs of the last
Polish generation raised on estates where life was unthinkable
without singing, dancing, and charades—in post-German Gliwice I came to know something of nineteenth-century Polish
gentry life, courtesy of Uncle Romek's imagination. While awaiting the end of the partitions, Poland danced, played games, flirted,
read, played the piano, and, upon occasion, conspired against
the invaders. Such estates vanished after the war, and the eastern
borderlands lived on only in memory, replaced by new borderlands to the west. Uncle Romek conveyed something of that lost
world's atmosphere.

●

The scholar and the artist, the scholar and the poet. A writer, a
poet is a holy fool who all too often turns up in public at his most
comic, hopeless, and grotesque moments (although, with any luck,
he'll have moments of greatness, too). He takes great risks, he
lays himself open to respectable, bourgeois opinion—and I don't
just mean the artist-rebel openly flouting social norms. No, I'm
talking about self-revelation, exposing your own condition in
the theater of a novel or a poem. Meanwhile, the scholar takes
cover in a library, concealing himself behind footnotes, never removing his coat or sport jacket. No one will catch sight of him in
dishabille, no one will reproach him with unreadiness.

●

When we told her—I'm speaking now of my other aunt, Maria's
sister, Ania—about Lvov, "What a lovely city!" we said, she answered drily, "What of it?" The brief phrase encapsulated all the
bitterness of the dispossessed. She spat it out like someone who'd
wasted her life, who'd ended up doing useless things in an alien,
ugly town. She spoke almost angrily—"What of it?"—as if she
wished she could kick us out. As if wanting to say, So this is what

you came for, to tell me what I already know? All too well. Through the window of her modest apartment an ash tree was growing so close to the building's wall that it might soon become her roommate. But she couldn't see Lvov. Even though the window, with the ash branches growing ever closer, faced east, in the direction of her lost city. But the lost city was blocked, in any case, by smokestacks, by little hills, by the towers of Krakow. We'd wanted to please her by praising Lvov, but we'd unwittingly done just the opposite. "What of it?" It wasn't her usual tone, warm and friendly. That "What of it?" was hostile, dry. She didn't need praise for the city she'd been missing for sixty years; she'd never gone back, of course, not even when things got easier, when the borders suddenly started to shrink like a cheap dress after washing. Her niece had once taken her to Spain— Spain! to the west, so far west that her lost city grew even more distant—but never a word about visiting Lvov, so much closer than Spain. It wasn't a matter of money, trips to Lvov didn't cost much, certainly much less than to Spain. My father never went back to Lvov either. To "visit" the place where an unhealed wound gaped would be like visiting purgatory, like visiting volcanoes (their interiors), like setting up camp on the edge of a crater spewing flames. The word *visit*, so frivolous, lighthearted, swift as a windshield wiper on a rainy day, presupposes a speedy return. There and back, a picnic, a walk, and then home again, maybe in time for the evening news. But if what you're visiting is home, then what do you call it? Making a pilgrimage to your own memory, to something that doesn't exist—is that a visit?

•

I think Aunt Ania reacted like that, drily, negatively, because she caught a whiff of treachery in the way that M. and I praised Lvov. "What a lovely city." The phrase was apposite in the mouths of strangers, those who had never been deported from the City. M. might confidently praise the City; she'd been visiting for the first time, that was fine, absolutely permissible, acceptable, even expected. Someone who'd come from there, one of the dispossessed, even in the next generation, didn't say, couldn't say, "What a lovely city." Anyone coming from Lvov knew perfectly well that it was, is a lovely city, but couldn't mention it; it was taboo. It goes without saying that people from other places, foreigners (foreign to Lvov, that is), had the right, no, rather the duty, to praise Lvov's beauty. That was their function, their modest task in the complex tragicomedy of the lost City. This was the order of things as long as those who truly knew the City remained among us. As long as the guardians of memory lived on, ever older, in poorer health, more hunched, more forgetful, enduring winter's frosts (never so frosty as in Lvov, though) and summer's swelters (but never so hot as in the City) with ever greater suffering. One must discreetly control the state of knowledge about the City for as long as possible. It seems to me, it always seemed, that my position among the dispossessed was unstable. Sometimes I was one of them; at others, I was not to be trusted. I had written a poem, "To Go to Lvov," that was generally accepted by the central powers of the dispossessed (there were, of course, no such powers, it's a figure of speech), and this weighed in my favor. My father, whose position among the dispossessed was solid, even indisputable, actually copied out the poem to show it to his fellow deportees. The poem apparently provoked no reservations. Although even here there was no absolute unanimity. A certain Lvovian, well advanced in years, once told me, spitefully, reproachfully—I'd just turned down his offer to buy a collection of periodicals devoted to the lost City—"Sir, I'm much older than you are, I lived many years in Lvov, which you barely know, and I have to say I never thought there was 'too much of Lvov.'" He was alluding to the poem's refrain, "there was too much of Lvov," by which he meant to expose, to condemn my pusillanimity and pettiness . . . That was one thing. But this was an isolated instance. Other, more fundamental doubts also surfaced. A key question arose: Should a poem like "To Go to Lvov" even be written? It might have its strong points, but isn't it a bit like saying, "Lvov, what a lovely city"? In other words, did the resettled, even in the next generation, have the right to speak of the lost City, and if so, how? They could of course write memoirs, gather photographs, they could even publish total kitsch, sentimental rubbish, about the City; this, paradoxically, could not damage the subtle, invisible politics of the dispossessed. Didn't the very fact of speaking about the lost City, speaking in verse, with poetic enthusiasm, place the author beyond the pale of the dispossessed? Didn't it locate him amid those foreign travelers from whom one expected praise, sighs, perhaps even raptures, which produced, however, no results, no lasting consequences? Tourists may go to Lvov one year, to Grenada or Buenos Aires the next, it can't be forbidden. They can't be relied upon, their enthusiasms are by definition short-lived, capricious. Buenos Aires might eclipse the memory of Lvov. Likewise Grenada. Tourists forget their trips after a year or two, their enthusiasm is confined to their most recent vacation and to planning the next. The dispossessed might have their various flaws and failings, but they could not be faulted for inconstancy in their longing for the City. Oh, no, in this there were no exceptions, here single-mindedness prevailed. Hence the aesthetics of the dispossessed advised mistrust of great emotions. Sentimental kitsch was another matter; it was largely the work of the dispossessed themselves. Kitsch was permitted, kitsch was welcomed, kitsch was a kind of familial dialect, countless volumes of memoirs written, so to speak, with the left hand, the hand nearest the heart, in a soft and swollen style, like the throat of a sick child, could do no harm, they played no larger role in the economy of exile. They didn't change a thing, not a thing, it must be so, they were indispensable, these thick tomes bursting with kitschy creations ("Ach, how I yearn for you, my beloved city," and so on), and hardly anyone opened them, they were beside the point, which was simply that the bookstores should stock thick albums clearly bearing the city's name on their spines, many, many such albums. And in these albums the lost City must be seen as idyllic, a place without persecution, where Poles, Jews, and Ukrainians lived linked by a bond of brotherly love. Clashes, battles, feuds, pogroms, went unmentioned. The central powers (the nonexistent ones) had other concerns, current problems: the dispossessed were growing ever fewer, they disappeared, they died, there was, alas, nothing to be done, they diminished, and those who lived on grew more hunched, ever smaller, ever slighter, they scarcely left home, and their memories likewise slowly vanished, dried up like the water in a pond. Successors must be sought out, trained, before it was too late. But it was already too late, and the powers that weren't had neglected the problem, they found no successors, they led no pedagogical drills—but how could they? they didn't exist—they didn't train the next dispossessed generation, and an age of amnesia drew nearer, an age of oblivion, the memory of the City slowly came to a close, and only the rustle of leaves, the rustle of dry autumn leaves swept along the sidewalk by a western wind, reminded us that we'd lost something precious, something life-giving.

•

Aunt Ania may have known nothing of the aesthetic quandaries troubling the dispossessed, she may have played no part in the cultural labors of its committee (once more: there is no such committee, the author persists in employing a fiction, a figure of speech); still she was, unwittingly, the voice of a typical, classic representative of that sad tribe, and her reactions likewise were absolutely classic.

•

As I described my grandfather and his bilingualism, I mentioned "German civilization." I read a biography once of the sociologist and philosopher Max Weber, and that book also painted a portrait of Wilhelmine Germany, a portrait of a boundlessly powerful country possessing virtually everything: great ironworks and burgeoning heavy industry alongside splendid universities with their world-renowned, black-robed professors, modern cities, networks of railroads, but also brilliant intellectuals, publishers, political parties, cultural societies, student unions (the fashionable *Jugendbewegung!*), and hundreds, thousands, of other marvels: countless symphony orchestras with their wind and bowed instruments, their percussion. Harps. Choirs. Opera scenes. Stock exchanges. Fire brigades. Solingen knives. Barges moving slowly along symmetrical canals carved courtesy of Euclid. Wealthy businessmen despising nations without statehood— even Thomas Mann commented in his *Reflections of a Nonpolitical Man* that the Poles were incapable of achieving lasting statehood. There was no Poland then: when Weber traveled to Poznan—which lay on the Reich's borders—he called it *stinkendes Loch*, a stinking hole. There was no Polish nation, there was virtually no industry, the three emperors sat on their lofty thrones, gazing down at the nation they'd divided. So did "Polish civilization" even exist? And if so, what shape did it take? Was it like an old cloth, a piece of antique fabric dotted with the black stains of anti-Semitism, ignorance, bigotry, but also with lovely stretches, scraps of cloth of gold? There must have been something in that old fabric since so many foreigners chose Polishness; my grandfather must also have faced that choice, he might have become an Austrian (or a German). He was perfectly bilingual, his mother was German, he studied German literature in Graz, but for all that he—like the much younger Jozef Czapski, born into an aristocratic, cosmopolitan family—chose Polishness. Did they choose only a dream? German civilization—it was a vast edifice, an enormous stockpile of building materials, palaces, and barracks, a fantastic warehouse of people and things, adorned moreover with the golden stars of Goethe, Schiller, and

Kant, who strolled park boulevards strewn with gravel. And on the Polish side—chiefly dreams, only dreams. Great poets, largely unknown outside Poland, and Frédéric Chopin. Stunning dissymmetry. Yet it's understandable—we're always seeking justice, the just state, and the countries, the empires that actually exist, that have achieved historical success, countries abounding in policemen and armies, universities, botanical gardens and geodetic institutes, are so taken up with daily life, the maintenance of basic order, that we view them as we view paintings in a museum, great panoramas, we mistrust their justice. They have, so we suppose, no time for ephemeral things, and justice is ephemeral. They're caught up in maintaining their armies, their police stations, in keeping their geodesists nourished, designing uniforms for prison and museum guards. But the dream is just—and portable, it can cross any border. The dream is invisible. The dream is justice—potentially at least. Those who live in dreams are convinced that they are—or rather will be—just. But on the Polish side, there were only little clusters of high-minded, disinterested intellectuals, groups, cafés bursting with poets dressed so as to ensure that no one would mistake them for anything but poets, an aristocracy, sometimes wealthy, but also largely self-absorbed, an illiterate peasantry, rain, November. It's something like Ireland on the eve of the twentieth century—compared to majestic, imperial England, Ireland was nothing, just poetry, a handful of romantic drunks worshipping opera and whiskey. Yet Poland and Ireland alike, impoverished, living only in dreams, attracted fanatical partisans and defeated bona fide empires. Certainly some people do prefer shadows to real powers. Perhaps some overarching hypothesis on the world's insubstantiality comes into play here as well. And perhaps some conspiracy of dreamers whiling away their best hours in libraries . . . In any case Poland and Ireland do exist now (as does Israel), they're quite real, and just as a fair portion of the English Protestants living in Ireland favored poetry over Britain's imperial might, so many of those bilingual German Polish speakers, like my grandfather, chose uncertain Polish dreaming over the vast edifice of imperial Germany. And over imperial Austria, it should be added, slightly smaller, but also impressive. And Russia, of course, though fortunately my family had nothing in common with Russia, apart from a shared admiration for its great writers and composers. They might leave Poland to study in Dorpat, in Louvain, in Paris, in Geneva, in Munich, in Graz—but then they'd go home. They would take the dream with them and return; some came back with the dream they'd taken still intact. Beautiful women also left, one of them dallied with a mournful Paul Claudel—he'd just been rejected by a monastery, by monks who'd realized he wasn't suited to monastic life. He met her on a ship sailing to China, he caught sight of her on deck with the sea wind blowing her long hair. Later he called her Ysé in his play *Partage de midi*. Some of them left for Paris, like Olga Boznanska, like Leopold Zborowski, like Bronislaw Malinowski. They left, they built bridges in California, there weren't many bridges back home, but there were dreams. Why do you need bridges when you've got dreams? Love and conspiracy and the uncertain dream, and on the other side the giant edifice of Wilhelmine civilization, the Cordeliers of military and police barracks. So it's probably obviously why they chose dreaming, poetry, and beautiful women over the households abounding in prosperity that are known as empires, those iron-handed nations possessing no mysteries, sated, sleepy as after a lavish dinner, cumbrous, lazily digesting their own selves, dull, triumphant—until the time arrives.

•

An interesting moment in a famous novel: in *The Bridge on the Drina* Ivo Andrić writes of the generation that came of age on the cusp of the First World War:

What other people of that race, in other nations and times
had achieved and attained over generations, through the
course of age-long efforts at the cost of life, or of sacrifices and renunciations greater and dearer than life, this
lay before them like a chance inheritance, destiny's peril-
ous gift. It seemed fantastic and unlikely, but it was genuine: they could do whatever they wished with their
youth.

This was the generation shaped by Friedrich Nietzsche: the
sickly philosopher, the neurasthenic who lacked the courage to
ask for the hand of the woman he loved and sent his friend instead, the traveler plagued by migraines, wandering from one
modest boardinghouse to the next, who played a part in the
"liberation" of an entire generation. "Liberation" in quotes, like
most liberations, but this one may have been even more doubt-
ful. Ivo Andrić wrote his great novel in Belgrade during the
Second World War—someone once even showed me the building where he had lived and worked. He grasped and named, so
it seems to me, that moment in European history when the topography of the usual narrow paths that had hitherto been the
natural terrain of each new generation, young people slowly and
cautiously following in their parents' tracks, suddenly exploded
in a revolution not so much political as mental. Just then young
Jews raised their eyes up from the Torah and began dreaming of
the great adventure that would lead them on to goals as yet
unknown; just then young Polish poets abandoned their odes
to the vanished fatherland and began penning hymns to the
Infinite instead. And young Serbs took to conspiracy and killed
the Archduke Ferdinand in Sarajevo.

A great part of that unsettled generation would be mowed
down by machine guns on the fields of battle in the First World
War, but we already know that. And as we drive along the

highway near Verdun, through the unending cemetery stretching across the undulating hills on which those young men rest, young men freed from the shackles of ancient superstitions and their own fates, a shiver of fear seizes us, a sense of history's senselessness.

Something similar must have taken place much earlier, at the moment when Napoleon appeared like a meteor on the heavens of European history and the young people of many countries prepared for a great adventure, fled home to join the army, while death whetted its scythe. But on hearing that Bonaparte had crowned himself emperor of France, his great admirer Beethoven crossed out the dedication to Napoleon on the score of the Third Symphony with such ferocity that he tore a hole in the paper. Dreams slipped through that hole.

•

For all that, so many chose not Poland, but Russia, Austria, or Germany. We prefer recalling those who chose the dream of Polishness. The others melted into the masses of Germany or Russia, germanized their surnames, started companies, became professors; some found success.

•

The writers of the West have prophesied the end of bourgeois life—for two hundred years now. In Poland, on the other hand, the problem of a weak middle class has been debated for ages.

Only what isn't real. Sometimes I thought you could only really love what isn't real: poems, paintings, the sounds of a piano drifting from the music academy, where a pianist, no longer young, a maestro, a stranger from another town, showed students how to play Chopin's Fourth Ballade. Love only what isn't real, but reality always resurfaced, in the shape of a trivial question about what to make for dinner (the ham's gone, we're out of tea), or in the form of menacing history: war's broken out, mass demonstrations have paralyzed the city, inflation has imperceptibly changed the appearance of shops and streets (though it left Beethoven's sonatas unscathed). And I could never understand how these two forces, the light element of music and history's heavy breath, coexisted. I've tried to write about it more than once, but even the most dedicated readers have delicately hinted that they've had enough, let's move on to something new, since these two worlds still cannot be reconciled or fused, they remain completely indifferent to my questions, they mock my inquiries, my worries, they likewise dismiss the protests of my scattered readers.

•

When I was a student of philosophy (not a very good one), I wrote a paper about something I called, as I remember, the "supra-empirical state." I struggled—clumsily, without the appropriate intellectual equipment—to grasp what Schopenhauer, again to the best of my recollection, termed "better consciousness." Schopenhauer meant those moments when the intellect rises above the usual struggles with matter, with the quotidian, and opens itself briefly to ideas, to beauty. I didn't know Schopenhauer yet, I was a practitioner, not a theoretician, but I had in fact experienced such moments of rapture, sometimes at a concert in the symphony hall, sometimes out walking, moments filled with a strange light, richer than the monotony of daily life, demanding expression, moments muttering in a language I didn't know and wanted to transmit in my first poems, also less than successful. The supra-empirical state, that's what I called those moments— my lack of philosophical talent is painfully clear, any reasonably competent philosopher would have burst out laughing at this student's struggle to grasp the fluid reality of experience . . . I was a practitioner, hands-on, emotional, not an ounce of the theoretician in me, forging concepts and categories was beyond my strength, I lacked distance, patience, the pinch of cynicism it takes to transport yourself from experience to the dry soil of ideas. The supra-empirical state! Professors of philosophy mock such tomfoolery. I passed, that's true, my thesis was approved, no doubt with a shrug or two. It couldn't do much harm.

•

Aunt Ania (my father's sister) was resettled, like my entire family. In the volume of memoirs my father wrote, at my request, after my mother's death—he wrote it at the typewriter, on second-rate paper that quickly yellowed—he confined himself chiefly to dry facts; the man who wrote such witty postcards clearly felt ill at ease with larger forms and produced only an extended curriculum vitae. In it he states that Ania, who had played piano since childhood, spent the Occupation preparing for the Chopin Competition, and at the war's end she met with a great, tragic disappointment: she had exceeded the age limit set for competitors. No one in the family had ever mentioned this. My father's story touched me. I instantly began imagining my aunt in Lvov during the war, in the house at 10 Piaskowa, which was and is a quiet side street . . . I imagined her practicing Chopin's ballades and Beethoven's sonatas; armed German soldiers patrol the streets, the Gestapo monitors each sign of life, winter draws close, Lvov's Jews perish, but in a small house set back from the street, among gardens, subtle sounds are born beneath her fingers.

But after reading those memoirs entrusted to yellowing paper some time later, Aunt Ania emphatically denied having ever dreamed of the Chopin Competition. I heard this first from my father, who passed the news on with a brittle smile. Ania, he said, insists that the thought had never crossed her mind, she'd "never come close" to the level that would permit such notions, which were utterly fantastical, her gifts were modest, she played chiefly for herself, and my father had dreamed up the whole business from start to finish. This came to me as a revelation, it showed him in an entirely new light—the light of imagination, which I'd never glimpsed in him. I'd always thought (in my arrogance) that I held the monopoly on imagination in my sober family. I asked her about this business some time later and received the same decisive denial. She played for herself, she said, she would never have dared to take part in any competition, where her humble efforts would be cruelly confronted by the virtuosic displays of pianist-athletes, let alone the Chopin Competition, scrutinized by the whole society, the government, the ministers . . . A competition at which the queen of Belgium had been a frequent guest. A competition serving as a sort of Olympics for young Polish pianists, the crème de la crème. I have no reason not to believe her. I must believe her. But if this is so, it means that my father, who wrote down his recollections while still in perfect command of his faculties, dreamed up the entire story for some reason. What's more, this would suggest a total upheaval in his mental life, in his whole spiritual makeup; he was so utterly straightforward, so guilelessly, organically veracious that falsehoods or fantasies were unthinkable on his part. So either his memory had already begun to mislead him (later, much later, it abandoned him irretrievably), or he, too, decided to enter upon the territory of imagination, which he had always strenuously avoided, and invented that story, which, if true, would have cast our family's entire Occupation-era odyssey in a slightly different light.

•

The author believes in the existence of a higher world, but cannot bring this world into being within his nation's, his family's, or even his own daily life. At most a few pages in his books mark efforts, always failed, always faulty, to attain this higher realm. However, without such efforts, the author would not be himself, would certainly not be an author.

•

The first poem I published was called "Music" and recorded an essentially minor episode that I'd witnessed at the Krakow Philharmonic: a musician fainted during a concerto. The concert was interrupted, an additional, unexpected intermission was announced. This shocked me. I still believed that music kept company with the highest realms of reality: that a black-clad musician fainted while within music, beyond the blight of ordinary time, defied comprehension, it was astonishing.

•

The oars of a wooden rowboat struck the brown water . . . Father possessed great energy as a young man, and he adored Sunday outings, greater and lesser expeditions, hikes over mountains and through forests. He always demanded company on these trips; he often took us to the village of Rudy Raciborskie, where an enormous park slowly eroded, and a palace and a monastery crumbled. You reached Rudy by way of a narrow-gauge railroad, which, unlike true railroads, left the intimacy of the town's outskirts intact; it seemed to tiptoe up the tracks, whispering apologies to the local inhabitants for disturbing their Sunday siestas . . . A strange world spread around us; Rudy held an old Cistercian abbey, half-burned during the war, ponds through which the Ruda River slowly drifted, and vast forests, while in regional offices crowds of little heads professed "Communism" (if anyone had asked what it was, I wonder what they would have said). Mother rarely took part in these Sunday outings; given the choice, she'd never have left the city. In his memoirs, father describes her horror the one time she had to spend the night in a hostel and sleep in a bunk bed; he also recalls that his mother, my grandmother, likewise stayed at home when my grandfather took the three children on extended walks through the outskirts of Lvov . . . On Sundays, the offices were closed, fortunately; only churches opened wide their doors. And in the middle, our little four-person family (Mother was with us even when she didn't come), working to keep up our prewar customs, convinced we were "different," since Father was a "professor." We had to be "different," otherwise we'd be swallowed up in the waves of the "uneducated masses," those who constantly, emphatically employed the repugnant word *kurwa*, "fuck" (the Polish curse could not exist without the energetic *r* that rolls on the tip of the tongue), who couldn't handle complex syntax and hence relied upon the parataxis so beloved among the modernists. We were in fact fairly poor and lived chiefly on appearances. The "professor" couldn't afford a decent suit. The "professor" combined absolute ignorance where money was concerned with a powerful moral instinct: the sum of these qualities condemned our family to a modest, irreproachable existence. On coming home from work, Father immediately changed into his most ordinary, well-worn clothes so as to save wear on his better things. Perhaps that's why the decaying park and crumbling palace made such an effective backdrop for our Sunday outings. It had nothing to do with the poetry of ruins, this poetry deals with solid, clearly defined remains, attractive, momentarily halted in their rush to obliteration. But here the palace continued to disintegrate before our very eyes. My sister wasn't much older than I was, just by enough to avoid these family outings and suggest that her friends made better company. I remained easy prey to my father's touristic appetites; I didn't complain, I didn't yet know that I had the right to complain, to protest. But he loved climbing mountains, and if that proved impossible—though mountains weren't hard to come by, an hour's ride in a run-down bus got you to the first gentle elevations, and just beyond, right after Skoczow, rose the loftier "mountains"—he would set off on extended hikes through the neighboring woods, which he ended up knowing so well that he might easily have given guided tours, and if for example Napoleon's army had blundered into

the vicinity, my father could have led it safely through the wastes
and wilderness.

•

Paul Valéry spent the First World War chiefly in Paris, although
he occasionally left for the provinces with his employer at the
time, the wealthy Monsieur Lebey; Valéry served as a kind of
secretary with ill-defined duties (he mainly spent his time preparing something along the lines of refined press briefings for
his employer). And he wrote and published his poem "La jeune
Parque," which was well received by the critics, so well that his
position as a writer changed completely from one day to the
next: he suddenly became a well-known poet. It never occurred
to him that the sufferings of war might form the subject of his
work. The thought never crossed his mind. It can't even be said
that he rejected it; it simply didn't "register," it was completely
foreign. The very act of writing "La jeune Parque" constituted a
kind of challenge to the drama of war, but only by contrast,
through the creation of pure, crystalline beauty, the work of a
free intellect. I suspect he would have been shocked to find that
later poetry might approximate historical reflection, that the pain
of history could saturate a line of verse, that a certain dry theoretician would openly question the status and sense of poetry after
Auschwitz. He would have been even more startled to learn that
the nature of Rilke's poetry could be questioned: How might
his poems have looked if he'd actually reckoned with the hor-
rors of trench warfare? The two great poets seemingly viewed
the World War simply as the next act in an age-old drama, the
eternal clash of battle, which might spare a generation or two,
but inevitably returned in full force; it was not a new, slow-acting,
and deadly poison injected into European civilization. Paris was
bombarded, the boundary between military action on the front
and the civilian population grew ever slimmer, but for all that,
the scholar's or poet's tranquil study remained worlds apart from

the trenches' muck. But Valéry did in fact write a piece called "Une conquête méthodique," which dealt precisely with a new element in history—the widespread militarization of German life. And of course just after the war, he published an even better-known essay, "La crise de l'esprit," which contained the famous phrase "Nous autres, civilisations, nous savons maintenant que nous sommes mortelles."

In other essays he traced the impact of modernity on the human mind. One splendid sentence reads, "Adieu, travaux in-finiment lents," "Farewell, infinitely slow works, cathedrals, whose endlessly slow growth lent itself astonishingly well to whatever changes and variations might occur—and which they them-selves seemed to create on high." In such essays, Valéry proved to be a remarkably astute critic of the changes that had scarred the face of European civilization, as he thought. But poetry was another matter: here he sought to prove that time could have no impact on a poem's lines, imagery, and subject.

·

I glance at the manuscript of my father's memoirs—the paper has already yellowed. If I were an archivist, a scholar, I'd be obliged to describe the object's physical appearance: all right then, the stack consists of 163 pages of yellowed, standard paper (poor quality, produced no doubt in Communist Poland, though my father was writing in 1991). The title page has been num-bered: *1*. In the upper left-hand side, the author's name, *Tadeusz Zagajewski*. The title is given below, underscored with a uniform black line: *From One Accident to the Next*. Below this comes the first chapter heading: *0. Introduction*. The zero before the head-ing indicates a form of enumeration used only in logic and the exact sciences. No humanist would put zero next to such a head-ing. The humanities don't have zero. The spirit doesn't admit zero. Homer didn't start from zero. Hofmannsthal didn't start from zero. I persuaded my father to write his memoirs, and he demonstrates in this way his distance from the endeavor, he shows that he's only a guest in a region inhabited, as he thought, only by aesthetes, where he is ill at ease. The zero at the start is also meant to mark his modesty. We're supposed to see the memoirs as virtually anonymous. *From One Accident to the Next*— that's how he saw his life, rationally, empirically, without emphasis or exaltation. In the book's opening, he retells a story our family knew extremely well, a story that demonstrates his uncommon reticence. In school he was once asked to write an essay describing the characters of Skierka and Chochlik in Juliusz Slowacki's poem "Balladyna." He wrote only one sentence: "Skierka was hardworking, and Chochlik was mean." (In the memoirs it ends "and Chochlik was lazy," but I remember only the first version.) His mother was furious; she thought her son was mocking the teacher, the school, national institutions. My father couldn't understand her rage, he saw it as an apt, witty depiction of Skierka and Chochlik. If one short sentence exhausts the topic, why write more? Why drag it out? It's the humanists who don't know when to quit. Father always viewed humanists with suspicion—although not without envy. But he was laconic, and nothing could change that. It was my grandmother's job to check how the children were doing in school, which is why she got angry and not my grandfather . . . I also came upon a piece about my father's grandmother, my great-grandmother, Maria Zborowska. Her deceased husband, Eugenius, had been a judge in Kolomyja: "We called her the big grandmother (the little grandmother was Otylia Ryckowa), she really was fairly tall, dark, always painstakingly dressed, but strong-minded, with very conservative opinions. I remember how outraged she was when our mother let my sister Maria attend a school party unchaperoned! But back then at every party you'd see rows of chairs with drowsy mothers keeping watch over their daughters."

Commentary: Otylia Ryckowa was my grandfather's aunt,

the sister of his mother, who'd died young; she and her husband, an Austrian army officer, raised him in Lvov.

And further: "Grandmother's house was beautifully decorated, with antique furniture, fine porcelain, silver cutlery, markers of apparent wealth that were actually just relics of former glories; in fact Grandmother barely made ends meet on her modest widow's pension. But holidays and birthdays were always splendid, in keeping with the old custom of 'helpings,' that is, you had to eat everything that Grandmother put on your plate. The story was that one of our uncles couldn't consume so many pieces of cake and stuck the extra pieces under the table, where they were discovered only later, while tidying up."

And again: "Our grandmother had three children, the oldest was our mother, Maria, Jadwiga (that is, our aunt Wisia) was the middle child, she was something of an original. She didn't much care for social life, but she loved reciting poetry, loudly, especially Tetmajer, playing popular tunes on the piano, and performing duets from operettas. She worked as a clerk in various offices, serving longest as a cashier in the Agricultural Bureau in Lvov. Jozef was the youngest child, a lawyer, he worked in the Lvov Office of the Treasury. He was exceptionally antisocial, self-contained, always sitting alone in his room. I remember my father would sometimes say he was afraid that I'd end up like Uncle Jozef, which turned out to be only partly true."

I'll stop quoting here; at other points my father returns to his "isolation," and to his own father's fears in this regard. His father, my grandfather, was a completely different type. Grandfather was a humanist: he would doubtless have covered pages with comments on Skierka and Chochlik. His voice boomed in the conversations and company he loved—and he wanted grandchildren. My father's love for solitude was clearly a genetic legacy from his mother. It "turned out to be only partly true . . . ," my father writes. He's thinking of what he called his great good fortune in meeting my mother, with her curiosity, her outgoing nature: once again opposite types united, as in my grandfather's marriage. Whereas Uncle Jozef was the family's famed eccentric, a homegrown Oblomov. On Sundays, when the entire family gathered for afternoon coffee, he paid no heed, stayed locked up in his room, and, if he had to use the bathroom, crept out in his pajamas only to scurry back, moments later, to the secret depths of his cave. What held his attention there? Did he just sleep all day, or did he harbor some secret passion, unbeknownst to his own relations? I'm also intrigued by the contrast between what Father calls the relics of my great-grandmother's former glories and her extremely modest material circumstances, her widow's pension. It strikes me as a classic motif in family histories: keeping up the appearance of middle-class comfort while living in poverty. Always the lovely teacups in the sideboard, the well-pressed blouses and shirts, the well-scrubbed floors . . . And the story about the pieces of cake stuck under my great-grandmother's table: Father told us about it several times, but in that version he was the one who'd done it, who'd stuck the cake to the table—I'd loved that idea of feeding the table . . . But in his memoirs he preferred to ascribe that harmless sabotage to someone else . . .

•

In Berlin, in a little cemetery in the city's heart, where Hegel and Fichte, Brecht and Helene Weigel, lie buried. Also Dietrich Bonhoeffer. So many ideas and ambitions for one graveyard. If they awoke from their eternal slumber, they'd no doubt have ferocious fallings-out. The birds sing on serenely, just as in every other cemetery, they have no clue about whose remains sleep beneath them, they don't know that great thinkers were laid to rest: Hegel, who had no biography, and Bonhoeffer, whose biography was cut short. And Bertolt Brecht, a marvelous poet and unpleasant person, enamored of ideology, whose grandfather (theoretically speaking) was Hegel. Another time in Berlin, many years ago, I set out with Wiktor Woroszylski and some other friends to track down what remained of the White Russian cemetery where Vladimir Nabokov's father was buried. We managed to find it, a sorry spot tucked under the vast viaducts of a highway crossing high overhead, under Gothic arches of concrete.

•

When I turn back to the yellowed pages of my father's memoirs, with their mathematically precise enumeration of chapters, headed by that primal zero, when I read about my great-grandmother and her apartment, designed partly to fool guests, to disguise her poverty, or at least her modest means, I try to imagine my family's life back then, before the Great War. Their Sunday-afternoon gatherings prefigured the Sunday-afternoon teas my grandfather hosted in Gliwice, though the cast had changed substantially: my great-grandmother was no longer alive, neither was my uncle Jozef, the one who'd conducted secret research in his room. A new generation had appeared, my generation, my cousins, my sister. And of course, there was my mother: for all her social ambitions, for all her assurance that she'd manage splendidly in any circle, familial or otherwise, something about her was brittle, as if she never really fit, she simply played her part; her animation masked some fear of others, of strangers. I suspect that her orations weren't born of strength, exuberance, joie de vivre. Once before the war, at Lvov University, she'd almost won a public-speaking competition for law students, defeating her male colleagues. (This was her greatest triumph; she often spoke of it, which meant that her audience—consisting exclusively of her husband and two children—tended to treat it ironically.) She'd almost won—her speech got the best response, the audience cheered, but the jurors finally decided that a woman couldn't win, and the top prize went to one of the men. But she triumphed nonetheless. People spoke only about her. No one agreed with the jury, she'd carried the day. She loved going back to that moment, our skepticism couldn't stop her (Oh, no, here comes the public-speaking contest again). Now as I watch— through the frail yellow pages of my father's memoirs—the family gathered at my grandmother's on Sunday afternoons, as I strain to hear their conversations, to catch the flies buzzing in moments of silence, as I think on the fate of my tribe, I realize, yes, of course, most of those who survived the war would number among the resettled, and the earlier Sunday gatherings would become something mythic, splendid, irrepeatable in a postwar world they saw as improvised, provisional, made only of cardboard. But I also can't escape the sense that even then, between the wars, they'd already been displaced; I don't envision them as self-assured possessors of the earth, Lvov's carefree proprietors, masters of fate, lords of life. Since there was my great-grandmother, cloaking her poverty in trappings of bourgeois perfection . . . Not to mention the crazy uncle who concealed some great secret in his room while lacking the least sense of basic decency, parading at family gatherings in his pajamas. Just like, twenty years later, our second-floor neighbor at Arkonska 3 in Gliwice, where all the residents had been resettled, except us children, and this neighbor likewise remained in his pajamas even when taking out the trash. If the weather was nice, he'd stay outside for a moment, greedily breathing the fresh air of spring or summer (he never went out otherwise, never left his second-floor apartment, why should he?)—in his case, though, so people said, this was an ideological choice, a protest against Communism, which he reportedly despised too much to put on appropriate clothing. He wouldn't get dressed for Communists . . . But what was Uncle Jozef protesting back in the twenties and thirties? Maybe he also saw his times, the interwar era, as a period of decline. Maybe he yearned for Europe, prewar Europe, the real Europe, not the one that emerged from the map after 1918?

I can't know. Maybe even back then he saw his times as make-shift, made of papier-mâché and cardboard . . . so perhaps they'd all really been resettled some 150 years ago—since some of them had once possessed smallish estates, had lived in modest manor houses with porches perched on two columns, a distant echo of Palladio's Renaissance structures, they'd held on to some scraps of land, perhaps a little forest, with hares and foxes, but then came implacable progress, meaning, for them, pau-perization hastened by failed uprisings and the subsequent confiscations, which meant that they lost everything and joined the ranks of the intelligentsia, of underpaid teachers, clerks, judges, doctors. Displaced for so long that no one could track down the beginnings. Displaced from displacement, always nostalgically looking back to the most recent incarnation of their perpetual displacement.

•

How to describe the way these two waves of reality, the world and dreams, meet, do battle, fail to reach agreement, conclude short-lived treaties that are immediately broken, how at dawn they stare at one another incomprehendingly, begin to build bridges again by evening, and then once more turn furiously upon each other, with a passion mixing love and hate, and after-ward, drift to sleep by the side of a highway leading nowhere, on an embankment where weeds grow with their heady scent.

•

I think about the displaced, about their suffering. If I were a historian, I'd conduct a study of the greatest, most tragic resettle-ment operations of our age. I'd speak, for example, of the Greeks deported from Asia Minor in 1923, the Greeks driven from Smyrna and the other cities where they'd lived for millennia. The Poles the Nazis deported from Poznan and Lodz at the Occupation's outset. The Germans deported from Königsberg,

Gdansk, Szczecin, Wroclaw, and Gliwice. But I'm not a historian, I don't spend long hours in the archives, I only write about what I've seen with my own eyes. I think about Aunt Ania, a slight old lady, so slim that the lightest breath of air might carry her away, about lonely Ania, who never made peace with her new surroundings and even now, at ninety something, remains a skeptical immigrant in her new town (new, some sixty years later!). About my father, constantly collecting—before his mind went—albums, books, and maps of Lvov. About my grandfather, how in his last years he confused the boundaries between countries and cities and thought that by some miracle he'd gone back to his Lvov . . . I think about their suffering, how they never made peace with the space of their workaday existence, its walls and trees. My father, an accomplished walker, did in fact master the outskirts of his new town, he knew the nearby forests inside out, but it sometimes seemed to me that he treated the local geography rather condescendingly—as if the true forests lay somewhere else completely (we all knew where). But I also think about how their torment, the loss they'd endured, may have been a kind of gift. If you look closely at people who've never lost anything, whose families have spent centuries in the same spot, the same village, the same town, the same house, if you watch them carefully, you'll see that they may not be so happy after all. They themselves don't notice their rootedness, to them it's self-evident, even boring. They yawn at the thought of their unparalleled stability. Such stability may be enviable, but it has no poetic merit whatsoever. Loss alone touches us deeply, permanence goes unremarked. It reminds me of that charming doctor from Israel—I met him a couple of years ago—who told everyone he met that his family had lived in Krakow for five centuries. Five centuries. Few families living in Krakow today could rival that charming doctor. But only the war's tragedies and the Holocaust meant that those five centuries held our attention—and even then only for a moment, since I noticed that the doctor's interlocutors dismissed his revelation after the first few seconds. Our attention is short-lived. Others' fates just engage us for a minute . . . our own never cease to absorb us. The displaced had lost much, but the paradox of life is such that only loss can give it meaning. An ideally untroubled life, a life guided by the calendar alone, may melt like a bit of ice placed in a child's warm hand. I remember what it's like in Tolstoy's epic novel: in times of peace, when ordinary life proceeds, governed by the seasons, harvests, rains, storms, balls, loves, aging, a generation's passing, the heroes begin, perhaps unconsciously, to yearn for war, for great purifying events (as in August 1914, when Europe, especially Germany, was seized by a short-lived euphoria when war was declared). Only when war reveals its monstrously destructive true nature do people start longing desperately for times of peace. The displaced live in times of peace but carry the war within them. Everyone else has long forgotten, but not they. The displaced—maybe not all of them—became artists, that's what it is. They didn't need to compose or paint or write, they didn't have to sign up for art institutes or conservatories, for courses in creative writing. They became artists by way of the turbulence, the mystery they bore within them. Ordinary neighbors, who'd never been deported, who'd never had to abandon family graves, family homes, native landscapes, the hills with perfect contours, pastel fields and meadows, idyllic, incomparably fragrant forests, streams in which the purest water flowed, ponds teaming with splendid carp ("The carp's just not the same these days"), just shrug their shoulders, thinking only of ordinary troubles, of health and prices. They are banality personified. The monotony of their existence bores them slightly. Although it must be admitted that finding people bored with their monotonous existence is not an easy task in Poland; you'd have to go to Canada. But the displaced are another matter, they carry secrets, they bear a loss, an abyss, a longing within them. They don't all write or paint, they don't have to, it's not required, there are no exams, no instructors (those parasites of art), but all of them are more or less possessed by their loss. They have enough to get by, their lives contain great stockpiles of meaning. Since every loss is also an opportunity. The displaced may suffer, but a certain secret order governs their lives. While gathering his books and albums about the city, my father may have envied inhabitants of the West's affluent, sated cities, people who'd never been driven from their comfortable apartments—but perhaps they should have envied him his lodestar, obsession, nostalgia, wound. They visited bookshops—if they did ever actually visit bookshops—and stopped short uncertainly, not knowing what to look for, they may have asked the salesclerks for advice, like those people who try to describe their readerly tastes to librarians: and, you know, happy endings, plenty of conversation, no gunfights . . . My father, seeking out old guidebooks and maps of the city, knew exactly what he needed. My generation had already lost this sense, I didn't suffer, I was an observer, not an emigrant. Although I'll admit, from time to time my friends do give me presents linked to the city: old engravings, maps, yet another book on our lost paradise, and it's not my place to set them straight, to explain that such things don't interest me. I'm free, though, of my father's passion, I don't have the slightest interest in accumulating Lvov artifacts: displacement isn't inherited, or perhaps it's passed on only vestigially. In childhood I observed that vast community of emigrants transplanted to Silesia, I saw the emigrants, often elderly, step cautiously on the paving stones that had so recently been German—and this undoubtedly marked me, it shaped my imagination without question, I don't intend to deny it. I watched them floundering through the post-German stage sets, moving like lunatics lost in the canyons of unfamiliar streets, and this marked me for life, I might even say it changed my life, it pierced me, it shaped me, that great, sad spectacle, that mournful parade; I might never have taken up writing if not for the unhappy exiles who didn't know if they were living in the real world or in some bizarre propaganda film shot by the Allies to demonstrate the joys of daily existence beneath the dictates of the Potsdam Treaty. If I hadn't witnessed that imbalance between people and walls, that fissure, that evident non sequitur, I might have embraced a less hazardous occupation, I might have become an engineer, as my parents wished—they viewed my future life exclusively as an exact repetition of my father's—or maybe a bank clerk, or an embittered teacher in some provincial outpost, a mediocre philosopher struggling to explain the difference between Plato and Aristotle to students who couldn't care less, who were caught up in dreams about their favorite movie or television stars. So there may be some link between what I saw as a child and what I do now, but I wasn't an exile. I'm not an exile. But I'm not settled either—it takes several generations to move from one condition to the other; there are intermediate transitional states, and I no doubt belong to one of them, to some stage without a name, it would be a shame to waste a name on it, since it's destined in any case to melt into something larger than itself . . . It's also worth noting —and I say this in spite of myself— that the settled types, who like using the word *always*, who lead their slightly dull lives beneath the sign of permanence, are the salt of the earth; they represent stability, continuity, while the displaced are only a caprice, an anomaly. But so intriguing!

•

A note from many years back: "Those fifty-year-old men who speak of the world with such fervor, competence, and conviction, as if they were its masters."

•

When reading Kafka: the world's strangeness. Whereas in some novels written much closer to our own time: the world made tame. But I still remember how much I liked the summaries preceding each chapter in old-time novels, where the author

revealed what would befall the hero over the next thirty pages or
so. We nodded off, serene in the knowledge that someone was
watching over us. Our guardian angel and a kindly old writer
with ink-stained fingers took turns by the child's bedside and
banished all demons and fears.

•

I should mention that when I was young, twenty-two or twenty-
three, a dark cloud hung over me, I might have become a typical
petty conformist. And not even out of careerism, dreams of sudden success, since I wasn't plagued by such ambitions; it was a
kind of carelessness that I still find puzzling today. And this was
partly due to poetry, strange as it sounds. On the one hand, I
was a philosopher of sorts, I'd gotten my degree; on the other,
poetry increasingly absorbed me. But my poetic side, so to speak,
had no social existence, I was rather ashamed of my writing, or
perhaps not of writing per se, those moments of writing that consumed me happily and absolutely; it was the appearance of writing, how my writing might be seen by others. I vaguely grasped
that a beginning poet was slightly comical, a cliché. We all wear
some kind of armor in society, the sturdier the better, and this
was no different in Communist times. A beginning poet doesn't
exist for others. A beginning poet has no social being, or plays a
pathetic, clownish role at best. A beginning poet stares enviously
at "patrons of the arts," "doctors," "associate professors." He
(or she) is just a chrysalis, from which some higher form of being
may yet emerge. I'd published only a few works, I lived less on
reality than hope, I often got rejections from the editors to whom
I'd sent my poems. I followed my peers' publications attentively,
and those of older poets a bit less assiduously. The older poets, I
supposed, must live on a different planet, they wouldn't understand my sufferings and dreams. Already, though, my "poeticity"
was corroding my "philosophical tendencies"—occasional bouts
of inspiration already took precedence over the studious discipline

of scholars pouncing on salutary citations in thick tomes with their sharpened pencils, I skimmed the tracts and treatises they assigned me. Once I attended a student philosophy conference in Zakopane and threw together at the last moment a chaotic paper adorned by some perfunctory reference to Marxist thought. Above all, though, the paper was simply vacant, a scandalous intellectual vacuum. But I felt justified, since I was, so I thought, a "poet" and was thus entitled to dismiss the rigors of scholarship. Fortunately, I soon abandoned such pseudophilosophy, I stopped pretending to be a "young scholar." The black cloud gradually dispersed. I think of all this, especially the talk in Zakopane, rarely and reluctantly, not without shame.

·

Stendhal in *Souvenirs d'égotisme*: "Le génie poétique est mort, mais le génie du soupçon est venu au monde" (The genius of poetry has left us, the spirit of suspicion takes its place—in my loose translation). Is it true? Yes, as to the spirit of suspicion, and it's also true that poetry and suspicion must always do battle, a vicious war in which prisoners are slain without mercy, flouting Geneva conventions. The spirit of poetry hasn't died, though; it may be weaker, it may disappear for days or weeks on end, but it hasn't abandoned us completely . . . At least that's how I see it. It may just be wishful thinking, perhaps the poets of various lands and languages are only shadows, and their festivals, fellowships, and glories are all mirages. But no. I can't think this way. The health of the spiritual world, its future life, depends on me, on us. We make decisions daily, we decide daily whether to raise the white flag of capitulation or a poem's bright tapestry.

·

I'm not displaced; but once I realized that my family tree was a tree of displacement, I also realized that the grain of unreality

I kept encountering grew from wanderings, uncertain tomorrows, from suitcases with gaping, hungry maws.

•

In December 2006, a well-known French poet paid a brief visit to Krakow; for discretion's sake we'll call him G. The Institut français asked me to participate in a discussion with their honored guest. The audience consisted of maybe fifteen people, mainly young, some of them no doubt students from the Department of Romance Languages. I asked G. about the hermeticism of recent French poetry, why it had become a kind of island on the map of world poetry. Did it set itself chiefly experimental, linguistic tasks, or, to put it differently, did French poets consider the idea that accessible poetry, dealing with recognizable "topics," constitutes only a kind of versified journalism? Some years back, I remember that another French poet, less well-known than G., told M. he couldn't help her translate my poetry, he didn't like it, it used too many dates ("Schopenhauer Cries," for example). And poetry is unconditionally timeless. But let's get back to G.'s evening in Krakow: He responded, with great conviction, that he saw things completely differently, that French poetry had many allies in its quests among American, French, and Spanish poets and was not at all an anomaly. He even invoked John Ashbery. He then turned to Polish poetry, so we'd know he took it seriously, followed it with great interest, acknowledged its worth. But one thing troubled him, he said: So many Polish poets still teeter on the brink of theology. Polish poets—of course not all of them—keep reckoning with God. He couldn't understand it. "Long ago we reached the conclusion, the basic conclusion," he said, "that God does not exist, and taking that business seriously is considered, excuse me, rather childish."

•

I was talking with a philosopher I know, and I told him about the passage in my father's memoirs where he describes the family gatherings at my great-grandmother's. The philosopher lit up at the bit about my uncle Jozef: That's fascinating, he exclaimed, your uncle Jozef, slightly insane, spending Sundays in his pajamas. I sense a deeper meaning in it, historico-psychoanalytic, so to speak. This happened in the twenties, the early thirties, right? This Jozef in his pajamas, surrounded by family members dressed normally, appropriately for the season, is like Poland under the partitions. A country that's lost its statehood, its autonomy, but hadn't completely vanished, it couldn't, it still had its inhabitants, its language, its rivers, it's like a man dressed only in pajamas surrounded by people shut tight, people in suits, frock coats, gowns. Free, sovereign nations are fully dressed, their frock coats are buttoned to the top.

•

In the monumental four-volume anthology of French poetry edited by Jerzy Lisowski and completed after his death, I find a poem whose history is somehow near to me; its author is Gilbert Lely, and the title is "Word and Cold." Gilbert Lely. Gilbert Lely was a writer linked to surrealism, known—as I read in the encyclopedia—for his erotic poems as well as for a highly regarded biography of Sade. But I know just the one poem, and that's all I'll mention here. A Polish version of this poem turned up in the anthology of French poetry, as translated by Konstanty Jelenski. I remember that Jelenski found this poem in yet another anthology, *Une anthologie de la poésie française*, published by Jean-François Revel in December 1985. The poem struck him, and he gave his translation to the Polish journal *Literary Notebooks*.

I'll give an excerpt from this—truly beautiful—poem, in which the author (speaker) visits his own grave as he strolls

through autumnal Paris. It's still empty, waiting in the cemetery
at Montmartre:

> Looking at my gravestone, with no year or name
>   etched in gold,
> A strange thought came to me; living, I have no covers,
> Persephone's recruit, momentarily on leave.
> Tomorrow I'll be bound in that Albigensian granite.
> Then I thought of my book: every sentence written
>   differently so many times,
> Since the unexpressed requires long resistance.
> And this poem's thought: less relentless than life, it
>   permits me to start yet again.

Now, reading this poem, I recall the exact location of the Montmartre cemetery, lying in wait beneath that famed Parisian
hill. Up above, buses deliver Japanese tourists, and other nation-
alities, too, who make the obligatory stop at the Moulin Rouge
cabaret. Still higher, at the very top, a crowd always gathers at
the place du Tertre, seeking some hint of a vanished atmosphere,
of an era when hungry young artists—some later became
millionaires—made their homes in this district. And now, in
the cold and quiet of white stones, smooth marble, the cemetery
waits patiently, like a spider hiding in the corner of an elegant
room. And Gilbert Lely, already old (his dates are 1904–85),
both a surrealist and a bourgeois (since only a bourgeois would
have his grave site waiting in this prime location), visits his future
and final address. Surrealist and bourgeois, not such an unlikely
combination, perhaps in fact ideal.

•

Konstanty Jelenski would himself die just a short while later, in
1987. I was visiting the United States when he died. He was
buried in a little cemetery above the Loire Valley, in the town of

Saint-Dyé-sur-Loire; in his diary Gustaw Herling-Grudzinski describes a stroll with Jelenski, who showed him his future grave site. The spot had been purchased in advance, prepared. That must have been when Konstanty discovered Lely's poem.

•

Somewhere I read a remark Schiller made about Madame de Staël: "Für das, was wir Poesie nennen, ist kein Sinn in ihr" (She had no comprehension of what we call poetry). It's intriguing. The old debate between Germany and France: Is poetry dark and mysterious? Or can it be strictly defined by way of rhetorical exercises? Can a formal definition sum it up, or does something vague, elusive always linger . . .

•

My father wrote that as a young man he "liked solitude" and that this tendency worried his parents. When I think of his life, which slowly draws to a close in unconsciousness, in the silence of a memory vanished forever, I realize that not only did he like solitude, solitude liked him, too. He had a wife, two children, he was a professor, he even joined the Solidarity movement in his later years. As a younger man, he had a group of friends who went camping several times a year in the nearby mountains. For all that, though, he was a lonely man, fragile and lonely. He was happiest in the mountains. We'd sit on a mountain meadow, with a sweeping view of other peaks, dark strips of forest, and the colorful blocks of houses in nearby villages, and he'd say nothing, just gaze in silence. And he was happy, I think, in that silence. Or perhaps not so much in the silence as in the gazing. He took in the horizon's broad circle, single trees, ashes and larches, then a valley emerged, and beyond it the gentle outlines of low mountains, with farther ridges growing ever bluer and more unreal, white strings of cirrus clouds in the sky, the occasional jet scrawling its unintelligible script across the azure. He liked late

September, early October, when fall streaked the edges of the leaves with red. He picked lofty mountain pastures, scenic spots that didn't draw crowds, and lost himself in contemplation. Although he never used the word *contemplation*, which he would have considered pretentious, an element drawn from some foreign language. As a "humanist," I might use such words; he refused. He just gazed. I suspect that in the mountains he found something that transcended daily worries and cares, the everyday choices he had to make down below. From those memoirs jotted down on yellowed paper, I know he rarely saw his life as the outcome of strong, unequivocal decisions, passions. Of course he was an engineer, a professor, he even had some success in this field, his students adored him. But in his younger days, he preferred history, and he returned to history as an old man, shutting the lid on middle age. I don't think he could have been a historian, he was too taciturn for that. But who knows, he might have achieved fame as the author of the world's shortest history books . . . He began a family—but he might not even have managed that without the active participation of his fiancée, my mother. My father describes, for example, how she turned up unexpectedly at the railroad station as he was leaving for the army; she came to say goodbye, though they hadn't planned anything in advance. And he was a good, a very good father, although he had nothing in common with those men who find total fulfillment in their family obligations, who seem to dissolve in them, like sugar in tea. He'd lost the city of his youth, and in some sense that formed the realest event of his biography. And even that grew partly from an "accident," a historical chain of coincidences, but it became a painful fact, unarguable, hard as petrified lava. He rarely spoke of it, since he couldn't tolerate effusions. He always loved mountains, he needed them; with his typical, literal-minded empiricism, he couldn't rise above life's troublesome ambiguity otherwise. We'd sit together for a long while in silence until he'd glance at his watch and say it was time to move on. He kept quiet, he liked keeping quiet, and that's why I'll never quite know who he was.

•

I spent a few days in Bologna last year along with the artists and gallery owners who'd come for the Arte Fiera, that great fair of contemporary art. Once I stopped by the local museum (Pinacoteca Nazionale), which holds Raphael's *Ecstasy of Saint Cecilia* along with a number of paintings by Guido Reni and Annibale Carracci, Caravaggio's onetime rival. It was a dark afternoon, the end of January. I have to say that I didn't share Cecilia's ecstasy; neither Reni nor Carracci belongs to my private pantheon. For all that, though, the old masters' gleaming canvases put me into a rather ecstatic frame of mind—I felt good in that museum with so few visitors (one of those small galleries where you sense a certain impatience in late afternoons among staff members anxious to get home to their families). Several small Renaissance paintings spoke to me, perhaps a few drawings, some fragments of sculptures, a whiff of times long past. At one point I found myself next to a window, and next to a whole series of windows. A window in a museum or gallery is always a great attraction— and likewise a threat to the art, since sometimes what's glimpsed through the window draws you more than the paintings and sculptures. But I couldn't resist a glance at the world. The museum window looked out on ordinary apartment houses across a narrow street. Museum buildings don't often keep company with people's houses; usually their windows open onto parks or gardens, onto open space, broad streets, panoramic cityscapes (to avoid temptation . . .). But it was different here. It was completely dark, and rooms' lighted interiors glowed alongside the museum. More than this—it was easy to trace the apartment dwellers' lives. Shutters remained unclosed, the time of shameful late-night mysteries had not yet come, Bologna's citizens readily displayed their late-afternoon and early-evening activities to passersby. In some kitchens they were making dinner. One person rinsed lettuce, another sliced onions. An old man shuffled around a large, peculiarly dark blue kitchen, like a priest in an empty chapel. On another floor, a young woman fed a baby. In yet another apartment, an enormous television screen displayed bright, living spots leaping nervously, as if in a film recording the transformations of exotic butterflies (the television was too distant for me to decode the meaning of these colored spots). An ordinary winter afternoon. The ill-defined moment between getting home from work and the evening meal. Between the dog and the wolf, as the French say. But I stood in a spot where the smells didn't, couldn't carry, in the gallery's aseptic space. And a sentence came to me: "They're just living." They're just living. I felt an enormous advantage over them, since they were just living. For a moment I felt more solidarity with the shining canvases, embalmed in artificial immortality, than with the people living on the opposite side of the narrow street.

•

For a moment I identified with the heroes of the shining canvases. For a moment only, it couldn't last, since I knew that any minute now I'd grow hungry, too, and begin to think about dinner, I'd return obediently to the ranks of ordinary humanity, return to smells and tastes, to measuring time by way of the rhythmic awakening of stomach juices. For a few minutes, though, I couldn't comprehend the ordinary eaters of bread, for a few moments I took the side of the two-dimensional people depicted by painters, people dead for centuries, still possessing faces—one of humanity's chief attributes, after all—but long since looking down on ordinary human fare with contempt. I liked that little eternity, I wanted to take part in it, in the pride of ideal beings. So perhaps Saint Cecilia's ecstasy had infected me after all. But it didn't last long, no, it couldn't last for long, soon I humbly rejoined my hungry, living brethren as we sat down to dinner.

•

"They're just living." I am, too. I live with them, and I'll die with them.

•

We don't know our parents well, we can't see them objectively (whatever that means) or critically. Which is to say, we may see them critically, very critically, but then we see not them so much as ourselves. At first they're our gods, but afterward we slowly, systematically come to resemble Feuerbach, we turn into agnostics or atheists. My father was rather shy, blessed with a marvelous sense of humor and a strong "sense of irony." For as long as I knew him, his mental powers were directed chiefly toward one encompassing end. Since at a certain moment, my father's calling, his life's mission, became comforting my mother, the constant, permanent, daily creation of an optimistic vision of events, a lens designed to neutralize her deep, deepest pessimism, her fear. I didn't know, I couldn't know, if my mother's anxiety derived from her earliest childhood—as more experienced psychologists would certainly say—or if it first arose in the dreadful period of war and occupation. I do know that my father was up to his task even at the darkest moment, one of the hardest moments in their life, right at the start of military operations. It's just air force exercises, he said, when bombs began to burst everywhere on September 1, 1939. My parents were living in Warsaw then, in the Saska Kepa district, and they were awakened by exploding bombs. Luftwaffe planes were bombarding Warsaw. Not at all, Ludka, don't worry, it's just exercises, nothing to upset us, calm down, it's just maneuvers, there won't be a war—these were my father's historic words, by which he granted his wife, my mother, an extra fifteen minutes of peace. He prolonged the interwar era by a quarter of an hour especially for her.

Then they tried to get to Lvov, they traveled for ages by train, and the train was bombed, too, so they'd run to the fields and lie down in them, in the furrows of autumn fields, listening to the Stuka's swelling wail as it swooped down with a bomb readied for them and potentially for me, too. My father's rhetoric must have undergone a dramatic shift then, he couldn't keep insisting that they were only exercises. Lying in a field in that September of 1939, dry, sunny, and lovely, he couldn't continue that masquerade with impunity, he couldn't behave like those academic philosophers who ignore their neighbors' suffering, there must have been a break in the discussion, deliberations were suspended for a while; it was a time, I think, when words didn't count for much, what mattered was dust and nettles and milk in a clay jug. And that the bomb should explode a hundred meters away. But then, after that pause, when they finally made it to Lvov and, having lost everything in Warsaw, went to live with my grandparents, I'm sure that my father returned instantly to his duties as a systematic beautifier of reality.

All signs suggested that my delicate mother was better suited to life in one of the quieter Swiss cantons than to the compulsive, accelerated course of recent history in our part of Europe; she couldn't bear the sight of the world she was forced to inhabit, she couldn't bear the sight first of Soviet uniforms, then German, and then Soviet again. She couldn't get used to the poverty of occupied and postwar Poland. And in occupied Lvov she saw things that no one should ever see; she couldn't forget the trucks carrying Jews to their execution. I don't know how my father shielded my mother then, what he said at those moments, how he lied; I didn't exist yet. I do know that—some time later—she cried while walking Gliwice's ugly streets after they arrived from baroque Lvov, which they both loved, in spite of the war and the

Occupation, and all the crimes and tragedies that must have scarred that lovely city. And my father needed to intercede again, he had to stand guard, play the eternal optimist who always calmed her as he had in Warsaw in September 1939; it's just exercises, flight maneuvers . . . don't be frightened. New topics appeared in Silesia, new opportunities to comfort and cheer my mother: we'll go back to Lvov any day now, don't worry, he'd say. And when the regime suddenly ordered an exchange of currencies, everyone lost money, including my parents, who lost the royalties my father had just received for a textbook he'd written— these royalties provided the only surplus in their exceedingly modest income—my father undoubtedly found some argument to shield her from the blow. But every day—I remember this distinctly—when he came back from the Polytechnic Institute in the afternoon, he'd bring in the local paper, settle into his armchair, and pore over that rag before lunch. I wondered why he wasted so much time on the one party's regional organ, a paper that mainly lied in the dry, ugly jargon of totalitarian states. I realized only later that this had nothing to do with ordinary paper-reading, with interest in the latest news; it was a demonstration intended for my mother, a magical routine. My father aimed to prove that this black-and-red newspaper could be mastered, its threat could be neutralized. By spreading its vast pages, the great black-and-red wings of the Prussian eagle—one wing displayed grim headlines of the day's political vendettas, while the other held soccer scores—my father symbolically killed the paper, he slayed the dragon, disarmed the mine; he showed my mother that nothing had happened, there's no bad news today, no currency exchange, no interrogations, no transports, no new war, no next resettlement, we won't have to leave this apartment, this city, everything will be fine, everything will turn out, the lunch will be splendid, the children are well, spring is near . . . He sang a sort of lullaby for her, sang without singing, without even moving his lips: Don't worry, I'll take care of it, the newspaper can't hurt you, look, I've got the upper hand. Everything will be fine, he sang (in silence of course), everything will be fine, don't be upset.

•

Two days in Berlin in July, a public conversation on how aging affects writing. I was set to appear with Antjie Krog, a poet from South Africa, and Johannes Kühn, a German poet. We were invited by the editor of *Sinn und Form*, Sebastian Kleinschmidt, my friend and a splendid essayist. I was surprised at first that he asked me to take part in a conversation on this subject— but then I recalled, with some distress, that I'd reached an age that gives you the right to answer such questions. I took the position that aging, for those who perform mental, spiritual labor— or perhaps simply for everyone—is like a duel, immensely difficult and inevitably lost, between the fading body and the spirit, which sometimes remains undiminished or becomes even stronger, or maybe even—at moments—is intoxicated by the thought of its increasing solitude. Abandoned by its faithful companion, the body, it grows ever lonelier, like those courageous soldiers in war films who single-handedly protect their squad's retreat, even at the price of death. The duel is always lost, yes, but the fight may be thrilling, inspiring, it may yield moments of true exaltation (in the beautiful, non-ironic sense of that word). Sometimes we happen to see, in reality or in some documentary, an old artist or poet, who walks with difficulty, but whose eyes still shine with spiritual presence, and this seems to be something magnificent, the frail body and in it, over it, right beside it, a little flame of fearless pride, the light of endless questing, wisdom, a challenge cast to sickness, weakness, age. Doomed to defeat, yes, since one day the light will die. Though we don't know even that, we can't know, another light may flare up then. We can't know, but we live with that hope. I argued quite eloquently, I thought. When I got back home to Krakow, though, I looked in the dictionary and realized that in German *duel* is *das Duell*, not *der Duell*, but I'd kept saying *der Duell* ... Over and over ... I'd used all the wrong forms. I'd suspected that I might make mistakes, I'd been anxious. Had my arguments survived my grammatical blunder? My fellow discussants tactfully (too tactfully?) ignored my error. From now on I'll remember: *das Duell*, not *der*. And I'm still dwelling on this mistake, I've given it a whole paragraph: it just goes to show that I still lack the wisdom I see in the eyes of some old men and women, I'm not even close ...

•

My mother required my father's unceasing labors to shield her from misfortune, the world's terrors. But one time—this happened before I was born—their roles were reversed, my mother protected my father. It was an unusual event: during the first Soviet occupation of Lvov, when the powers back then were hunting down so-called escapees, that is to say, fugitives, that is, people fleeing Hitler's invading forces in central Poland, who were, as a result, "unregistered" in Lvov. Mandatory "registration" formed the cornerstone of Communist policy vis-à-vis populations. Anyone remaining "unregistered" was not a full person. Hence the "unregistered" were, if discovered, subject to automatic deportation to Siberia or Kazakhstan; few ever returned. Since my parents arrived in Lvov after fleeing Warsaw, they were technically "escapees," condemned to deportation. They finally got "registered" in Lvov, and shortly afterward two Soviet soldiers, undoubtedly linked to the NKVD, the Soviet secret police, turned up one evening at my grandfather's house on Piaskowa Street. They had an order to arrest only one person, my father. Why only one, we don't know. I found my father's hypothesis in his memoirs: a few days earlier my mother had been chatting with a couple of Soviet emissaries at the gate, and, so my father writes, they must have taken a liking to her, she made an impression. Possibly—only if such low-ranking officials could make such decisions—they wanted to sentence my father (who was not yet my father) to deportation so that they could seek my mother's favors afterward. In any case two Soviet soldiers (not the ones who had been chatting by the gate) came in the evening to take my father. Then my mother played the greatest scene of her life. She wouldn't let them take him. She produced a document showing that he wasn't a fugitive, an "escapee," and declared unequivocally that he wasn't going anywhere, they had no right to take him and that was that. They had no right. Forbidden. End of discussion. At first they yelled, it's impossible, they've got orders, they can't change them, but finally they left empty-handed. My mother scared them off. And they didn't come back for my father, who wasn't yet my father, in the days that followed. It must have been the only such incident in the forties . . . Ordinarily frightened of everything, this time my mother was magnificent. My father, whose job it was to shield her from the world's ugliness, was saved by my mother.

•

A brilliant, if minor, invention: while listening to our CDs, we can push a little button called *random* or *shuffle*, that is, the button of chance. We're seated in our armchairs, holding the remote, a device designed to facilitate our laziness, but which also aids those inclined to contemplation, and we become demiurges possessing power over matter, over art, we push the button called chance and a masterfully ordered work of art turns to rubble. Everything changes. Venerable symphonies begin dancing to a different beat. Bach, great, pious Bach, who sings his cantatas by way of patterns and models that musicologists dissect in learned studies, suddenly shifts direction, grows younger, amazes us. The adagio doesn't have to wait its turn, it can open a symphony, a string quartet, a sonata—the poor adagio, always, almost always second in line, like a poor country cousin, the adagio, forever yielding pride of place to the energetic allegro vivace, the adagio, doomed to the proofreader's role in musical history, finally wins first prize, thanks to the button of chance.

•

In my father's memoirs I find another episode, tragic, from the time of the German occupation. Once, while my parents were still living at the family house on Piaskowa Street (they lost it shortly afterward, just when the resettlement of Lvov's Jewish population had begun), an acquaintance of my parents', a Jewish woman, came to ask if my parents could hide her and her child. My parents said it wasn't possible, they couldn't trust their neighbors. To reach their house you had to pass through a narrow corridor of sorts, with a fence and green belt on one side and another small house on the other. And these neighbors, whose eyes you sensed while passing their windows, were the ones my parents couldn't trust. They mistrusted their neighbors, who kept watch over everything, whose house was the neighborhood Gibraltar. I can only imagine how difficult this must have been for my parents. And I think, too, of the fate of the woman who sought their help. But the neighbors really couldn't be trusted; the next day the Gestapo turned up at the house on Piaskowa Street, looking for Jews.

•

Too late. Sometimes I wonder—and it's not simply a symptom of my conservatism, my opinions, but a genuine worry—if I wasn't born too late. With my passions, my predilections, with the strange sense of mission that visits me, luckily, quite infrequently, with the doubts that visit me daily, isn't it too late? Does the world of thought still exist as it once did, the world of warring ideas, heated polemics, positions, convictions, writers who show no mercy to their intellectual opponents, but who reach for ink, not firearms, in the heat of battle? We're told that in virtually every arena there comes a moment defined by the preface *post*. Mass culture, with its phenomenal indifference to fundamental questions, produces those journalists who have taken the place of critics and essayists, journalists employed by the newspapers (though "paper" newspapers will soon vanish, along with their phlegmatic authors) to write about new books, concerts, and exhibits; and they must be given a special supplement for withholding their own opinions (if they've got them), their feelings, their antipathies, their passions, their criteria. You get the sense that they're paid not to go beyond a basic summary of the book, a blunt description of the concert, a bare-bones account of the exhibit. Is it too late to make a suggestion, to propose that we try over the years to express the thing that seems, in our moments of melancholy, a mere pipe dream, to do battle with ourselves, make mistakes (I've made lots of them here), misstep, exaggerate, write poems, sometimes weak ones (plenty of those, too), sometimes failures, to arrange our life around this passion? Will someone respond to us, however feebly, apart from those kind readers who sometimes show up at our poetry readings to provide support and occasionally confide that some word of ours helped them in a dark moment? But their comments, moving, sincere, remain in the private, amateur sphere, they change nothing in the official world, where such admissions go unheeded, are dismissed, mocked as mere "gush." Too late? But I know that I'm not alone, I'm tied in many ways to unknown friends (or perhaps foes) working in all kinds of disciplines. I come across such people particularly in the United States, poets, but also musicians and philosophers, and though we don't always get the chance really to talk— sometimes we're passing by in time, in space—still I remember their existence. It's worse in Europe, which seems rather disaffected, caught up in various intriguing political projects intended, inter alia, to mask listlessness, fatigue. So it's too late? No, absolutely not. Not so long as we live, as a certain sentimental hymn runs.

•

"In the duel with the world you should always take the world's part." At first I resisted this aphorism. Yet another case of Kafka's masochism, I thought. More precisely, I mocked, yes, I see now how you turn against yourself. It's easier to write it than to do it. Later I understood, though, that Kafka's idea could be interpreted in various ways. For example, "take the world's part" could mean that we shouldn't be governed by our impulses, whims, which are—may be—blind, arbitrary, short-lived, childish, frivolous. The task is rather to understand what the world is, how it's structured, what it expects of us, what it might offer. Only then, when we've learned to recognize, however imperfectly, the world's nature—it is blind and deaf, mindless and cruel, or rather it can be cruel, of course, but it also emits a splendid spark from time to time—can we begin to act, new initiates into the world's secrets. Only then do we start imperceptibly to take our own part. We may also come to understand that there is in fact no conflict between world and us, we're made of the same substance, the same cosmic dust.

Moments of joy; but also the danger produced by a false poem, by what the English language calls *cant* ("insincere and sanctimonious speech, chiefly moral, religious or political in nature," the dictionary informs us), that is, duplicitous rhetoric, a kind of propaganda. Cant may turn up in poetry, and Polish priests rely on it all too frequently in their preaching.

•

Listening to Bach, Mozart, Shostakovich, Lutoslawski—does it really take courage? Cioran felt otherwise, Bach gave him courage, Bach made this radical skeptic believe in God momentarily. But a different phenomenon grows stronger with every passing year: anyone who admits to listening to "classical music" (in quotes, since neither "serious" nor "classical" music quite fits) runs

the risk of being called a snob, of setting himself above the rest.
A strange accusation: How do you set yourself above others by
way of something they don't even acknowledge? Many of my
friends prefer the easier music that could once be called "young,"
but not anymore, it's gotten fairly mature, now that old men such
as the Rolling Stones have decided to die onstage, swaying like
their guitars, now charged by nuclear power plants. Sometimes
you hear: classical music is so far removed from life . . . But
where is life if not in this music, which links inner rhythm, the
soul's rhythm, to the voices of the outside world? In *The Demons*
Heimito von Doderer says of one character, "It seemed to him,
that he now knew what reality is, and its measure must always
fluctuate, the degree of adaptation between the Internal and the
External." This degree of adaptation, the eternal dissonance
between inside and out, the soul's romance with the world, this
ceaseless, fertile mésalliance is measured in music and poetry;
music and poetry study the proportions in which the Internal
and the External mix. The phenomenal popularity of what was
until recently called youth music derives partly from the weakness
of serious contemporary music. Rock music unquestionably trans-
mits a powerfully ecstatic, Dionysian charge. But the young
Nietzsche—far more trustworthy than the half-mad author of
Ecce Homo—tells us in *The Birth of Tragedy* that the Dionysian
element in art is in perpetual dialogue with the Apollonian. And
in rock music the eternal conversation of Apollo and Dionysus,
the splendid dialogue of passion and moderation, feeling and
form, grows silent, we hear only the wail of an Asiatic deity in
tight jeans (along with the little bell that signals growing profits,
dollars flowing into the cash register).

•

I hear a polemical voice: So we're listening to some Asiatic deity
in tight jeans? But rock music is ecstatic on some level, however
low; it reveals Dionysus's presence in our world. But primitive?

Do you really think that the ancient, original Dionysus of distant legends, that newcomer from Asia, dealt only with an infinitely refined range of sounds? That, dressed in a suit, shirt, and bright tie, he attended the conservatory, took courses on composition, studied with Nadia Boulanger, showed some interest in dodecaphony, and pored over Adorno's letters by night? I'm afraid not; what speaks in you is simply the thin-skinned snobbishness of an intellectual who doesn't really understand art, who can't accept its explosive, archaic passions, art is a volcano on which your type tries to plant fine intentions, a moral summons, and can't come to grips with its wild flights. Such people say: Humanism, progress, morality, and art doesn't argue, it's indifferent to whatever labels, however noble, they attach—a galloping colt could care less about the name the sire's owner gives him. Of course the music is primitive, it holds no surprises, it doesn't "renew the language of music," it doesn't strike experts with its subtle structures. All that is true enough, but what do you expect from Dionysus?

•

The two-volume correspondence of Rilke and Nanny Wunderly-Volkart, the wealthy, influential wife of a Swiss industrialist—it's some of my favorite reading. Only the poet's letters are included, since his correspondent decided that her answers didn't merit publication. The name Angela Guttman often figures in these letters. Who was Angela Guttman? In brief, she was one of the poet's protégées. It's often said of Rilke, rather maliciously, that he had a knack for acquiring patrons among the rich; and there's some truth in it. But it's easy to forget that in the long chain that links human conditions from high to low, from emperors to beggars, great corporate executives to the newly homeless, Rilke shows up somewhere in the middle. The author of the *Duino Elegies* helped others in his turn, took them up, supported them, brought them to the attention of his own patrons. Angela

Guttman was one such person. Everything we know about her we glean from Rilke's letters. So who was she? She seems to have been a woman with an unusually ardent inner life, and at the same time a writer who couldn't get publishers interested in her work. You'd guess from the letters that there was no love affair this time, that Rilke was simply taken with her personally. But you'd be wrong, the biographers inform us that there was an affair, most likely brief, which quickly became a friendship, protective on the poet's part.

Angela Guttman must have possessed, as I've said, enormous inner strength. Rilke often mentions her in his letters to Mme Wunderly-Volkart, he tries to direct this benevolent lady's attention to his exceptional friend, who lacked all means of support. But Rilke didn't just feel sympathy; he admired Angela, he sympathized with her personal and financial difficulties, but he admired the strength of her personality. Something he said in one of the letters particularly struck me. He says that Angela lives constantly, permanently *im Geiste* (in the spirit). That is, she remains in an unrelieved state of great spiritual tension. He adds, "Das ich noch nie, außer für Momente, erreicht habe" (it happens to me only at certain moments). So the great poet envies an unknown woman, ignored by her contemporaries, unremarked in the cultural history of her century. And what does he envy? Her unceasing life *im Geiste*, in the spirit, in ardor. But it was not Angela Guttman who wrote the *Duino Elegies*. So who was she? She must have been an ecstatic, otherworldly individual—and highly intelligent, too, since she impressed Rilke. Can we draw any bold conclusions from this, make any far-reaching observations? Probably not. But something about this unlikely juxtaposition of a great artist and a virtual unknown is compelling. So perhaps I might risk the following reflection: It may not be such a good idea to dwell always, exclusively, in "the spirit," in a state of unvarying exaltation, rapture, with no experience of emptiness, melancholy, even despair. Living in the spirit

only now and then is doubtless difficult, distressing, restless—
but it may also be more creative. You enter "the spirit" only briefly,
but with the passion, the joy, the energy, that accompany any
meeting after a long absence, a prolonged separation. And you
depart immediately after, not without sorrow, regret, perhaps
even with the mistaken, mostly mistaken, impression that you'll
never return, the spirit's flame has been dowsed forever. This
would mean that less is more, that retrieving "the spirit" only
every so often—for all the momentary pain of parting—is
more fruitful than taking up permanent residence in rapture,
since the person living in a palace is less likely to admire and
describe it than the modest visitor, well-worn suitcase in hand,
to whom the master grants a brief stay before sending him on
his way. That way may lead to the next palace—but not immediately, he must cover a long, gray, dusty road before catching
sight of the next splendid edifice, whose master will once more
open the gates for our traveler. And each time he leaves one of
these wondrous dwellings, he misses it, and in his longing he
sees once again, more clearly, what precisely he has lost. And
he'll live in that longing, which seems to be the form best suited
to our existence.

•

"We don't expect that from Dionysus." It reminds me of a certain
micro-event that happened to me twice, almost identically, in
Western Europe, once in Paris and once in Holland. Someone
came up to me after a reading—I don't remember the name or
even the face, just the overall sense—and said, "We expect something different from you Eastern European poets than from our
muted artists; we want strength, energy, inspiration, we've got
irony to spare, enormous stockpiles of irony, from you we need
enthusiasm, faith . . ."

•

A dream I had a while back just came to me. The dream gave a single direction: Write about delicate people. Nothing else. No principles, no ideologies. Just that message: Write about delicate people. I thought about my aunt Ania, her life. About so many others who existed lightly, who never took first place in the contest of life.

•

But we shouldn't get carried away about Dionysus, or rather, about the Asian deity's similarity to those men in leather shirts clasping electric guitars, with their agents and bulging bank accounts. A wild god and those masters of life and drugs, who cling to their golden microphones for decades while making wise investments—the comparison can only go so far. Dionysus may not have studied with Nadia Boulanger, but he never did business with Wall Street either.

•

A few days ago in Gliwice: a reading in the cultural center of the Silesian Polytechnic Institute, a June evening, chilly but sunny, and long, endless . . . The center is housed in a villa on a park's edge, in a green space that also hosts multitudes of singing black-birds. The black, poisoned river, the Klodnica, that runs along-side is, astonishingly enough, surrounded in summer by lush greenery, as though the poisons it bears not only hadn't harmed the plants and trees, but actually served as potent narcotics, nour-ishing foodstuffs for lindens and alders. Walks along this black river played a major part in my childhood, and I still remember this contrast between the dead water and the thriving, triumphant weeds that flaunted their rude health along its banks. My grandfather, a retired teacher, often took me on these walks—but does a teacher ever forget his pedagogical drive, can he truly retire? My grandfather often taught me, lectured me, even here, along the pitch-black river. I recall him once using his cane, with its tip capped in protective metal, to pull one plant out of a thick clump of weeds, a seemingly ordinary plant in no way distinguished from its vulgar neighbors; he said, Did you know that this is hemlock (or poisonous water hemlock, as the botanical dictionary notes pedantically), and did you know that Socrates died by drinking an extract made of this, of hemlock? And do you know who Socrates was, and why he was forced to drink this? Then he told me about Socrates, about his trial, about why he didn't defend himself, he could easily have fled, but he refused, and my grandfather told me about Socrates's death, and his last wish, to sacrifice a rooster to Asclepius. Because of this, the black river always reminds me of Socrates, his trial, and his brave parting with this world. And since that time I've never ceased to be astonished that such an ordinary spot, an embankment along a black river, poisoned by Silesian industry, could yield hemlock, a plant of Greece, of antiquity, of legend, which killed noble Socrates, to be sure; still, some of his nobility took root, paradoxically, in the hemlock itself, a weed among other weeds.

·

I knew in advance that it wouldn't be an ordinary evening. I was a little nervous. I didn't fear attacks, hostility; I'm not a troublemaker, after all. If anything worried me, it was emotion, sentimentality. My own emotion. My own sentiments. The audience wasn't large, but it wasn't particularly small either. It was neither too young, nor too old. I understood immediately that this audience was, in some sense, nearly ideal. It was my audience. Maybe even too ideal. As I read poems featuring the names of certain individuals, no longer living, who'd once been connected with the institute, I would ask, Do you remember Professor Romer? The answer: Yes, of course. I'd look at their faces. And Professor Mazonski and his wife? Yes, of course. I knew then, I guessed, that they knew my parents, not firsthand, they certainly weren't

among my parents' acquaintances, I would have known, but they
were part of the same community, the community of the resettled, transported to Silesia after the war. Yes, this was my audience, my ideal public, at least for the poems tied most closely to
my childhood. I was touched. In fact I knew almost no one in
the hall (not counting three former schoolmates who'd greeted
me at the outset), but actually I knew them all. And they knew
me without knowing me. The reading went on for a while, it was
still light outside, a blackbird's melancholy song drifted through
the open window now and then. At the close, as per the protocol
of such events, I asked for questions. There weren't many, and
they weren't as interesting as I might have guessed, given the
audience's close attention. But that's how it usually is. The questions were bland, they failed to convey the tension I'd sensed
throughout the evening. And then I remembered yet again why
I'd had to leave this city. This city, which lives for the institute,
for calculations, chemistry, physics, mechanics, for constructing
bridges and viaducts, planning catwalks through coal mines, for
the graphs and technical drawings once plotted on purple carbon paper, and now on purple computer screens, couldn't speak.
All the more because earlier, before the war's end, it had spoken
German, and then, after a brief Russian interlude, that is, after
the Red Army's occupation, it was forced to switch to Polish. It
was forced to change everything, grammar and vocabulary,
it had to tackle a Slavic language, capricious, sometimes soft,
sometimes strangely unyielding, and this was difficult. Painstaking and painful. The city was no longer young, and learning
languages, as we know, comes easily only to the young. It was
mute. It was a good, decent city, full of decent people—not all of
them, to be sure—regardless of whether they were displaced,
resettled, like my entire family, or locals, indigenous. Over the
years these two groups had intermingled, intermarried, yielded
children, grandchildren, who no longer knew if they were resettled or locals. But it couldn't speak. And even back then, when I

was a student at the local high school, the Rymer School on Gornych Walow Street, I yearned uncertainly for this. I wanted to speak. In my silent city, in my silent family, in my good, kind, taciturn family, where good conduct, decency to others, counted, but speaking didn't, in my family, which firmly believed that those who speak reveal their weakness, turn into blowhards unworthy of ethical recognition, since you should simply hold your tongue and help others, in spite of all the aspirations of my tribe, I wanted to learn to speak. I have no idea where this desire originated. That's why—so I realized back then—I had to leave for Krakow, a city of expression, or at least a city, so I thought, that invited expression, embodied expression, that spoke through the facades of its old houses, even trumpeted from the tower of St. Mary's Basilica. I wanted to flee a mute city for a city that talked, that spoke through its poets, its university, its theaters and concerts, even its palaces and homes. I wanted to choose speech, but I kept something nonetheless of my Catholic family's taciturnity—which was, I suspected, not entirely free of Protestant influences derived from the German side of the family. I shared their mistrust of easy, unregulated speech, unmotivated, shapeless. And a mistrust of oratory, in which music prevails over sense, the intelligence of words. As a student, I often took the train from Gliwice to Krakow, and I remember jotting down in my black notebook an aphorism that filled me with pride for a week: "Orators commit suicide shooting themselves in the mouth." The sentence doesn't particularly impress me now . . . But perhaps I mistrusted speaking generally. Perhaps in my heart I remained a faithful son of my tongue-tied city, a city of technicians, engineers who smile skeptically at the great torrents of humanistic eloquence. Perhaps without even noticing that those torrents, those streams, have gone dry.

•

Vladimir Jakelevitch on music: "Music shows us that the essence of being is ungraspable, unnameable; it confirms our sense that what is most important in the world cannot be articulated . . ." And further: "It's always the case: the moment a concert ends, the hall fills with feverish chatter. Isn't that the public's way of avenging itself on the music that sentenced them to two hours of silence? The pent-up words burst from every larynx like mountain streams. The bow work in the violin section is dissected, the pianist's slightest gesture is discussed, the soprano's sharp notes come under attack . . . Such analyses serve chiefly to free us from the music's magic, to which we refuse to submit; they also help to undermine the primordial stratum of innocence that leaves us open to enchantment. These are among the methods that our dreadful intellectual sobriety and pedantry employ to take vengeance on stillness and silence."

Splendid words. Since what moves us most deeply in music can't be caught, cornered in words—unless of course we resort to that wonderful French trick and talk of some je ne sais quoi, before happily returning home, convinced in spite of everything that we've managed to pin down music's essence. What I like most in Jakelevitch's essay: the comment about "the primordial stratum of innocence that leaves us open to enchantment." A marvelous formulation. That innocence reaches us more easily when we're alone, listening to music or reading poetry in our own room, and we admit this innocence, for a brief while we achieve pure receptivity. But a concert, with its double nature, the impossible contradiction between innocent attention, the innocent opening of ourselves to something greater, and, on the other hand, the temptation to irony, to jokes, to the mockery that marks any large gathering—it wounds the very substance of the music. Yet concerts are a time-honored tradition, they're an institution that may undergo the occasional crisis but shows no sign of making way for some other, still undiscovered means of communing with music. Perhaps this contradiction between innocence and irony underwrites the institution's success; innocence can't exist in the world in its pure state, it must hide itself inside a carapace of wit, it must experience some corruption, however slight, if it is to survive. Just as some peoples believe that food should be wrapped in nettles to preserve its freshness.

•

George Seferis admits in his diary that he had trouble accepting Cavafy's work, even though outside observers saw him as continuing the work of the great Alexandrian in key ways. Seferis viewed him as a prosaic, sober poet, perhaps even too sober. In the end, though, he yields to the charm of the Alexandrian recluse, acknowledges him as his master. Cavafy's poetry is both extraordinary and troublesome. If great poetry consists chiefly of two strata, one earthbound, sober, and the other, distressingly different, inspired, even ethereal, eluding definition, then the empirical, earthbound element prevails emphatically in Cavafy. He is the Balzac of modern Greek poetry. Like a good novel, his work holds countless intrigues, powerful passions alongside ruses and stratagems. Cavafy's reader leaves his poems feeling that everything has already happened; it's a poetry of the past perfect, in the love poems and historical poems alike. His work, as we know, is usually divided into two: there are the poems that take as their subjects figures, sometimes fictitious, from the Hellenistic and Byzantine eras, and there are the erotic, homoerotic poems, whose heroes are young men, anonymous inhabitants, like the poet, of modern Alexandria. These heroes exist completely outside of history, in the capricious space of the city's seedier districts. Such wisdom here! Chiefly the wisdom that comes from defeat. You could read Cavafy's poetry as a splendid treatise on failure, a discourse on disaster. The Alexandrian poet found a positive side, even a kind of comfort, a sweetness, in defeat. Vanquished peoples tower over their vulgar conquerors intellectually—or so they like to think. Humiliated time and again by

their invaders, Poles in the Russian Partition found relief in thinking, speaking, and writing about Russians from a position of supe-
riority; not an admirable trait, but the psychology behind it is clear
enough. Cavafy's poems often present the stages of Rome's con-
quest of Hellenistic cities and kingdoms, frail states unable to resist a young, expansive empire. But these frail cities and kingdoms
produced refined philosophers and poets, gifted with sensitivity
and erudition. The Romans possessed great, valiant legions and
splendid swords, but they had to learn refinement from the
Greeks, and they knew it. And the Greeks knew it, too. Well
then, in such a case defeat may be accepted with shoulders slightly
shrugged: the vulgar conqueror will have to take lessons from
me . . . He'll learn to read Greek, since Latin literature is still in its
infancy, it relies on borrowings from Greek authors. Young intellectuals flocked to Athens just as—even now—they head off for
Paris. Cavafy achieves an unusual feat: he shows that being con-
quered is better than conquering. He spoils the victors' pleasure,
ruins their mood. The peace that comes from accepting defeat
philosophically is far more dignified than frenzied triumphs . . .
Please note, though, that Cavafy doesn't have a single poem
about Greece's greatest defeat, the Ottoman captivity, the fall
of Constantinople that precipitated four hundred years of Turkish occupation, oppressive, gray, hopeless, historyless, dividing
Greece from living European history even more completely than
the Partitions did in my own country. Almost four hundred
years of darkness—though the Mediterranean sun kept shining,
dolphins continued to frolic in the sea, and the olive trees refused to relinquish their hardworking ways. But not one poem
on this subject from the Alexandrian's pen. Cavafy was a poet
of defeat; he discovered many shades of pleasurable melancholy
in painting the psychology of failure and the relativization of
loss. But he lacked the courage, or perhaps the imagination, the
heroism, to describe the sorrow of four mute centuries under

the sultans' rule. Poetic alchemy clearly isn't omnipotent . . . It shrinks from certain substances, from complete humiliation.

•

I wanted to leave "the mute city," I wanted to speak. That's how I naively saw it—all I had to do was move to another city and I'd start speaking. Maybe I thought that I had to reverse the curse of resettlement that marked my family. But what did I want to say? Did I know? Do I know now? When I was young, I thought I knew. It's increasingly difficult for me to come up with a "program" these days. The very word *program* stirs misgivings in me. To say, yes, that's at the root of everything. But what should you say? Deep silence usually precedes the writing of a poem. And some of that silence usually enters into the poem. That's the difference between poetry and rhetoric, public-speaking competitions. The silence that precedes the poem may be intoxicating, it may seize the world's wholeness more completely than the poem that emerges later. But it can be a moment of great despair. Writing a poem (if only a few lines —a whole poem seldom comes of a single séance) is linked with a certain loss, and also grief, since the well of silence must be abandoned. And that's the great problem facing anyone who writes, who tries to write poems. Only when the sad weeks of true, mute silence begin, when you can't write, do you begin to understand that only this first silence, which fosters poems, is happiness, while the other, empty silence can be a curse. If at the same time you admire music because it says nothing, the matter becomes still more troublesome. In poetry you can't "say nothing." On the other hand saying something that could exist as a text outside of poetry causes further difficulties— since how can you praise something that's already waiting in the world of discourse? I also know that completely incomprehensible poetry, poetry aspiring to music, holds no charm for me, or for most other readers. Academic, rhetorical music likewise leaves me cold. For example, yesterday's jazz concert, a big band from Germany made up of fantastic musicians; you could tell they were first-rate musicians, superbly trained at various academies. But something was missing. The great black jazz musicians may have lacked this meticulous training, but they had something else, they were driven by hunger, they hungered for expression, they had something to say, they told us of their childhood in the slums, they lamented and rejoiced by turns.

•

To write—on the best days writing, energetic, joyful, comes close to creating your own self, it gives an extraordinary sense of mastery over your own life, you define yourself anew, as if almost nothing before were worth recognizing, as if you were charting a new future. On worse days it's a battle with depression. On the bleakest days you just try to save yourself. What remains of the great projects from the good days? They dissipate into space. The tremendous plans, the expansive hopes from those moments when everything starts afresh, all quickly deflate, leaving you to protect your abruptly diminished realm in despair. It's as if a great ruler, the master of a vast empire, suddenly found himself defending a tiny, provincial fortress with minimal stores of water and food; it can't hold out for long . . . Unless the wonderful days return and the tremendous plans shape your imagination once again. The writer, the poet, is insignificant in this endless cycle of expansion and contraction, enthusiasm and aversion. If politicians or judges gave way to such vacillations, everything would fall apart, we'd be afraid to leave the house at night . . .

•

An odd moment: just after I'd finished high school, during the graduation ceremonies, our homeroom teacher, an unpopular

Polonist named Professor Markow, handed me my diploma and said, "Adam, I'm sure you'll be a fine engineer."

•

I remember a comment, a hypothesis I found somewhere in Julien Green's diaries (he was paraphrasing someone else's theory): the great flowering of Elizabethan poetry and drama derived from the violent, brutal rejection of everything Catholic; the monasteries were shut, including those of the contemplative orders. That great energy of contemplation couldn't simply vanish, dissolve into thin air, such things don't happen, it had to go somewhere, and it turned to poetry . . . I like that idea, though I'm afraid that my scholarly friends, historians of culture, Renaissance specialists, would stare at me in shock if I dared to advance it at some seminar or conference.

•

The loneliness of leaders. Sometimes I try to imagine what they read, what books the great political leaders might pick up. I don't mean the abhorrent dictators, the rulers of totalitarian states, vicious authoritarian despots, the tyrants of lesser or greater nations, but genuinely great leaders. I'm not sure such leaders even exist at this historical moment, probably not, but they did exist, fortunately enough, not so long ago, during the Second World War. Poets and novelists are reluctant to remember this . . . As a rule, they prefer condemning the whole sphere of politics, and, more generally, all action within the human collective; they hide happily in art, music, poetry, painting, they like creating the illusion of a world that doesn't extend beyond the walls of the library or concert hall. Danilo Kis—a superb Serbian writer and a charming person who lived in Paris for a while and died too young—published a book of essays, *Homo Poeticus*, in praise of an art that closes its eyes to the reality in which contemporary social and political action unfolds. Paradoxically enough, since his own work took modern European history, the war, the Holocaust, Communist dictatorship, as its chief subject. My much-mourned friend Joseph Brodsky believed only in poetry, although he occasionally made brilliant comments on politics and history— he was phenomenally perceptive. These finally concerned him less, though, than the refined poetic forms one generation transmitted to the next as its most precious legacy. For Brodsky, verse structures formed something like humanity's most potent DNA—from Horace to Auden was just one step.

You find something similar in the wonderful Austrian writer Thomas Bernhard; he admired Schopenhauer's notion of an absurd human fate for which the only possible recompense was art, above all music (and compassion, as every encyclopedia reminds us). The wavering between a purely aesthetic vision and some kind of political passion shapes Proust's great novel. The pages of *À la recherche* . . . leave no doubt as to where their author stood in the fierce battles on Captain Dreyfus's guilt. As to Proust's vacillations—the ancient quarrel between the artistic realm and the political (or more generally, the historical) shows no signs of ending soon, and the task of mapping out their respective territories and competencies with surgical precision appears to be well-nigh impossible. In this case vacillation reveals an intellectual vitality that refuses to relinquish either part of a complex reality. For all that, Schopenhauer, a splendid, suggestive writer (his pages on music are unforgettable), was profoundly mistaken. He mocked love (nature deceives us). He placed no stock in history. He wished to divide all human affairs, with their tangled dramas, tragedies, errors, with their days of happiness and disillusion, with their despair, their dreams, from the sphere of art, the passionless contemplation of the world's essence. But it can't be done, if only because art constantly mixes with life's reality, grows from it and returns to it, sometimes even alters it, shifts it, molds it in its own image. And this is why we live in art only for brief moments, crucial moments, rich in meaning, but fleeting—and then we return to the disorderly world, where we can't help noting that we'd much prefer to dwell once more in regions where someone at least tries to bring about some kind of order, a decent human order, than in the chaos of bloody dictatorships or the ominous anomie of unstable wastelands. We live on the border between "life" and "art," we migrate between them, drawn first to one, then to the other, as though wild nomadic tribes held us captive, tribes favoring each empire by turns. We can't take up permanent residence on either side of the thin boundary.

•

So what should those extraordinary individuals, the *real* leaders, read? I was raised on literary culture, which has its bona fide heroes, truly remarkable, in which Kierkegaard and Kafka, Dostoevsky and Celan, receive their due. But if I try to think myself into the minds of those who bear the responsibility for a whole nation, if I imagine the nightly vigils of someone facing the monumental challenges of, say, a Churchill, would I really recommend *Fear and Trembling, The Sickness unto Death, Notes from Underground, Metamorphosis*, wonderful texts, books, categories, images that are our hymns, the hymns of our introspection, articulating our uncertainties, our mistrust of all authority? I wouldn't dare. For the time being, these great leaders—do they exist?—must reach for Thucydides, Plutarch, Livy. And of course Homer and Shakespeare.

•

I should mention that there were years when I listened obsessively to the music of Mahler. I remember talking with Americans my age—this was the spring of 1981, at the MacDowell Colony in New Hampshire, where I spent three months, my first stay in the United States. I asked them—who shaped you? I was such an ardent Mahlerite back then that I'd raise the question chiefly so that I could announce that I myself was "shaped by Mahler." We sat at a little table in the large living room at the MacDowell estate (it was just after dinner). It was May or maybe June. I now see my declaration as an obvious exaggeration, I had other masters after all. But I was completely taken with Mahler for many years, drawn by the powerful contrasts in his music, the coexistence of street music, the well-known echoes of the military bands that likely marched by the home of the young (and unhappy) Gustav in Moravian Jihlava, and the purest elegiac note in his long, wonderful, endless—like June evenings—adagios. I was astonished that someone could live at the juncture of what can't be joined, in greatest sorrow and ecstatic joy, rarely stopping for transitions, at the dark corridors between a symphony's movements. And that music could express humor, circus irony alongside great seriousness, both jokes and the quest for the absolute . . . And that such varied ingredients don't shatter the symphony, it remains a single musical home, it doesn't lose cohesion. I still listen to Mahler regularly, I've stayed faithful—I listen to the Ninth Symphony most often, and also to the fragments of the Tenth, reconstructed after the composer's death. I still consider the *Song of the Earth* one of the greatest works in the entire library of music—but I no longer initiate conversations meant to demonstrate who formed whom.

•

A moment many years ago in a Parisian café where I sat with Tzvetan Todorov and C. K. Williams discussing a reading that was about to begin. Jazz drifted from the speakers: Billie Holiday was singing, I knew her soft voice well, but then, that day, that moment, I was spellbound. I was sorry we couldn't linger in the café, endlessly listening to Billie Holiday, her voice, casual, friendly, sad.

•

What I wrote on the eve of my father's ninety-fifth birthday: My father was born in Lvov, he studied at the Lvov Polytechnic Institute, he worked in Warsaw for two years right before the war, in a factory producing the engineer Jaskolski's radio transmitters. Then after the war he became a professor at the Silesian Polytechnic Institute; the Automation Division was ranked first nationally as a result of his work. He spent the Occupation in Lvov. I occasionally meet his former students on various continents, they all speak of him with warmth and admiration. In March 1968 he tried to defend his students, and he paid the price, he lost his position as dean and director of the institute. When he stepped down as dean, his students gave him a bouquet with two hundred roses; I met one of the students years later, he described how the passersby stared on that gray Gliwice street on catching sight of the gigantic bouquet, like a multicolored Birnam Wood, only this time it didn't proclaim the tyrant's fall (not yet), just gratitude for a decent person. He was an adviser for the Solidarity movement, he greeted the birth of a free and democratic Poland enthusiastically, I've heard that he was asked to run for the Senate, but declined. The Third Republic (to say nothing of a Fourth) didn't shower my father with honors, but he was unconcerned; the thought of orders and honors never crossed his mind. And his marvelous sense of humor must also have helped to keep such thoughts at bay.

My father no longer remembers anything. He's lost his memory. I can't write him a letter. He didn't know that Sunday was his birthday. He won't know how many people think of him with admiration. He usually doesn't remember me either. He's been a widower for sixteen years. He's a good, modest person; he's lost his memory, but I haven't lost my memory of him.

He's so modest that he only told me relatively recently what he'd done during the Nazi occupation. To keep quiet for years in a country where every family apparently hid a hero of the resistance—so many hidden heroes that we're shocked that the Wehrmacht held on as long as it did—is quite unusual. But he finally said, You know, I worked for the Underground Army in Lvov. I didn't have anything to do with weapons, ammunition, nothing like that. So what did you do? Nothing much, I fixed radio transmitters . . . I'd take a transmitter home if it broke, and I'd fix it. So how did you get them home? I just carried them in my briefcase, they'd already been miniaturized back then. So he'd just walk through the city with a transmitter in his briefcase, passing German patrols at every turn. And in the house on Piaskowa Street, a few steps from Lyczakowska Street, right by St. Anthony's Church, he'd get to work—I picture him sitting evenings by the light of a little lamp, near covered windows, checking something in the textbook, soldering wires, fixing the transmitter, thanks to which two cities beginning with *L* could carry on a conversation. Lvov was linked to London.

And then came the long years in Gliwice, and at the institute there, he became, willy-nilly, a model of professional respectability and political decency. He never joined the Polish Communist Party. He was, so I'm told, demanding, but fair to his students. Of the newcomers from Lvov—assistant, associate, and full professors—he was among the youngest. Few of them must still remain. My father, who rarely complained about anything, lamented for years that he had no friends left from his own generation, they'd all passed away.

He always walked quickly; it was difficult keeping up with him until quite recently. People often recognized him, nodded or smiled in passing. In the little world of Gliwice, consisting chiefly of one street, Victory Street, he was well-known (I use the past tense since he doesn't leave home now). His former students greeted him, colleagues of long ago, his many acquaintances. But he remembered less and less, and he told me that he no longer knew who was saying hello—like a famous actor who can't acknowledge all his fans.

·

The MacDowell Colony, a venerable home for creative work, founded in 1907, is apparently the oldest such institution in the United States. In 1981, it initiated a special stipend (aided, I think, by the Rockefeller Foundation) designed to support several visiting writers from Central Europe. An invitation, completely unexpected, found me in Berlin. The recommendation letter, that indispensable element, that cornerstone of every American cultural institution, had been written by Zbigniew Herbert, who was also living in Berlin at the time . . . I'll never forget that first evening—I'd flown from Paris to New York, then to Boston, and finally took a bus to Peterborough, New Hampshire, where I arrived late at night after hours of riding through the inky darkness of provincial New England, as if en route to a different life— only to find myself in an old neoclassical building, in a reserved bedroom brimming with antique furniture; the floorboards creaked beneath my feet. At last, my strength exhausted, I lay down on a bed made differently from European beds, with enormous quantities of superfluous pillows (I had only one head after all), and it seemed to me that I'd landed on Mars—although it felt oddly familiar, more from dreams than from reality, perhaps from a Ukraine before my birth, a provincial manor smelling of hay and the long-gone Commonwealth. On the first day, after breakfast, I met the other participants and got to know the house routine: the artists and writers, musicians and filmmakers, all had their own studios (the studios were scattered through the woods like chapels), but breakfast and dinner were taken together. Dinners particularly served to foster a flourishing social life, they ran on, splintered into smaller groups and endless discussions. But come morning, routine and work again. If indeed everyone did work. I wasn't convinced . . .

But I didn't mean to talk about all this, I just wanted to mention one colleague, also there for a longer stay (the Americans ordinarily came only for a few weeks). This was the singer Karel Kryl, famous, even legendary, in his native Czechoslovakia. I'd already heard of him, his fame, his position, before we met at MacDowell. I liked him right away, we became, if not friends, then friendly during our stay. Kryl, who'd been living for many years as an émigré in West Germany, in Munich, was a political singer, lamenting the tragedy of the Warsaw Pact's invasion in '68, the fall of the Prague Spring. He worked for Radio Free Europe in Munich, and for this reason, I suspect, he never entirely lost touch with his Czechoslovakian audience. Bavaria was so close to Prague. The beer tasted the same in both places. But here in Peterborough, New Hampshire, in this picturesque town set amid hills, lakes, and forests, where the birds were different from in Europe—when it grew warm, there were even hummingbirds, gorgeous, gifted with tremendous intellectual concentration—Karel Kryl was utterly helpless. His visit was, I think, a great mistake, a gigantic misunderstanding. Karel was deeply depressed. Just imagine a *legendary* singer cut off completely from his public, from the people for whom he was a legend, for whom he sang. How can you be a legend if nobody knows? Being *legendary* must be exceptionally difficult in any case, all the more so if no one knows you. This separation from the audience that admired him, that knew all his songs by heart, was a cruel blow.

Although for someone who simply watched events, that is to say, for me, it was also fascinating: it revealed the utter relativity of fame. Famous people are better off sticking to their own city, their own neighborhood. God forbid they should head off for another continent. Unless they're international rock stars . . . Many years later, right after the attack on the World Trade

Center, when television stations across the globe sent their reporters to New York, I caught sight on my screen of an immensely famous French newscaster, who'd become just another anonymous reporter on a Manhattan street . . . Pedestrians passed him by without blinking; he must have suffered terribly. For the American artists at MacDowell, Karel Kryl was just a short man with a sad face who wore thick-soled shoes and spoke bad English. Once he sang a few songs for the MacDowell guests—there was a piano, we had occasional concerts—but it didn't change much. Songs torn from their context, and sung of course in Czech, meant nothing to their American listeners, however well-disposed. I experienced something a little similar myself, although on a much smaller scale; not being a famous, much less *legendary*, poet, I couldn't know anything like Karel's grief. I mainly just worked there, wrote, locked in the chapel of my forest studio—at lunchtime a jeep carried lunch baskets to weary artists, which a foundation employee silently deposited on our doorsteps, so as not to disturb our labors—and I expected no applause from my American colleagues. But one of my new acquaintances asked if he could read some of my poems. I had a few, maybe a dozen, translations of my early poems—Anthony Graham's work—which I gave him, and after a moment I noticed the disappointment he was trying to conceal. They were "political" poems, angry poems from the seventies. Wrenched out of context, they clearly meant little to my acquaintance. He didn't say so, but I understood perfectly the question he didn't ask: "This is it?" Voices from then-suffering Central Europe fell on deaf ears in the forests of New Hampshire.

Karel Kryl died of a heart attack in 1994, in a hospital in Passau. I never saw him again after those three shared months in the New Hampshire woods, among crimson cardinals and pensive hummingbirds.

•

I can laugh at the resettled, mock their rituals, their outpouring of literary memoirs, their fondness for kitsch, their sentimentality. It's easy to satirize the perfect idyll that exiles find years later in their vanished homeland—but I never think of that lost city without pain. It pains me to know that I never lived there, the great vacuum of what never was, the childhood that should have been and wasn't, that had died. Even the teachers I never had fascinate me, in the great school building, I don't know which, districts don't affect those who've left, but I would certainly have gone to one high school or another, the steps would have been freshly washed in advance, with the metallic ring of the water bucket the cleaning lady set on the marble incline. I'm convinced that those teachers would have been more interesting than the teachers who bored us to death in Gliwice. I often think of it. The life I didn't have there, the loves I didn't meet, the familiarity with stones and trees, with streets I'll never know. The scents of that city, scents in which East mingled with West, black sunflower seeds with creamy, peeling halvah and the delicate perfume of old pianos, well acquainted with the music of Bach and Schumann. The pianos' yellow teeth. All those houses and the countless objects that their owners thought about, like an anchor keeping them safely, peacefully in Lvov. The heavy chests and vast cupboards were meant to be an anchor. But they weren't. With so little water, the city had no place for anchors. The harsh winter and then the spring's sweetness, when the earth opens. The clean sky in May. And the horror of war and occupation. Exterminations, terror, first Soviet and then Nazi (but I didn't endure it, didn't see it). The city's hills and the many spires of its churches, Catholic and Orthodox, the green-patina-crusted cupolas of its tallest buildings, the symphony, the theater. These buildings, solid, weighty, were meant to be anchors. Dandelions' saffron on the meadows. Family graves in the Lyczakowski Cemetery—such as the tombstone of Stanislaw Zborowski, lawyer and poet, who died young, mourned by many, and couldn't know that the next generation of his family would produce women living nearly a hundred years, as though some invisible hand of statistics wanted to compensate for his untimely demise. The old market placed on a gentle slope and the wall of the Orthodox church in the town's very center, a wall permanently pocked by an artillery shell, a trace of the fratricidal Ukrainian-Polish battles of 1918. And the beautiful Armenian cathedral, like entering a Coptic church somewhere in Egypt. And where you could hear unembellished Eastern songs praising the Armenian Lord. Discreet synagogues, which always said they were houses of prayer, not the house of God, and didn't want to bother anyone, a little anxious. That which no longer is. Sundays, when the Austrian officers went strolling in dress uniforms, and the servant girls watched in adoration. The sabers of Polish officers, silver braid on the collars of their jackets. And then the leaden winters of the Occupation. All that past stored in the trees, in the swallows' whistling, there and not there. The Jesuit Garden, whose name entranced me as a child, since two incongruities clashed in it, the indefatigable fertility of flowers and bushes met with Jesuit discipline, with rhetoric honed over centuries, with black cassocks. In the garden, birds and lizards, the unruly pupils of Jesuit professors always disappearing into thickets, untrackable—and alongside them, the monks seeking their young charges. Prosperous fin de siècle dwellings testified to the city's success as the nineteenth century neared its conclusion. Sunburned suburbs opening to Ukrainian steppes— those touching spots where the city first shrinks to the size of little one-story houses and then suddenly becomes a village. A small sky-blue tram clambers up to the High Castle, slipping on the narrow tracks. Wild cherries in the Kaiserwald, whose taste surpassed that of all other fruits. I might be someone different if I'd grown up looking at Lvov's hills and not the towers of Silesia's coal mines. I'd have looked at Orthodox churches and Uniate shrines, I might have understood difference differently.

And myself, too. I can't know. What can we know about emptiness, absence, that which wasn't?

•

Music reminds us what love is. If you've forgotten what love is, go listen to music.

•

The ancient Japanese poets who wrote haiku—we see them as remarkably serene, permanently lost in cheerful, carefree contemplation. But it could have been completely different, they might have been nervous, anxious, fearful, and, who knows, the moment when they composed the poem we read so many centuries later may have been the only moment of inspiration, calm, in the gallop of their difficult, dramatic lives.

•

I walked through the Planty Gardens; a little girl zipped past me on a scooter and at that moment I grasped the essence of motion. But I can't explain it.

•

On the Mediterranean beaches of France, in summer, you hear one cry repeated endlessly: *Elle est bonne.* That is, It's good. Meaning the seawater. Cautious, modern inhabitants of cities thus assure one another that it's safe to go in the water, they won't be stunned by its arctic cold. But in its essence this cry affirms the world, nature. *Elle est bonne.*

•

Yesterday, at an exhibit of Stanislaw Ignacy Witkiewicz's photography. We call him Witkacy, compressing his three-part name, we embrace the abbreviation that makes a jester of the thinker. But Witkacy himself liked playing the jester, as his many photographic self-portraits amply demonstrate. He mercilessly reveals his missing teeth, his advancing age. He was always playing dress-up, and he drew others into his games. In one photo he keeps company with Bruno Schulz, the timid schoolmaster from Drohobycz. There are also many society figures, Warsaw ladies, well-known gentlemen. Most of the pictures were taken in Zakopane, sometimes outdoors, by mountain streams. There, in this idyllic landscape, Witkacy carefully set up his various grimaces and arranged his friends' features as well. Born in 1885—the perfect year for an artist of the European avant-garde—Witkacy personifies the modernist dilemma through his great ambivalence toward the changes in civilization conveniently embraced by one term: *modernity*. Everything changes, Witkacy says—although those changes were still almost imperceptible in Zakopane. But he'd seen Petersburg, after all, the capital of a rapidly modernizing power, he'd recognized the threat of war in Russian uniform. He must have been the only real initiate into the tragic mysteries of modernity during his games with younger friends. Witkacy's thesis on the disappearance of metaphysical feelings formed the fulcrum of his "system." My feelings are mixed as I look at these pictures. I don't actually like this man who refused to go to the dentist, he must have been a true despot, I sense, in his dealings with male and female friends alike. I'm not convinced that his friends actually enjoyed the company of the Zakopane tyrant. Some of the faces they make look forced, pretentious, at times his models seem unhappy, even close to tears. But I also sense his tragic nature, the tragedy of someone possessing great knowledge, great self-knowledge, but who doesn't have a clue what to do with this knowledge in Zakopane's microscopic realm. Of course he wrote those breathtakingly original plays and novels, he painted, he was splendidly talented, erudite, as befits a philosopher-artist, a writer's son. He created a multitude of things, but did it all as if with his left hand, always a bit carelessly, like a dandy who turns up at an embassy reception in a new tuxedo, but with dirty long johns poking from under his pant legs. He was a brilliant jester, like Kierkegaard's luckless clown, crying, "Fire, fire," at the circus; no one takes him seriously, the spectators just laugh, expecting clownish pranks, the laughter roars in an audience about to be devoured by flames. I'm not overly fond of him, but I understand him. I understand his fear, I'm convinced by many of his arguments. Metaphysical feelings—are they really almost gone? Of course not. It's our task to make something of them. Each of us decides at every moment, they don't exist outside us, they're not the dissolving glaciers of Greenland, whose fate we feel so painfully. They're not an autonomous continent slowly melting into the ocean. We are these metaphysical feelings. They've been under threat long since, for centuries, but someone has always saved them and still does. Those who maintain such ideas now are called conservatives; the modernists were in a better position, they held impeccable avant-garde credentials while by and large subscribing to conservative views. They created a new era in art while looking back with regret. Rilke, who loathed the great modern city. Eliot, who mourned the hierarchical world of ardent Christians. Yeats, who admired Byzantium. And with them, Stanislaw Ignacy Witkiewicz of Zakopane. The self-portrait, at least a certain kind of self-portrait, seems to emerge at a relatively late phase of the disappearance of "metaphysical feelings," or, more precisely, of the growing fear that such feelings inspire in alert observers who aren't sure if they should despair or simply seize a marvelous opportunity for play. Or perhaps, embracing the principle of great ambivalence, they should experience great despair while devising splendid entertainments. They happily do this by streams, on riverbanks—there are several such photos— possibly to spite Heracleitus, although of course Heracleitus is really laughing at them. The rivers themselves have absolutely no sense of humor.

•

Paola Malavasi was a charming young Italian woman, gentle, smiling, shy, intelligent. She taught Greek and Latin at a high school in a small town just outside Rome. She was a poet. I got to know her during one of my visits to Rome—she came to the modest little hotel near Roma Termini where M. and I were staying. She wanted to interview me for some little journal, I forget which one. She liked my poetry, which she knew chiefly through English translations. Of course I don't remember what we talked about, what she asked. She then told me that she'd translated a dozen or so of my poems. She'd translated them from the English, but, she added, a Polish friend had helped her check the English versions against the originals. Some time later the translations appeared in the monthly *Poesia*, edited by Nicola Crocetti, in Milan. I saw Paola two more times. First in Rome, where we agreed that she and her friend Ennio Cavalli would meet us at the corner of the little street, via Ofanto, where Miriam Chiaromonte, the widow of the great essayist Nicola, lived. (She lived at number 18, on a high floor in one of the tall, substantial houses prized by doctors and lawyers.) In the event, Ennio came for us in a Jaguar, and we drove a long while to his little apartment in the Roman suburbs. Why do I bring this all up? Because Paola died suddenly, her heart stopped. She was forty years old, she died in Venice, in the morning, one Sunday morning in September. She hadn't been ill, she died without giving notice, without taking leave. She made a French exit. After our second Roman meeting, we saw her once more in Castrocaro, a town in the Emilia-Romagna region famed for its curative waters. Ennio had organized a small poetry festival there, and we spent a few days visiting neighboring towns, and giving readings, whose organization changed slightly each time. Every day we'd hold a little council; Paola would sometimes

bring her son. A Roman actress was also with us, she read the
Italian translations. We visited Forlì and Cesenatico, on the
Adriatic, but didn't make it to Rimini, Ennio's hometown (also
Fellini's). One of our readings took place in the large hotel where
we were staying. In the hotel elevator you could see that the top
floor held the "Mussolini" penthouse. The building next door
was a spa, with baths and springs. The hotel guests returned to
their rooms in white bathrobes and afterward dressed and went
down to the hotel restaurant, which served ample meals with
good wines, to erase the bitter taste of the local water. Why do I
bring this up? To keep Paola Malavasi in this world a little longer, to see her once more, alive, kind, cheerful, charming. Which,
while she lived, seemed quite normal. Delightful, but normal. It
seemed normal that Paola was living, that she was kind, intelligent, warm. Everything changed when she died. Partly because
she vanished so discreetly. Now we all know, those of us who
knew her, how exceptional she was, we know too late. But it's
always that way; you don't venerate the living.

•

It's fascinating, the ritual by which a new artist comes to be accepted; it can take years, even decades. There's nothing more
difficult: being recognized, accepted. Who serves on the tribu-
nal? We're not entirely sure. Critics, readers, some timid angel
occasionally turns up in the mix. The jury deliberates slowly,
convenes rarely, forgets its duties for months on end, the decision
it's called upon to make. Each new poet is treated with great
suspicion. One of the key questions to be addressed by this peculiar judicial body reads as follows: Isn't he simply pretending? I'll
try to explain. A new artist—we'll confine ourselves to poetry—
proposes a certain tone, speaks of rather unclear things, not entirely obvious, a little hazy, joyful sometimes, sad at others, on
the melancholy side overall, but each time surpassing the limits
of the ordinary, obvious themes and moods to which journalists

and behaviorists give ready assent. So precisely the excess of tone (but this shouldn't be immediately understood as praise of "high style") that is the very heart of poetry becomes acutely problematic for our invisible jury. Our jury, if it has convened—which, as we know, happens rarely—will raise the question: Is she or he (the candidate) simply pretending? Since what could possibly be the source of this excessive tone, this extra something introduced into the general social conversation? The jury has no answer. Opponents of the new talent then respond: he (she) is pretending. Pretending to have gained admission to some other region. How could he (she) possibly have been admitted to a different domain, since he (she) is just like us? Attended the same schools, read the same books, saw the same movies. The poet is just pretending, standing on tiptoe, seeking applause, a typical snob. But supporters of the new poet (new, although this poet may be seventy-five and still be the subject of juridical battles, battles as lazy as they are frenzied) refuse to yield, they respond: True enough, he (she) went to the same schools, saw the same movies, but maybe something happened, something changed. Something shifted one night. We can't know, but let's give this candidate a chance. There are weak poems, conventional, to be sure, but some have their moments, lines showing that something's been seen, experienced. They hold images, metaphors suggesting that something's happened, something's opened up. The candidate's opponents protest instantly, they roar with scornful laughter. Don't be ridiculous, it's all smoke and mirrors. This poet went to the same schools, watched the same television shows. He (she) is simply pretending, wants to take us in. Dresses in robes borrowed from dead poets, just one of us, who went to the same school, followed the games of our own incompetent soccer team, we wept together, loathed the political system, shouted, prayed together, drank second-rate beer, how could a new artist have emerged among us? And the argument drags on, few notice, since who on earth pays attention to such things?

•

Music—organized by melody, harmony, but sometimes we're most struck by the mass of sound, the absurd (intellectually speaking) accumulation of noises, the magnificent, physically compelling actualization of the instruments' power—as sometimes in Bruckner we feel the bows vibrating, the cellos' heavy hair swimming alongside the bass cry of the trumpets and trombones, sometimes in Wagner, or more recently, in the first movement of Henryk Gorecki's Third Symphony, when slow as the dawn, the orchestra's cocoon unfolds—or, a different metaphor, we can imagine the hull of a massive ship emerging, slowly, from the mist. This incredibly sensual, palpable wall of sound stirs our entire body, but remains unseen. And perhaps it's precisely this contrast—between overwhelming presence and invisibility—that moves us, leads us, momentarily, to another world, another way of being that we can only visit.

Once more on the show of Witkacy's photographs: They aren't simply self-portraits; one shows the image of Jan Leszczynski, a philosopher who was twenty years younger than Witkacy. As a young man, he must have been fascinated with the figure of Zakopane's diabolical jester. He was Witkacy's philosophical interlocutor. Leszczynski died in 1990, at the age of eighty-five; his correspondence with Witkacy, *The Monadism Controversy*, appeared some twenty years later. The photograph shows four people: the Master and Jan Leszczynski are flanked by two other friends. It's a summer day, everyone except Leszczynski is dressed rather lightly, without topcoats, only Leszczynski wears a coat and hat. Why do I mention this? Thirty-five years later Jan Leszczynski advised my master's thesis in philosophy, and always, summer and winter, he wore a light loden coat, even on the warmest days. The Leszczynski I knew was utterly subdued, absent, silent. He may have been my adviser, but we never had a real conversation. I can't even quite imagine how such a conversation might have looked. Leszczynski—Professor Leszczynski, I should say—was a shadow among people. He always kept still, and if he did speak up—as for example at his own lectures, when he had to say something—he spoke in a quiet monotone. He lectured on classic problems of epistemology, he analyzed, as I recall, Descartes's views, the Cartesian quest for a stable basis for thought, but he spoke of this so dispassionately, flatly, that the theory of cognition struck us, his audience, as the dullest field in philosophy.

Professor Leszczynski was dead inside; wrapped in his loden coat he passed through Communist-occupied Krakow like a ghost—or a spy. Thoroughly familiar with Witkacy's prophecies on the death of metaphysical feelings, he knew absolutely that life had no worth. Unlike his old friend, Leszczynski didn't take his own life, at least not in the physical dimension. Perhaps curiosity kept him going. Faithful to his old friend's teachings, an expert on his philosophy, he may have wanted to demonstrate how accurate Witkacy's prophecies had proved; he became a kind of emissary, an ambassador of sorts. Back when I was working on my thesis, I saw him as an old man; soon I'll be the same age he was then. Professor Leszczynski might have found satisfaction in his role as Witkacy's secret envoy—the prophecies had been fulfilled with some accuracy. Witkacy had failed to predict one thing, though: the rebellion against Communism, the revolts against a gray totalitarian state. And he didn't anticipate that the intellectual resistance might be motivated, at least partly, by those slighted, stifled, suppressed "metaphysical feelings." It quickly turned out that the democratic system for which the bold opposition had yearned so ardently was not especially well-disposed to Wikacy's "feelings"; just the opposite—not that it persecutes or condemns them, it simply doesn't have time, it's not remotely interested, it drowns them in a sea of indifference, as mean people drown blind kittens in a bucket of water.

But Witkacy also failed to predict something else. In each

generation and almost every nation, regardless of system or
century, men and women turn up who can't imagine life without what he called "metaphysical feelings"—even though they've
never heard of the Zakopane playwright and thinker, they've
never used this phrase, which might strike them as pretentious
or superfluous. And they clearly don't feel the need to weave
elaborate theories in the grand style. It's enough just to listen to
music, to keep asking questions for which there are no answers,
to remember paintings seen in a museum, to note the earth's
quiet at dusk, birds' voices in May, to shiver at the thought that
they're alive, that the gleam of each new dawn is an endless
promise.

•

I realized that I'd taken that "Isn't he just pretending?" from
Witold Gombrowicz, I got it from a well-known letter in which
Gombrowicz provokes the subtle Bruno Schulz, asking how
he'd react if some "doctor's wife from Wilcza Street in Warsaw"
dismissed his artistic efforts in exactly this way: Schulz "is just
pretending." But the question was interrupted by the Second
World War: Wilcza Street was reduced to rubble, then rebuilt
after the war, the fictitious doctor's wife could have died in the
Warsaw Uprising, Bruno Schulz was shot in his native Drohobycz,
Gombrowicz ended up in Argentina. Still, Gombrowicz's amus-
ing idea survived the war. I don't think it's only doctors' wives
from Wilcza Street, the half-imaginary jury that evaluates new
authors asks exactly the same question . . .

•

Great moments, instants of elation, of short-lived certainty, light,
faith: they seem—since such things are fleeting by definition—
to dissipate somewhere on the fringes of memory, after a certain
point we cease to take them as seriously as they deserve (and
as we do when they suddenly appear before us). Moreover, the

ubiquitous mist of irony, the modern world's innate skepticism, mean that we scrutinize these moments critically after they've gone, as if we didn't trust ourselves, we want to discard them, cast them aside, we refuse to let them complicate our lives, which are tangled enough as it is. But these moments form the base, the foundation of everything. Attacked on all sides, defenseless (since they'll vanish), their sense is extremely difficult to extract, they may suffer corrosion by way of the ever-so-intelligent irony that permeates us even when we reject it "in principle." We can't tell our friends and acquaintances much, there's something obscure, mute, about these moments, for all that they speak so clearly to us while they last. But how can you talk about them over coffee or tea, or a glass of wine, since—regardless of the age's prevailing philosophical climate—the very fact of meeting friends for dinner predisposes us to good humor, to high spirits, which, vivifying and indispensable as they are, have nothing to do with the real situation of those friends having such a splendid time. But writing about these great moments is also not quite the thing . . . And even if it were, it wouldn't work. Since even the great mystics couldn't tell us much . . . There's no ready form in which to grasp them, express them. I've noticed, though, that a kind of innocent conspiracy has taken shape in our times. People who listen to Bach attentively—and it can't be done without experiencing those great moments now and then—have found a shorthand, a code, they don't speak of brief moments of faith, they simply say, "I was listening to Bach." There are of course those aesthetes who venerate Bach, whose music is just one more artistic pleasure, whom they place alongside Prokofiev, Britten, or Respighi (the dreariest of all composers). So bearing this in mind, I'll introduce one caveat: Not everyone who talks about Bach belongs among the initiates. But some do. And they're not necessarily musicologists, not at all.

•

After all, the question (Isn't he just pretending?) isn't new, and it seems to be universal: in Julien Green's diary (entry of January 9, 1932) I stumbled on the following: "With her usual acute intelligence, sparing no one, Gertrude Stein speaks cruelly of a certain painter, whose sketches she's actually purchased for her collection. She wonders if he's really what he makes himself out to be, if he's as *unreal* as he implies, or if his mystery is simply deft pretense. And she compares his case to the long-standing problem of the Church: Is it dealing with a saint or merely with a hysteric?"* Julien Green was a discreet writer, he doesn't give the name of the artist he's discussing, but who knows, it may be Salvador Dalí, who was living in Paris at the time (and Green belongs to the cluster of people who helped the young, impoverished artist by contracting to buy his work regularly). Each new author, painter, or composer must prove that he "isn't just pretending." How is this done? Convincing people, connoisseurs, is hellishly difficult. In principle almost impossible. Acknowledging a new artist is like the birth of a myth, and myths aren't born every day, their quantity is strictly limited, like the number of chairs in the Académie française.

•

The thesis I completed under Professor Leszczynski's direction (direction! this supervision was in reality pure fiction, a professor who was just a shadow, who'd never actually lived, and who certainly viewed me suspiciously, I might well be a *typical new man*, void of substance, how could he possibly help me?) bore the title, I'm ashamed to say, "On the Cognition of One's Own Body."

•

* Translations from Julien Green's diary are from the Polish, not from the original French text.

I used to like thinking that in my sober, taciturn family, which like an old but industrious apple tree had for several generations continued to put forth teachers at various levels, from elementary school to higher education, in various fields, solid, hardworking people devoid of fantasy, I was someone completely different, I possessed an artistic temperament. In families full of unstable characters, alcoholics, pathological liars, people no doubt dream of stability, pedantic predictability. However, I sought not bourgeois propriety, but imagination, the courage to cast off a life measured by small steps up the professional ladder. I found someone like this: our distant cousin Leopold Zborowski, a poet and art dealer, whom the great artists had painted, among them Modigliani. But I kept on looking. I came up with the idea of a fictitious relative, for example, my father's brother, who might be, so I imagined, a composer (but of course that's why I'm a writer, I can fill in the gaps in my real, silent family, add peculiarities). I made up a biography; like Witold Lutoslawski, my nonexistent uncle would have scraped by during the Occupation playing hits on the piano in a Warsaw (or Lvov) café. He would have broken with his family, gone to Paris, studied with Nadia Boulanger . . . But someone in the family, on my mother's, not my father's, side, had actually lived differently, not like all the rather conventional teachers. My mother had a sister, Janina, who was seldom mentioned. My mother's family was decidedly right-wing, nationalist; my mother took these reactionary tendencies with her when she left home. Fortunately, though, her new family, that is, her husband and her children, submitted her to a thorough-going reeducation, and little remained of her early views later on. But Janina had died of tuberculosis while young, before the war. She spent her short life chiefly in Zakopane's sanatoriums, where she moved in Communist, intellectual circles. She doubtless broke with her family, she certainly couldn't have stomached their politics, their petit bourgeois lives. As with many tuberculosis patients, her illness was a curse, a burden, a battle, but also a kind of opportunity, it tore her from a circumscribed world of routines. A flame burned in her, the flame of tuberculosis, which consumed her, but also tore her from a banal existence, helped to open her imagination. It was the bitter gift of an accelerated life, speeding to its end, like a film projected at the wrong speed. Perhaps she knew Witkacy . . . She certainly befriended many artists. I don't know if she dabbled in the arts herself. Her husband was Czeslaw Wieteska, who shared her Communist sympathies. Zakopane's artistic circles must have revolted her ultraconservative family . . . Czeslaw Wieteska—who also suffered from TB—was a novice theater director connected with Leon Schiller; he was his assistant. Wieteska didn't survive the war. He was detained by the NKVD, the Soviet secret police, in Lvov, apparently at the same time that Aleksander Wat and other intellectuals were arrested after a staged provocation in a café to which they'd all been lured. He had a high fever when they took him, he'd caught a bad flu. He likely died just after his arrest. Yet another life ended too soon, in dreadful circumstances. Although we'll never know what images, what dreams, accompanied his death. Perhaps they held great sparks of joy, self-fulfilling wishes. We can't know. In any case, when my reactionary grandmother stood in line before the Brygidki Prison in Lvov—where she encountered Wladyslaw Broniewski's first wife, Janina—to give her son-in-law a packet of food (and it must be said in her credit that, for all that divided them, she tried to help her poor son-in-law, who was already a widower and would soon turn to dust), she waited for a long time in the freezing cold before being told: He isn't here. We don't know anything about him. Next. And my grandmother went home. So ended the rebellious, artistic strain in my mother's family.

•

And here's Wilhelm Windelband—in the encyclopedia photo, he doesn't seem to have a neck at all. He must have been short

and stocky, an enormous black beard, like an ominous cloud of
hail, overgrows his broad face. Truth be told, he looks just like
every other scholar of the era. They all had gigantic beards (as if
trying to hide their faces). Windelband. This was the name of a
certain philosopher, a neo-Kantian. He really lived. The young
Osip Mandelstam probably heard him lecture on Kant in Heidelberg (Mandelstam hadn't yet been admitted to St. Petersburg
University, which maintained a quota on Jewish students). Windelband may also have encountered Stefan George, the poet and
shaman, on Heidelberg's streets. The bearded Wilhelm Windelband went down in the history of thought for his ideas on clas-
sifying the sciences, which he divided into the nomothetic and
the idiographic. The first of these seeks out general laws (chemistry, physics), while the second, comprising the humanistic disciplines, concentrates chiefly on particular, individual facts, events
that resist generalization. We attend most carefully in this case to
the event's specific timbre, its irrepeatability. We try to grasp what
can't be grasped: individuality, a singular, unreproducible essence.
I remember this much from my studies. Poor humanities, timid,
uncertain, desperate—like a young scholar who fears both his
students and his superiors. The unhappy humanities, envying the
success of the nomothetes . . . They, too, would like to establish
laws, discover regularities, evoke mathematical symbols . . .

When I turn back to the books of Jaroslaw Iwaszkiewicz, particularly his stories, his travel essays, his diaries, I experience shock,
a splendid, positive shock; here's an absolutely *idiographic* writer, a
student of specifics, a connoisseur of buildings, pictures, people's
faces, without the slightest regard or sympathy for theory. He
specialized in individual things, individual women and men,
he understood perfectly that only this exists, only this single white
poplar with a broken branch and a yellow dog with a reddish
muzzle, wagging its tail, well-disposed to all, and a little black cat,
brashly tackling every tree, and the cute little boy with big eyes
riding a scooter, who chatted with us politely as we strolled around

Kosciuszko's Mound (he said his name was Franio), and that old woman whom we see on our street in Krakow, stooped over her cane, clinging to her cane, barely able to navigate the sidewalk, but retaining the shape of distant things, the shape of long-gone beauty, the trace of a nobility, something that I'll never know.

That's all there is, just particular people, particular things, poplars and beeches, black lilac bushes, and the mind that watches them, and the sorrow that everything ends. People, men and women, each and all, closed in their own lives; we see them only for a moment, on the street, as they're getting back, heading home, rushing, almost running. Some carry bags of groceries, potatoes, bread, apples, tomatoes, ham, cottage cheese. They have to nourish their distinctiveness. They hurry, run, so as to hide once more in the dark drawer of their distinctiveness. There's also memory, which works so imperfectly to preserve the particularity of those who've gone, which weeps as our dear ones' features, the melody of their voices, begin to fade. And imagination, too, memory's cousin, which likewise despises abstraction. Imagination is like a widow, dressed in black, who sits in a deep armchair, trying to resurrect the dead. Then silence falls. Still later, much later, writing comes, which aims to grasp something idiomatic, unrepeatable, singular, in indicative sentences cast upon people and things like a lasso tossed at a wild colt by an amateur cowboy. Indicative sentences are artless, designed to record the simplest observations: the moon is pale, the linden tree is green, the river is shallow, Anna went to school, the marquise left the house. And with this tool, so primitive when compared to the instruments of astronauts and surgeons, writers set out on their great expedition into the jungles of life. It's both foolish and sublime. Writing, which undertakes something impossible, completely impossible. It may at times plaster over the holes in reality, but only by way of its own passion for reality. For this alone redeems it, its infatuation with the world (unreciprocated, as we know, since the world thumbs its nose at literature).

Writing loves the world, or hates it; some writers, for example the Austrian Thomas Bernhard, wrote only with rage, fury; Jaroslaw Iwaszkiewicz cherished particulars almost hysterically—hysterical outbursts of love, for people and places, favorite dogs, works of art, punctuate his work. He reproached himself at the same time for his "poverty of thought." In an essay on Venice, for example, he writes, "I talk nonstop, since chattering helps to conceal my poverty, the poverty of my country and my thought." Poverty of thought, what a misconception, since someone who longs for particulars and seizes them in his writing is thinking in the best possible way ... Blessed poverty of thought. And how did Iwaszkiewicz live when he managed to tear himself from his work? I'll never forget how courageously he and his wife helped Jews during the Occupation, they saved both Jews and friends who didn't wear the yellow star. By the war's end, dozens of people, survivors, fugitives from ruined Warsaw, were living in their great house. Their estate became a vast Noah's ark (though unlike the biblical patriarch, the Iwaszkiewiczes didn't confine themselves to preserving only two of every species). Their estate, Stawisko, became a fixed island while floodwaters rose all around. Iwaszkiewicz loved German poetry and music, he even had some contact with George's circle in the late twenties. But he hated the Nazis' barbarism, the contempt they displayed for the Poles during the Occupation, for a time he even wrote the word *German* without a capital letter, violating the rules of orthography ... Orthography, what's orthography to someone who loves particulars? Particulars take no notice of large and small letters.

After the war, he became an *homme de lettres* known for his opportunism and for his political naïveté, doubtless partly feigned (in brief, he thought that gum-chewing Americans posed a greater threat to future civilization than the Soviet secret police). He proclaimed himself an ardent Communist sympathizer and benefited accordingly—he not only kept his great house, his palace, he could heat it, repair it, maintain it. But this doesn't change anything. Maria Dabrowska remembers him as follows (this comes from her diary entry of March 30, 1954): "There were toasts, one raised by Iwaszkiewicz. Every time I hear him speak officially I'm filled with revulsion, his groveling, his obsequious preening. I'm ashamed of him, and of writers generally."

But she also thought and wrote about him—in the same diary—with respect, even admiration. Time passes to his advantage: fewer and fewer witnesses remain to his cowardice, his evasions, his siding with the political powers that be and not with his fellow writers (although he sometimes came to their defense when the worst threatened: arrest, destitution). An opportunist, to be sure, an exemplary, ideal opportunist—but what a writer! There was no question of ideological collaboration, of embracing Marxism. Marxism held no appeal for him. It didn't recognize particulars, it suffered from a cirrhosis of particulars, and particulars killed it in the end. Iwaszkiewicz was a man of enormous culture, of *idiographic* culture, so to speak. When I read him, I perceive the abyss that divides us from his generation of writers (he was born in 1894). Iwaszkiewicz's education was worlds apart from that of later generations, my own and those that came after. This isn't the standard conservative lament on the decline of classical culture. Iwaszkiewicz admitted that he found Greek civilization incomprehensible—he commented once, in Sicily, in Agrigento, that the Chopin waltzes he heard played by some young girl through an open window while passing by a row of houses moved him far more than all the majestic Greek edifices in the famous Valley of the Temples.

We rarely consider how much we've lost by way of the systematization of intellectual life over the last century. In an age of ideology, systems, endless -isms, have taken hold everywhere, even, or rather especially, in universities. All varieties of Marxism, but also psychoanalysis, avant-gardism, structuralism—the poor man's Aristotelianism—and its multiple offshoots preceded by that fatal prefix *post-*, not to mention all the modalities of "post-modernity," sects and subsystems, each of which possesses its own Parisian prophet (and they all lived in the same neighborhood, the Latin Quarter, and met at the same café). Some systems, such as psychoanalysis, may be useful in practice, as a kind of art for dealing with people, helping them, guiding them, healing them. But all systems are finally a mental poison, the rotten apples of the mind's life. Systems have turned us into slaves, dwarfs. The disinterested contemplation of life is a different matter, as for example in Paul Claudel's "Second Ode," where the author exclaims, "Oh Credo full of things seen and unseen." That's finally all that counts: disinterested contemplation of the world, brimming with admiration or revulsion, or both together. Systems don't permit disinterested contemplation: they're sieves, they sift, segregate, eliminate, smooth, simplify, diminish. Systems are like mnemonic devices, ideal for accelerated evening courses . . . A person who masters any one of them—it demands just a few months of intensive cramming—will be liberated from true knowledge, from authentic, free, gleeful erudition open to reality, but open as well to dozens of varied traditions, hundreds of different painters, composers, writers, united by nothing, almost, except perhaps their unconditional refusal to be tidied within a single system. Each sought truth at first hand, painfully, in joy and disappointment, in depression and inspiration, and each paid a different price for this quest. Some of them met, even became friends, such as Delacroix and Chopin; some knew nothing about each other and still don't. Those who seek only peaceful contemplation of the world don't form creative societies, don't carry membership cards. They don't want theoretical justification for their works. In his splendid poem on Chopin, Gottfried Benn says, "When Delacroix pronounced his theory, he grew anxious, / since he had no way of justifying nocturnes." It's extraordinary: Justifying nocturnes! Justifying ballades!

Iwaszkiewicz traveled a great deal, mainly in Italy, but also in Denmark and Poland; and in every town, whether famous, such as Venice, or obscure, such as Sandomierz, he had his favorite spots, strolls, paintings. No system unified these towns, each had its own scent, its weeds, its bonfire smoke, its swallows and sparrows, its little cafés, its regional museums, its hours of grief, its happy moments. In each one person rejoiced and another despaired. Each had its local lunatic and at least one lovely, noble face. Iwaszkiewicz loved individuality. He was an exceptionally sensual writer, his heroes are consumed by love, love creates and destroys them, time and the world's neglect destroy them. One weakness in Iwaszkiewicz: at times death comes as predictably, as automatically, as a hotel breakfast, as if summoned by the author, not by fate. Iwaszkiewicz had a great gift for death, it occasionally helped him to solve his writerly dilemmas, it simplified quandaries resisting resolution. This happens, for one example, in his glorious story "Anna Grazzi"—glorious, but neatly wrapped up with a death *ex machina*.

He had a superb writer's memory, he returned to distant experiences, moments when he'd caught sight of something lovely, particular, expressive, to the great or minor revelations that every traveler experiences. He loved music above all and knew it well. He was apparently a decent pianist himself. Music is idiographic by nature. Music enters Iwaszkiewicz's writing even when it goes unmentioned. Music, which is particularity's queen, its victory over the dreariness of theory, which opens only to those who know how to listen. Music kills systems. So why should Nabokov, that great connoisseur of the particular, be absolutely deaf to music? We don't know. Iwaszkiewicz read writers who are almost forgotten today—Chledowski, Kremer. He recommended Eliza Orzeszkowska's letters to everyone. He was obsessed with Kierkegaard (whom he translated)—another foe of systems. I found something similar in Paul Léautaud, the French diarist, eccentric, and cat lover—I used to read him fervently (though not anymore). Léautaud, a truly second-tier writer—he flaunted it—attacked the postwar writers, the generation of

Sartre and Camus. He complained that the reins of literary power had passed to philosophy professors, pedantic monomaniacs, weak stylists, as he thought, with no access to the riches of artistic French, blind to the world's multiplicity, to the unforeseen, to wildness, to the extraneous, the tragic and the comic; they'd stifled the living voice of human individuality, the voice of particular, irrepeatable expression, idiosyncrasy. Iwaszkiewicz thought exactly the same thing. In one letter from his American travels he said, speaking of France, "It slowly forgets its noblest experiences from the Occupation and, consumed by fear and ambition, gives . . . the impression of an invalid. All its contemporary literature reflects this condition. In Paris I read both Sartre and Camus. Very gifted, but oblivious to the writer's true calling." (I'd gladly take up Camus's cause here . . .) And what is the writer's, the artist's, true calling? Iwaszkiewicz often considers this difficult question (any system would give its perfectly codified, boldfaced answer on the spot), for example, during another trip, this time in Sicily, in Syracuse, near the spring of Arethusa, with its shallow, dark water overgrown with papyrus. He thinks of Karol Szymanowski and writes, "I see the face and gestures of that man, who transformed all his love of life and all the inadequacy of human striving into sound, so as to measure that life, comprehend it, and give it a final, artistic justice, justice in beauty . . . not a quantifiable, mathematical justice to be weighed on Archimedes's scales, but that most essential justice, so when a person hears, or sees, reads or views it, he says to himself, This is truth, this is life, this is love, this is death." And when we read Iwaszkiewicz, we can say nothing more, since we haven't learned anything new in the many years that divide us from his moment, the moment holding his travels and struggles, his discoveries, his sufferings, we still can't explain anything. We can only repeat, Here is truth, here is love, here is death.

•

Iwaszkiewicz once said that he "hated Galicia" (although he had fond memories of Krakow, he liked coming here). He also "hated Vienna." He "hated" city life, a cramped existence in apartments, he spent a lifetime remembering the past, the legends of the Ukrainian estates of his childhood (though his own parents occupied a fairly low rung on that world's social ladder). In Leningrad, he was disappointed on visiting the apartment of Aleksandr Blok, whose poetry meant so much to him; disappointed, since the apartment's on an upper floor and there's nothing special about it, not even a fine view. He was shocked to find that Blok's imagination could be cooped up in an ordinary apartment. Estates, palaces, the Ukrainian steppes' expanse, the fields of Sicily—yes, poetry could function there, but not in some mundane fourth-floor apartment.

•

Another note from Julien Green's diary, this time from April 21, 1935. The writer is in Rome, on St. Peter's Square, where crowds are, as usual, cheering for the pope—Pope Pius XI at this time. So among the thousands cheering, Green passes by "hundreds of German Catholics crying *'Heil'* and raising their right arms." He doesn't even comment on the pleasure the German Catholics apparently thought they were giving the pope by this Nazi greeting.

•

One photograph in the Witkacy exhibit shows a man in a pilot's cap, inscribed *Elzenberg, aviator*. This must be Henryk Elzenberg, the philosopher, whose place in literary history is due chiefly to his role as Zbigniew Herbert's friend and teacher. He wasn't permitted to teach much in the Stalinist years, but a circle of students, including the young Herbert, surrounded him just the same. He wrote many works studied by specialists; but the greatest of them are his intellectual diaries, which were published under the title *The Trouble with Existence* in the late 1960s; they've lost nothing of their power today. It's an exceptional book. Elzenberg was influenced by a range of traditions: nineteenth-century historicism, Eastern philosophy, he found masters from Goethe to Gandhi. In *The Trouble with Existence*, he reveals an encompassing intellect, unprotected by any kind of philosophical armor. Just the opposite: these are the notes of a defenseless man, who spent fifty years scrupulously recording his observations, his doubts, he comments on his rich, wide-ranging readings, reacts to historical events. He engages with the classic questions of the philosophy of culture, but also with dilemmas less frequently encountered in the history of systematic thought. One such problem is the link between poetry and life: Does a person preoccupied by poetry, imagination, inevitably stand at a remove from life? . . . Elzenberg doesn't have a clear answer to the question, he struggles with it constantly, coming down on the side of life one time, and defending the imagination the next. During the First World War, he comments that poetry has won in the debate with life, since the drama of war has shown what life can be in its "amplitude, richness, tragedy, splendor." But this observation comes early on, when the terrors of trench warfare hadn't yet been disclosed. During the Second World War, while living in hell (since Nazi-occupied Poland was hell), he continues his reading, the patient recording of his thoughts. He never doubted the value of contemplating art, of ideas and literature, and this at a time when other writers and thinkers, stunned by the war's catastrophes, the Holocaust, spurned the entire history of European culture, choosing nihilism instead—like offended children. He managed to keep his intellectual independence amid brutal historical realities; he continued to comment on his reading as the Battle of Stalingrad raged. He didn't construct a philosophical system, he didn't advance a single "central metaphor," he never entered the pantheon of great philosophers—but he left behind a book whose greatest virtue is its "softness," its rejection of final conclusions, its ongoing, daily reckoning with the world. In Elzenberg's diaries, it's as if each night erased his earlier meditations and opened all his doubts anew—is this the philosopher's defeat? He started fresh each day, as if he didn't allow himself to read the earlier entries, as if he had to address the fundamental questions ab ovo. Is this defeat or triumph? Does he simply equivocate, is he incapable of taking a clear-cut position, staking his claim, and energetically defending his territory? I'll admit, sometimes his endless questing does bother me. At other times, though, I'm convinced that he won a great victory, precisely because he achieved two things: he didn't find the answers, but he never forgot the questions.

•

In the preface to Iwaszkiewicz's *Diaries*, the author cites a marvelous aphorism taken from the critic Karol Irzykowski: "Anything can be lived through to the end, nothing can be thought through to the end."

•

We spent a few weeks in the little town of Leuk (the Canton of Valais, or Wallis, in German), in the Rhône River valley courtesy of the Spycher Literary Prize. The valley of the young Rhône is remarkable. The world could have begun in this place. Some trace of that primordial chaos before the world's creation seems to survive here, at times some vast cliff rises in the wrong spot, a stream descends from too great a height. The valley is enormous; gray-white clouds drift slowly at its highest point, hawks glide a little lower, while ants and humans scurry about their day's work on the valley floor. Painstakingly tended vineyards climb the slopes, their tracks and patterns as regular as a French orthographic dictionary. The medieval town of Leuk, tiny as a village, lies twenty or thirty meters above the Rhône in the German-speaking zone. This is Rilke's domain; Leuk is located midway between the tower of Muzot, where he wrote the *Duino Elegies*, and the church in Raron where he's buried.

•

Guillaume Apollinaire died on November 9, 1918—he was only thirty-eight years old. His organism, weakened by the heavy injuries he'd sustained at the front, couldn't withstand the Spanish flu. He lay dying just as the First World War concluded, and witnesses recalled how crowds filled the ravine of boulevard Saint-Germain—where the poet occupied a top-floor apartment—and chanted, "À bas Guillaume"—Down with Guillaume—meaning Wilhelm, the German kaiser.

I've long loved—along with "Zone" and a few other poems—one work of Apollinaire's particularly, "La Jolie Rousse," "The Pretty Redhead." It's one of his last works, a kind of testament. I'll quote it here in Roger Shattuck's translation:

Behold me before all a man of good sense
Knowing life and of death what a living man can
    know
Having experienced the griefs and the joys of love
Having been able to assert his ideas on occasion
Knowing several languages
Having travelled a good bit
Having seen the war in the Artillery and Infantry
Wounded in the head trepanned under chloroform
Having lost his best friends in that frightful struggle
I know of the old and of the new as much as one man
    alone can know of them
And without being uneasy today about this war
Between us and for us my friends
I pronounce judgement on this long quarrel of tradition
    and innovation
        Of Order and Adventure

You whose mouths are made in the image of God's
          Mouths which are order itself

Be indulgent when you compare us
To those who have been the perfection of order
We who seek everywhere for adventure

We are not your enemies
We wish to offer you vast and strange domains
Where flowering mystery offers itself to whoever
          wishes to pick it
There are new fires there and colors never yet seen
A thousand imponderable phantasms
To which reality must be given
We would explore goodness a vast country where
          everything is silent
There is also time which one can banish or call back
Pity us who fight always in the front lines
Of the limitless and of the future
Pity our errors pity our sins
Behold the return of summer season of violence
And my youth died like the spring
O Sun it is the time for flaming Judgement
                    And I wait
To follow for ever the sweet noble form
It assumes in order that I may love it alone
It comes and it attracts me as a magnet does the needle
                    It looks for all the world just like
                    My redhead darling my beloved

Her hair is really gold you'd say
A flash of lightning which endures
Or flames which dance a proud pavane
In roses as they slowly fade

But laugh laugh long at me
Men from anywhere above all men of this place
For there are so many things I dare not tell you
So many things you will not let me say
Have pity on me

This striking poem is difficult to interpret; we have an avant-garde poet begging for forgiveness, for mercy, when the standard avant-garde tone is arrogant. Apollinaire was torn between tradition and modernity; he adored older poetry and knew it well, yet he advocated novelty, the renewal of artistic expression, he recalls the once-famous battle of the Ancients and the Moderns. But here, in this poem, he stands at the world's center, at a crossroads. It's a late poem, as I said, the poet had been seriously wounded at the front (the line about trepanning refers to this), he doesn't have much life left. What does it mean to stand in the world's center, between archaism and modernity? Perhaps it means that someone who's known true suffering no longer treats the slogans of ambitious young artists with deadly earnestness. Someone who stands between life and death no longer places faith in programs and manifestos.

•

Yesterday on an evening walk. I stopped by the Gothic Church of St. Mark, one of the oldest in Krakow, and spent a long time watching the swifts. They must like that old church with its dark bricks; they make their nests there, it's their building, their home. At dusk they lovingly circle the church's walls, they move with phenomenal speed, whistling shrilly, accelerating at moments, ignoring the human world completely. They look like they're storming the church, a besieging army, exceptionally mobile. I share this sensation for a moment, I assume the viewpoint of the swifts careening through the ever-darkening air, I look up, not at the passersby, I admire the agility of these black arrows aimed capriciously at all points of the globe. I know that they're just hunting insects. But now, at dusk, as they ensnare the church's bulk with their trajectories, I forget this, I hear only their whistling, I admire the patrolling swifts, who perform their daring loop-the-loops through ancient Krakow's narrow streets like Europe's greatest circus artists, and later, when the long, patient work of dusk concludes, they vanish in the darkness, as if dissolving into the night.

•

If I could write novels, I might try to write a book about a man who wants to live his life only in brief, intense moments of mystical revelation, while neglecting everything that happens predictably in endlessly repetitive days and weeks, he views those days and weeks as insufferable drudgery, as the dreary cotton wool with which life is stuffed, in which, so my hero would think, things happen only for banal, dramaturgical reasons—since we can't live exclusively in moments, after all, Darwin would never permit it. The man wouldn't necessarily have to be a practicing artist, a thinker, he might simply confine himself to intense experiences. He might also make notes, hoping that they would one day lead to his *Hauptwerk* (Witkacy's term). His philosophy proves its worth, such as it is, only in times of relative peace, but then war breaks out, ominous SS uniforms appear, or the only slightly less ominous uniforms of the NKVD, the Soviet secret police. And our mystic finds himself caught in a trap. He's being destroyed by the monstrous, primitive machine of modern history, which disdains even the subtler approaches to time measured in days and weeks, not to mention those ecstatic seconds. Henryk Elzenberg, who knew and admired Marcus Aurelius's *Meditations*, would be a prime candidate for the novel's hero. In some ways he lived through aphorisms, in aphorisms, and not in the systematic continuity of events. In 1938 he commented in his diary, "War draws closer and closer, it will erupt any day, without warning. We must be mentally prepared. It will reach deeper into life than the last war. It will undermine *everything*, destroy the ground beneath our feet. It won't leave us the kind of peace that the earlier war did; you could still fall in love, argue, make up, write articles on philosophy, present them at the Academy, get a fellowship to Vienna and spend weeks on end looking at paintings in galleries and reading books about Rembrandt . . . For those who've staked their cards on thought, on art, this may be the *end*—literally."

•

A few more words on Iwaszkiewicz's *Diary*: In the early sixties, Iwaszkiewicz spends some time, as usual, in his beloved Sandomierz, and one night he hears a teenaged boy playing a harmonica. Some girls listen raptly. The famous writer, nearly seventy, a dignitary high in the regime's graces, is gripped by envy—he envies Sandomierz's young inhabitants, he envies them the evening, the dusk, their youth, that harmonica, a symbol of freedom and gentle inspiration.

•

I don't know much about Elzenberg's life under Nazi occupation. I know only that he managed to survive. And I know that he lived in Vilnius then, that he taught secretly, that he got by on temporary jobs, he worked, for example, as the night watchman in a carpentry factory. This struck me as a revelation: the thinker as night watchman, a watchman with a meditative disposition, who likes contemplating the night sky. As Elzenberg himself once remarked, every writer faces a choice: Should he tell the stars about his generation, or tell his generation about the stars? . . . During his stint as a night watchman, he could talk with the stars at his leisure. He certainly didn't travel to Vienna, didn't linger before the paintings of old masters. But he survived. And in spite of all, he didn't abandon his beloved diary, in which he stubbornly, systematically, perhaps not daily, but regularly, composed his endless letter to us, to coming generations. So he couldn't actually serve as my novel's hero—the war didn't shatter him, Stalinism didn't crush him. It might even seem, for all my unwritten novel's early premises, that his aphoristic way of life permitted his survival, or at least abetted it, that the indispensable drop of nonchalance shaping this man who lived in moments increased his chance of survival in a time of mass repression, tremendous danger . . . It's as if someone chasing butterflies had missed a mass arrest by accident or luck, since he's been following the insects' chaotic flight, which is nothing like his persecutors' harsh, monotonous march.

But chance destroyed many other aesthetes and mystics (it can be hard to tell them apart); they blundered, lost in thought, they walked into a roundup, they stopped by a friend's place, where a trap lay waiting, an SS officer was having a bad day and didn't like their looks on some Lvov or Warsaw street. And their chance of escape was near zero if they were Jews.

Elzenberg, who came from an assimilated Jewish family, survived the war only to fall prey to the next ideological system; he became a subject of the Soviet empire. Yet even then, in those dark years, he found friends and students, among them the puckish young poet Zbigniew Herbert. Elzenberg wasn't allowed to teach from 1950 on, thanks to his "incorrigible idealism" (as *Wikipedia* puts it). He lived to see 1956, though, and the relaxed restrictions on scholarly and intellectual pursuits. He died at the age of eighty, in 1967, having witnessed the success of his greatest publication, the work that gathered and preserved so masterfully the fruits of so many moments of meditation. No, I won't write a novel about him.

•

I don't know if I remember this correctly, from my late childhood, from the time when I first began to recognize, to suspect, some kind of doubleness in the world's nature: it's not just the perfectly obvious, empirical layer, the opulent, imperial layer that dominates life's chief currents, that makes up all the basic components of a relatively stable life, including trams and trains (even when they're late), newsstands and flower shops, schools and drugstores; something else lies concealed beneath it, something unnamed, without which quotidian ordinariness would wither, shrivel like a scrap of paper cast into a fire. I lived about a six- or seven-minute walk from the local library, I was a passionate reader, mainly of novels, which were all, without exception, clad in dark brown wrapping paper, as if someone had put them in uniform, hoping to standardize their unstandardizable variety. We had lots of books at home, too, but I thought I'd already read them all, as Mallarmé says in "Brise marine" ("j'ai lu tous les livres"). The books at home were too comfortable, too familiar. I wanted independence. The library was housed at the time in the town hall; a sturdy plaque on the wall informed us that King John III Sobieski had spent the night here on his way to save Vienna. The king, I thought, had slept in my library. And all the dark brown books seemed vaguely regal as a result. I went to the library every day, almost every day. I find it hard to believe how quickly I read back then, usually skipping the nature descriptions. I gather from talking to my friends that this wasn't particularly unusual; I conclude that my friends likewise devoured books and ignored nature descriptions. Trees and meadows, lilac bushes and the little birds that lived in them, failed to capture our attention. Maybe we thought that we had so many birds and bushes all around us that we could just toss them right into our reading, as a cook tosses salt into a pot of macaroni. I said a six- or seven-minute walk, but it wasn't a walk, it was anarchic wandering. I loved the moment of leaving the house, as soon as I was old enough to go out alone, the moment of happiness, freedom, when for an instant my family seemed like a prison that I'd just escaped. And then the moment of carrying the newly borrowed books back home, which no longer seemed like a prison, as if my absence had purged it. A newly borrowed book promised extraordinary adventures. I still remember the thrill of pleasure and expectation produced by a freshly checked-out book, the anticipated surprise. More thrilling even than a book from a bookstore, newly bought—which brought with it a sense of responsibility for my new possession. The library, on the other hand, is a realm of free love, offering unencumbered romance, fleeting affairs, fickle reading, sometimes rapture, sometimes boredom, but always that option of quick changes. No one checks, fortunately, to see if we've actually read the books we've taken home. At times the books brought the mobile surface of events to a halt. And not just the books. At times all reality seemed to stand still. When I ran from the house out to the street, I was free, open to every adventure. Others apparently couldn't see these adventures, they took place only in my inner world. Heavy cumulus clouds paused, watches stopped. We all lived in the dusty history of the weekly film chronicles; the narrator's energetic, joyful voice embodied the glorious nature of our age, it grows, thrives, rises, blooms. Luckily, this universal melody could be evaded now and then, you didn't even have to leave home. Sometimes just sitting by the window would do, watching a storm cloud, blue-black and ominous, as if it had just sailed in from ancient Rome. Or catching sight of a neighbor who'd gone outside in his pajamas. Or—I'd moved from the window— sometimes a violin would play a sweet tune on the radio, for an instant its promises would shatter the all-too-palpable reality of an autumn afternoon. The radio's voices were marvelous. As long as you couldn't see the actual people through the brocade covering the speaker. They were voices with no faces. Television destroyed this unwritten contract, it added faces and even bellies. I liked the radio dramas, where desert winds howled and violent seas raged. I suspected that the ocean crashed in a tin bucket and the wind whistled through an actor's lips, but it didn't bother me. These were fixed points, spots where the bus of dailiness stopped. Points of momentary freedom. That might return.

•

A few days in Paris—this time in April, when the city is loveliest, when the majestic green reaches the peak of its botanical dignity, when plane trees rise triumphantly above the boulevard Saint-Germain, above the noisy cars filling the streets, as if the trees had realized that they are the city's long-term residents, unlike those tin phantoms doomed to end their brief days in vast, rusty graveyards. The poetry fair (Marché de la poésie) was being held in the place Saint-Sulpice; I'd been quite skeptical of this event previously, I had my doubts about its artificial concentration of poets. I'd given it wide berth while I'd lived in Paris, but everything changed this year, I was a visitor from Krakow, I inhaled the Parisian landscapes and scents. And in the bookstore la Procure, two smiling young men working the cash registers, probably students—it was afternoon, there weren't many customers—were both reading passages from Rimbaud, savoring them, which struck me as more convincing proof of poetry's presence than the official book fair with its wooden stands and scores of rare editions, with its poets patiently waiting at little tables, placed on public display, for sale, waiting for someone to come up with a newly purchased book, requesting a dedication. But I, too, kept watch at a little table for an hour, I, too, was for sale.

•

The Luxembourg Gardens spread right beside us: one of the magical forces that make Paris one of Europe's few eternal cities, retaining—since when? the Revolution? perhaps the great reconstruction dating back to Napoleon the Third and Baron Haussmann?—a stylistic unity rarely seen elsewhere. The Parisian cafés, with their stone floors littered until recently with cigarette butts, but also the plane trees on the boulevard Saint-Germain: a nervous city, paced in the wintertime by students clad in corduroy jackets and office workers in suits, both groups alike without overcoats despite the sharp air, wearing only those red scarves tied in a knot whose secret other cities haven't mastered. The red cashmere scarf is a telling symbol: Paris is a southern city, don't be fooled by the cold, the snow. The Luxembourg Gardens formed the backdrop for a scene that took place in the thirties, as Raymond Aron recalled many years later. It was a lovely spring day, Aron and his wife went for a stroll and found Simone Weil sobbing in one of its avenues (Aron and Weil knew each other well, they'd worked together at the École normale). "What's wrong?" the Arons asked. "Do you mean you haven't heard?" Weil replied. "The Shanghai police have opened fire on the workers!"

•

I was listening to Tchaikovsky's Violin Concerto; I don't know it well, I'd long since rejected the composer programmatically, too sentimental, too easy. But I've grown more tolerant with age, now I realize how many wonderful pieces he has. And listening to the middle segment, the "Canzonetta. Andante," I remembered what Sviatoslav Richter told Bruno Monsaingeon: he was supposed to perform a concerto in Leningrad during the siege. He'd come to a city where so many had perished from bombs and missiles, and from hunger and exhaustion in the winter, frozen corpses lay piled by the walls of houses or on the bridges above canals. And in this poor, tortured city, which was fully equipped for sound (it's a little known peculiarity of the Soviet Union: every street had its own loudspeaker, which could instantly transmit the ruler's mood to his subjects' souls), every speaker was broadcasting the Violin Concerto's slow movement, the "Canzonetta. Andante." I can't forget it. The juxtaposition of that

brave, dying city, where the sick and elderly paid with their lives
for their military leaders' decisions, with the violin's slow song,
the contrast between the stench, the bleak streets, the ruins, and
that sweet cantilena stays with me. That lovely melody from
every street post, every speaker. In that dead setting.

•

It was really just like that: sometime in the midnineties, in
May, in a Tuscan village where impossibly swift swallows flit-
ted through narrow streets, we ended up in a crowded café—we
wanted something to drink—and at the next table I saw a
German tourist reading a little book, whose title I spotted when
he turned his head for a moment. (I'm not the only one who likes
finding out what other people read on their vacations.) It was
Mysticism for Beginners (*Mystik für Anfänger*), a how-to book for
spiritual searchers (the very idea's a little silly, to tell the truth).
I won't bother copying out the poem that bears the same title, but
I experienced an epiphany: poetry is mysticism for beginners.
That German tourist traveling through Tuscany with his funny
little book helped me to realize that poetry differs from religion
in essential ways, that poetry stops at a certain moment, stifles its
exaltation, doesn't enter the monastery, it remains in the world,
among the swallows and the tourists, among palpable, visible
things. It describes people and things, participates in their concrete existence, walks streets wet with rain, listens to the radio,
goes swimming in Mediterranean inlets. It's a little like those
politicians who like to remind us how close they are to ordinary
life, they know the price of butter, bread, and bus tickets; and
like those politicians, poetry can be less than truthful, since it
yearns at times for *something different*.

•

Rue Servandoni, right by the Luxembourg Gardens. One of my
favorite Parisian streets, or rather side streets; quiet, almost always

empty. One building bears a plaque informing us that the Marquis Nicolas de Condorcet spent the last months of his life in hiding here; he'd been sentenced to death by the Revolution. In the end, he left his hiding place, was recognized, denounced, arrested, and shortly afterward died in prison under uncertain circumstances. In the months preceding his arrest he worked on his final project, *Esquisse d'un tableau historique des progrès de l'esprit humain.* The Revolution's thugs were out to get him, and he writes on progress! He listened for footsteps echoing in the quiet side street, but retained his faith in progress. He kept one ear open for his persecutors' footsteps, while the other heard the ever-advancing music of the future. He witnessed the terror unleashed by the Jacobins, but never lost his faith in human perfectibility. I don't know what to admire more, the courage or the blindness of the philosopher hiding in a house on Servandoni Street.

•

One of poetry's limits: I had a friend from the university, Hanka Kozarzewska from the town of Nysa, whom I hadn't seen in many years. When we finally got back in touch a little while ago, she asked me to review a book of poems written by her father, Jerzy, who'd passed away. She told me her father's remarkable story; I came upon it again in the biography of the poet Julian Tuwim by Piotr Matywiecki, who draws chiefly on the account of Tadeusz Januszewski. So Jerzy Kozarzewski, an officer in the National Armed Forces, a radically nationalist, anticommunist underground movement, was sentenced to death in 1946 by a Communist court. Five other people were sentenced along with him. Without other options, his desperate family turned to Tuwim, who had just returned from his wartime emigration, hence the Communist regime treated him like the Archangel Gabriel. They gave him an apartment, a villa, a chauffeured car, he appeared constantly in the press and on the radio, he was granted access to those at the pinnacle of the party hierarchy. He was an invaluable ally for the new ruling class; an immensely famous poet before the war, he had undergone a political sea change during the war years, he came out in support of the extreme left and decided to return to Poland—unlike most of his generation—thus legitimizing the new system. Tuwim's mother had been murdered by the Nazis while her son was in New York (the family was of Jewish descent). The National Armed Forces wasn't known for its philo-Semitism. Tuwim nonetheless decided to intervene on behalf of the condemned man and the other five individuals. His plea to Boleslaw Bierut, the head of the government, has been preserved. This is an excerpt: "For two weeks, since I accidentally discovered that I could help to save these people, I've been walking around like a madman. I'm not even afraid to admit that some kind of mystic aura enveloped me . . . since how could I possibly justify my presence on earth more profoundly than by returning life to those facing death? Since what is the poet's mission, in the final, essential sense of that word? It is to do good. Sometimes this good is called beauty, sometimes knowledge, sometimes truth. For two thousand years that good has summoned people in vain from the cross."

As the authors I draw upon comment, Tuwim expressly stated his aversion to nationalist views; he wanted only to save these young people's lives. And something extraordinary occurred: Bierut pardoned them. Tuwim had saved them. In the midfifties, when the political climate changed, they went free. My friend went without her father for several years, but she didn't lose him. He died in the last century after a long life. Here we come up against one of poetry's boundaries. Tuwim was an inspired, uneven poet, lofty, but with a marvelous sense of humor (though the two elements rarely meet in his poetry). After the war he made a deal impossible for a true artist; showered with money and honors, he was cut off from ordinary human solidarity, from those living in a city of ruins where human remains still turned up in buried basements, from all the people who lacked villas, fine apartments, chauffeured cars, telephones linking them directly to Bierut. He was cut off, in other words, from the great mass of those around him, and yet he did something splendid. He gave sense to the unfortunate fact of his artificial elevation by saving the lives of these six people. He was given to understand shortly afterward, his biographer writes, that there would be no more pardons, that he hadn't been brought to Warsaw to bother the authorities with his humanitarian interventions.

●

Speaking of the good, goodness: in his *Notebooks*, Cioran observes that goodness is a wonderful thing in human beings, but he immediately adds that it can never be combined with strong intelligence. If this were indeed the case, the world would be a terrible place. Fortunately, this comment belongs among the mistakes that occasionally punctuate the work of the great misanthrope. One example will do to debunk his thesis: Jozef Czapski. Or to name someone truly famous: Friedrich Nietzsche, who proclaimed the will to power and contempt for the weak, but was honest, gentle, and good in his daily life (Cioran himself mentions this from time to time). And Cioran was afraid of loneliness, though he celebrated it in his writings. Writers shouldn't be taken on faith.

●

An entry in Jozef Czapski's diary (from November 4, 1961). He'd just seen an exhibit of Mark Tobey, the abstract expressionist, and after quoting the title of Simone Weil's famous collection, *La pesanteur et la grâce* (*Gravity and Grace*), he says this of the American painter: "In that *grâce* of Tobey, in that contemplation fed by religious syncretism . . . there is a kind of distance from the real essence of our life, our globe. I suddenly felt that this does not even tempt me, that my world is in gravity, in masses, in heavy matter, which we should transform, à la Rembrandt, but not forget, as Tobey does." His comment, so powerful, is close to me: the sense that art should not, must not, divorce itself from *la pesanteur*, from what is painful, even ugly, that every quest for clarity, radiance, must proceed through full consciousness of what constrains us. This might be one definition of rapture: rapture means to forget pain, ugliness, suffering, to focus only on beauty. But purely rapturous works provoke only my opposition or indifference. Precisely the endless battle between heaviness, suffering, and illumination, elevation, forms art's essence.

•

Swifts also like the basilica of St. Catherine's Church, a huge Gothic cathedral whose history abounds in dramas, fires, and even earthquakes; thus the structure was never completed—there is no tower, it's a vast hangar. More swifts gather here even than at St. Mark's. Their flight is chaotic, partly collective—they happily serve in patrols of ten or twelve birds—and partly individual, single swifts keep shooting off from the flocks of their black brethren. They circle through the warm air, they whistle, and their whistling sounds rough, strange, otherworldly; Kaspar Hauser might have whistled that way.

•

Gloomy circumstances of a historical nature lend weight to Czapski's notebooks (Czapski hints at this in the comment I just cited). The massacre of Arabs in Paris took place on October 17, 1961. The Algerian War was raging at the time; dozens of, perhaps a hundred or more, bodies ended up in the Seine. Historians say that police dumped the murdered Arab protesters into the river from the beautiful Pont Saint-Michel in the heart of old Paris. The massacre is one of the most shameful episodes in postwar French history. The prefect of police at the time was the infamous Maurice Papon, who had so energetically collaborated with the Nazis during Vichy—he was the secretary general of the prefecture in Bordeaux and helped to deport more than sixteen hundred Jews. Czapski had this massacre fresh in his memory (though the French papers reported it only later and never gave the full dimensions of the crime) as he discussed Tobey's elegant art. He most certainly didn't expect a literal, faithful depiction of such a tragedy. But he didn't want "contemplation fed by religious syncretism" to divorce itself entirely from the world's pain, its ugliness. The knots binding pain to beauty should never be undone completely . . .

•

In Berlin, in my beloved Gemäldegalerie, the heir of a quiet museum in Dahlem, which few tourists visited in the old days, when the city was divided into two civilizations. Zbigniew Herbert was one of these rare tourists, he visited the museum repeatedly; he brought a notebook and sketched the paintings he particularly liked. Today that collection occupies a huge building in the heart of Berlin, right by Potsdamer Platz, but it still doesn't draw many visitors for some strange reason, unlike the Louvre, where you can't find a spot to stand among the throngs of tourists from every continent. The museum building was perfectly designed. An enormous rectangular hall, completely empty—if you don't count the discreet water feature in the center—creates a meditative space where you may order your thoughts, on a polished wooden bench, if you prefer sitting. From the hall you enter galleries brimming with masterpieces. A different picture catches my attention every time. For example, Poussin's dark, matter-of-fact portrait of himself as a serious man, a professional artist. Or Brueghel's little painting depicting two monkeys chained to a wall while a great port bustles in the background, boats sailing, birds flying. (Wislawa Szymborska wrote a wonderful poem about it.) This little work demonstrates not only great craft, but great wisdom. "About suffering they were never wrong, / The Old Masters," Auden writes in "Musée des Beaux Arts," a poem inspired by the Brueghel painting depicting the fall of Icarus. The two monkeys aren't looking anywhere, their gaze is fixed in the niche that has become their cage—they pay no attention to the port, the boats, the birds. The old masters understood the meaning of captivity: indifference to the world, the boats, the birds, enclosure in diminished space. Or an even smaller painting, a late Rubens work, a landscape with a gallows. A castle rises in the distance, silent, monumental. The wind rocks the trees and the white hanged man. The clouds are dark, dreary, but there's a glimpse of light at the painting's right edge. We don't know if it's sunrise or sunset.

•

One key question that every reader of poetry or poet must face from time to time: Does the light, the poetic force without which no great poem could take shape, exist only in our imagination, in intense, blissful fantasies of inspiration, or does it have some counterpart in reality? Is it only a leap of imagination, a holiday from the ordinary, a festival of language, or does it uncover something that is usually concealed, but truly exists? Much depends on the answer to this question. If questioned, I myself would say, I have my doubts, I worry at times that this light is only Saint Elmo's fire, glowing on the masts of our imagination. But ultimately, were I freed from my doubts, rooted in a pure and powerful place, I'd reply, what is most remarkable, wonderful (and rare) in poetry derives from reality, from a dimension that seldom reveals itself, from some radiant part of the planet.

•

Every time I'm in Paris, I think about the twenty years I spent here, twenty years give or take a month or two—a year or two, if you subtract my trips to the United States from the Parisian total. I went to Paris for M.—I was not such a young man, but I still seemed to be governed by impulse, and not by careful thought. Some literary friends active in the opposition back then couldn't understand my motives. "That's no way to shape your biography," I heard. "Love, sure, but at your age?" "We need you here, not over there." I didn't dismiss these voices, but I couldn't obey them either. I knew I'd never be a political activist—but I could write anywhere, even abroad. I went to Paris, which had already ceased to be, as Jerzy Stempowski had noted much earlier, the Central Laboratory of European art and poetry. (Stempowski couldn't forgive France, which he had once loved and to which he remained grateful, for the decline symbolized by Vichy's infamy as well as by the bloody epilogue to French colonialism.) When I was living there, Paris was known chiefly for new, or revitalized, methodologies in the humanities. The great, internationally famed Methodologists were already ailing, aging, proclaiming their last lectures, passing on. The Methodologists had embraced leftist ideologies in their youth, but returned later in life to humanist views: they defended human rights, they spoke up for the Vietnamese boat people and Polish "Solidarity." I never acquired a taste for their work, even though I had friends (or rather acquaintances) who insisted that the Methodologists continued the great French humanist traditions. But wasn't it also a methodologist—who happened to be a great poet, too— T. S. Eliot, who said, "There is no method except to be very intelligent"?

Paris loved methodology, though—and novels. The Methodologists were like tailors who don't make clothes, they just crafted treatises on beautiful apparel. Or at least like the needle from the Arabian proverb: it dresses the whole world while staying naked itself. In reality, though, Paris loved only novels. The Methodologists were intended for export, they were meant to impress North and South America, Asia, and Europe, all of Europe,

Southern, Northern, Western, and Eastern, also known as Central, along with Australia and New Zealand. But I don't recall ever seeing someone engrossed in a Methodologist on the metro. No, in the metro cars I encountered only thick novels. The novel industry has been around for some time now; who was it who wrote about customers lining up in nineteenth-century Odessa for a new shipment of Parisian novels clad in yellow dustcovers? I even suspected a secret agreement between the Paris metro management and the publishers pumping out vast quantities of popular novels in yellow or bright pink dustcovers virtually unchanged since Balzac's time. Since passengers on public transportation required novels. The metro lines grew ever longer, new stations sprang up, new connections—this was why the novels kept getting thicker. It sometimes even happened that readers absorbed in the thickest novels didn't get off at the last stop, they just kept reading. Almost no one wanted poetry, poetry was no help with duration, with narrative, it provided only great moments, lightning bolts, but moments and lightning bolts went unacknowledged, they were considered erratic, impractical; narrative alone was held to be therapeutic. Narrative healed wounds, bandaged less-than-successful lives, mended cuts and bruises, depression. Narrative offered thick slices of sense, it was like a huge holiday ham, pink and fragrant, it could last for many afternoons and evenings. It was like the Himalayas, the Andes. Narrative cast bridges between the difficult days of the week; narrative drew on the world of dreams, it told of love, of betrothals, it led its readers to the wedding day and then discreetly withdrew. Moreover, a thick novel read in the metro seemed part of home, it transformed the unfriendly train into a kind of household annex. The lightning bolts of poems required healthy readers, who were hard to come by. Lightning bolts heal no one, they may even kill. A lightning bolt can't feel like home.

For all this, many things in methodological, novelistic Paris enthralled me, I can't pretend to have been offended by it. I was often a solitary wanderer there, mornings and afternoons I worked at home, in dreary, suburban Courbevoie, I wrote, or tried to write, sometimes I could only read, listen to music, wait for better times, times of enthusiasm, of writing; after lunch, though, I almost always took the suburban train into the city, regardless of whether I'd managed to ignite imagination's bonfire earlier that day. It took only five minutes to reach the Gare Saint-Lazare, once painted by Monet (the painting in which a cloud of smoke presses against the station's glass vaults), and from there I set out to the various districts.

I observed Parisian houses and churches, streets with dramatic profiles—for example, the picturesque ravine of rue de Lille, which served in spring and summer evenings as a kind of telescope focused on the west. Rue de Lille is a perfect example of Parisian construction; two rows of stone houses stand so close along the narrow street that they really do look like an optical instrument. If you stood at the corner of rue de Lille and rue des Saints-Pères and gazed westward, you'd witness a splendid vision: the street brimming with multitiered cumuli, and at its end, beneath an impressive white-gray mass of storm clouds, an enormous, rosy sun drifting slowly toward Spain and Portugal. The sky over Paris—not counting the dark rainy days with their solid, low overhang of clouds—takes shape from the Atlantic's relative proximity; that ocean may no longer bear splendid sailing ships on its waves (Delacroix mourns their loss movingly in his journals), but it still sends its squadrons of cumuli to Paris, which become en route majestic schooners, frigates, and brigs. Thus what had been supplanted by modern technology, which favors low-lying steamers and flat vessels driven by diesel engines—Delacroix wasn't alone, many artists and writers longed for the beauty and charm of a world powered by wind and white sails, the tradition of Magellan and other great seafarers— returned to life almost daily in the high Parisian skies as peerless regattas of towering ships constructed now only of water vapor, of illusion. And these cumulous sailing ships no doubt vanished, dispersed as soon as they passed beyond Paris's borders, like troops after a parade celebrating a national holiday, a king's or a president's state visit.

I got to know both new and eternal Paris, the Paris of the Montparnasse Tower, which crushed that once-brilliant district like a giant tombstone for Europe modernism, I viewed the Paris of patient plane trees and the rare remaining medieval streets that Baron Haussmann's scissors had spared. That baron— whose aristocratic title was rather dubious—reshaped over half the city to suit his pompous taste, he was ubiquitous, much more so than Baudelaire or Rimbaud, since, unlike bureaucrats or police prefects, geniuses don't leave traces in the material world. I viewed the Paris of nearly forty bridges, amorously spanning the river's banks, bridges arched like cats above the Seine's mobile mirror. The old Paris still existed, the lovely Île Saint-Louis (with its incredibly expensive apartments), cafés, and little squares dappled with restless poplar shadows, little restaurants with red-checked plastic covering their tables, and near the Sorbonne, students discussing the nature of substance just as in Abelard's and Héloïse's time, though the spirit of Christianity has long since fled. Paris still had its Notre Dame, it had its churches, walls, towers, though it had almost completely lost the ether that once filled it. The boulevard Saint-Germain, a center of eternal Paris; the street deceived with its beauty, it seemed that it might turn human with the slightest effort, it was so densely innervated by its bookshops, cafés, elegantly dressed intellectuals, even the plane trees growing by the bookshops didn't seem like ordinary trees circled by ordinary (extraordinary) magpies, they certainly read philosophical treatises and discussed them on sunny days through the rustling of their intelligent leaves.

But eternal Paris could be deceptive, its charm didn't vanish even under Nazi occupation. After all, Capt. Ernst Jünger, a druggist's son—like Haussmann, he might also have liked to be called a baron with his aristocratic inclinations—a writer whose essays and journals I'd liked so much (although their indifference to the weak, the suffering, always bothered me), had strolled through eternal Paris in his Wehrmacht uniform, fortunately not eternal—although, as M. remarked, very becoming, unfortunately, like all the uniforms designed by the Nazis (which in turn further complicates the ancient quarrel between ethics and aesthetics). Jünger also admired the trees and walls of the city that I viewed years later, virtually unchanged. He knew more about trees than I do, much more; he particularly loved the paulownia trees, with their early-blooming violet flowers and their large leaves, he loved the place des Ternes, surrounded by paulownias. He explained that this tree, of Chinese origin, was named in honor of the Russian princess Anna Pavlovna. Jünger botanized in Paris while genocide was being perpetrated in my own country. Jünger's journals are a triumph of classicism, a discrete, economical aesthetics that ignored amorphous, inelegant events unworthy of a refined author's attention. Although I'm not being completely fair: Jünger discreetly tried to understand evil. But has anyone managed to understand evil? I still like reading Jünger's journals, they still fascinate and irritate me, as for example when their author claims that a large group of German soldiers took the Jewish side in the Warsaw Ghetto Uprising, a claim unsupported by any historical source; fifty years later, when a reader asked him to substantiate this information, the hundred-year-old writer repeated stubbornly that he'd heard it from a new arrival from the East. Was this the same Paris? Mine had been scrubbed by André Malraux, it was the color of calcified cocoa, no longer the black that you see in the films and photos taken before the great cleanup.

•

Emil Cioran was still living in Paris then, I even met him, I visited him just once in his apartment at 23 rue de l'Odéon, on the top floor, which you accessed by way of a miniature elevator (so small you could scarcely breathe), but nothing came of it, it never went any further. He was already quite old, and I, with my damned shyness, couldn't imagine that he might want to be friends. I saw him later a couple of times, after he'd been stricken by Alzheimer's, that pitiless disease. His faithful life companion, Simone, now led him, uncomprehending, along the same streets that the acute, ironic flaneur had once paced. I turned my eyes from them; the contrast between the earlier Cioran, with his vital intelligence, and this man's blank gaze was too much to bear. I remembered the accounts left by those who'd seen Nietzsche in his last years, who had encountered not the brilliant philosopher, but a demented patient babbling incomprehensible syllables. Fortunately, though, I had Jozef Czapski, who combined goodness with intelligence, Czapski, who lived in Maisons-Laffitte, who also fell slowly, inevitably prey to old age. And I also had other, younger friends, I had books and walks, since Paris, in both its eternal and everyday incarnations, never lost its fascination, I never ceased to discover new routes, to seek out traces of the past and signs of modernity, since both interested me, I wanted to see both, new buildings and new squares, the slightly socialist realist place de Barcelone, but also the marble tablets commemorating the countless eccentrics, omnivores, and geniuses who'd tried at one time or another to conquer Paris, though few succeeded, not even Mozart or Wagner; both suffered here, they never guessed that one day elegant marble plaques would bear witness to their unsuccessful stays, although, in keeping with the principle of universal hypocrisy, not a single word betrays the failures they endured in Paris. Chopin had better luck; I liked to sneak into the square d'Orléans, in the ninth arrondissement (to sneak, since the composer lived in a house located in the midst of a building complex whose gates were guarded by a rather unsympathetic Cerberus), and to look at the fountain singing in its monodic monotone, closer to Gregorian chants than to Chopin's dramatic ballades. The square d'Orléans was apparently the composer's last Parisian address; he died, though, in Delfina Potocka's apartment on the place Vendôme.

•

I barely knew, didn't meet, Parisian poets. Things got off to a bad start early on, soon after I arrived in Paris, at the moment when M., who wanted to translate my poems into French, asked a certain poet, my contemporary, for help, without suspecting the obstacles she'd meet. He requested the extant translations and promised to get back to her about collaborating in a couple of days. When they met again, he informed her that he couldn't possibly work with her, since he didn't like the poems. Because, he said, these poems contain historical time. Look, for example, he said, at the poem "Schopenhauer Cries," it gives the Gdansk philosopher's dates (1788–1860). It's unacceptable, he said, poetry lies beyond time. Poetry liberates us from time, from history. We read and write poems to escape time. Poetry is pure, virginal. The introduction of historical time diminishes, demeans it, which is why I don't like these poems and can't collaborate with you. Let's be absolutely clear here: I refuse to translate poems containing historical time. As I recall, he made this declaration sometime in 1983 (we'll smuggle historical time in again). At least he made it openly. Time had corrupted me, and I had corrupted poetry. French poetry—for the most part—didn't want time, didn't want history, didn't want Vichy, didn't want genocide, didn't want treason, didn't want aging, Alzheimer's, didn't want me.

•

In the Krakow English-language bookstore Massolit I recently happened on a little book describing the life of the Polish boy who'd inspired the beautiful Tadzio in Thomas Mann's famous novella *Death in Venice*. The book's author, Gilbert Adair, an American from New York, went to great lengths tracking down the fate of this boy. Adair discovered, among other things, that the same boy, at an even earlier age—he was only six—had made a great impression on Henryk Sienkiewicz! It's long been known that the boy was the model for Mann's character, that Mann actually encountered an aristocratic Polish family in Venice and succumbed to "Tadzio's" great charm—he fell in love, although, as his biographers stress, this was, as always for Mann, a cautious, purely platonic fascination; he made no effort to meet the hero of his future book. The boy's identity first came to light in the 1960s. His name was Wladyslaw, not Tadeusz, but his family called him Adzio, hence the name the German writer gave him. Wladyslaw Moes was a baron, an *authentic* baron (unlike the Parisian prefect Haussmann, who just liked the title), and spent the first half of his long life in luxury. There was nothing of the artist, the intellectual, about him. He liked horses, races, elegant attire, balls, parties, cards. He was, in short, the ideal incarnation of an aristocrat in the more vulgar version favored by writers of popular fiction—sometimes, as it turns out, they're right. He apparently had no interest in bona fide "high" literature, he didn't quest after "metaphysical feelings," politics likewise held no interest; he lived in another world, the world of careless pleasure. He knew, though; he discovered much later that he'd been the model for the beautiful boy in *Death in Venice*. More precisely, he didn't seek it out; rather, the news reached him, since I doubt he actually ever tried to discover anything about himself, about himself in Venice, in the hotel on the Lido, where he must have felt the fixed, watchful gaze of that short, middle-aged gentleman, an elegant member of the German bourgeoisie. He doubtlessly felt flattered once the information finally reached him. He was an ordinary man, what the French call *un homme moyen sensuel*, who suddenly found that he contained mythic potential. He must have stood long before the mirror, seeking to find traces of that mythic being in his face, without success . . .

Later, much later, when articles revealing his name began to appear in the European press, when he'd been found out, his true identity had been deciphered, he tried to file a lawsuit defending his privacy—as if his anemic privacy required defending, as if the relative immortality offered by Mann might in any way threaten his fragile dignity. After the war he lost everything he possessed, he scraped by on a humble translator's earnings; only his knowledge of languages, his French, now betrayed his better days. It was in short a difficult existence, not tragic, but sad—through a distant observer's eyes, it might seem that the vacation on the Lido had been the high point of his life . . . and not just because it has been preserved in world literature. Later, in 1971, Visconti shot his film, with its obsessive repetition of the "Adagio" from Mahler's Fifth Symphony, and a beautiful Swedish boy playing the role of the young Pole. Photos of the actual boy from the time of his Venetian vacation also began to appear—which must have vexed the aging Wladyslaw Moes if he saw them, and if he still cared about the legend of his early years, since they came accompanied by malicious comments: he hadn't been so good-looking after all, the young Swedish actor beat him hands down . . . But did early twentieth-century photographs tell the truth about human faces? (I'm taking up the baron's defense.) It must have been painful: they wanted to destroy his last remaining treasure, the legend of his beauty, his charm . . . But something else struck me even more—"Tadzio" had spent the Second World War in a German Oflag, a POW camp for officers. "Tadzio" as a German POW! We have to imagine this man, the former ephebe of Mann's novella, a rather dissolute aristocrat, in a German prison camp. Yet another encounter with Germans, different this time, plebeians, speaking a debased language in which the word heard most frequently was the monosyllabic *Raus*. I also imagine the unchanging routines of camp existence: rutabaga soup, mess tins, dingy darned sheets, the rare letter from home, dreary coexistence with the same companions in misfortune, seen, and thus perhaps loathed, daily, frost, snow, heat, the four seasons circling monotonously around the barracks like a flock of vultures, the lack of privacy, not a single moment to step aside, to hide. Horse races, banquets, elegant outfits, smoking jackets—forgotten, unreal. And even earlier, the luminous Lido, games on the beach, a brief moment of happiness we know only by chance, thanks to the gaze and gifts of Thomas Mann.

As we know, Mann spent the war years in California and had of course long ceased to think about "Tadzio"; that episode now belonged to history, to philology. Decades later Tadzio had become a literary character, something along the lines of Tonio Krüger, Clavdia Chauchat, or Little Mr. Friedeman—all of whom existed, however, exclusively on paper, unlike the man who had inspired Tadzio. The famous novelist continued to encounter other handsome boys, to observe them carefully, and to record these meetings, never leading to any kind of intimacy, in his pedantic diary. And "Tadzio"? He survived the war, left the camp for home, but this home had been confiscated by the Communists. Only poverty remained, a gray quotidian, chasing after a job in one of the Western embassies in Warsaw, since they remained islands of another world, tolerated by the odd types from the Central Committee, uneducated people with square skulls who filled the blank spaces in Marx's utopia (the underdefined spaces, as the Krakow philosopher Roman Ingarden would say). Finally, near the end, illness, stays in sanatoriums, hospitals, packed wards (like the camp barracks), and the last day, death, about which we know nothing, so we can't say if it suddenly lit up the life with a glow even brighter than the Lido, or if it simply carelessly snuffed the flame of an already dim candle before heading off to the next patient.

•

So many years in Houston—if you add up all the trips, it comes to over five years, but never longer than four months at a time, a single semester (always the spring). The first time I went, I had only the weakest impressions of the place, I pictured a brown desert, a wasteland. I had to go, I had to accept the invitation that Edward Hirsch sent in the summer of 1987—since we had nothing to live on in France. I still had no idea how important, how sustaining, this American adventure would be. My English wasn't exceptionally good at this point, but from the outset I conducted so-called poetry workshops, that is, I assessed the poems of young American writers, I had to suggest corrections, changes. I took an English-German dictionary with me on the first visit, since I spoke German well and couldn't find an English-Polish dictionary in Paris. It took me some time to realize that excellent English-English dictionaries could be purchased for pennies. I studied the students' poems the day before classes with the help of my yellow dictionary. I experienced great crises—was I up to the job? In such situations you sometimes forget what you're capable of, your inner resources. Gustaw Herling-Grudzinski quotes Lichtenberg, who supposedly said, "Experience isn't much use, since we see each new lunacy in a different light." In the world of introverts, this might be rephrased as follows: we see each new difficulty in a terrifying light, since we don't remember that we've dealt with similar dangers in the past. And our "inner resources," if they actually exist, don't as a rule exist for us ourselves, they make themselves known only around others, hence they're easy to forget when you're sitting in an empty room biting your fingernails from stress.

Edward came to pick me up at the airport, as he did for many years to come. He usually took two books with him, in case my flight was really late; one might not be enough . . . And they were always books of poetry, or about poetry. The first time I flew from Paris to Houston I had a stopover in New York and picked up some new vocabulary en route (in Newark, the flight to Texas was delayed, and someone said, "They screwed it up again"). The next day I had one of the worst migraines in my life, I didn't fully realize where I was, but through the windows of the sizable apartment I'd been given, I saw gigantic trees, evergreen oaks overgrown with Spanish moss, like ancient bison. I quickly realized that Houston was a very green city, and that those evergreen oaks were its claim to fame. And that little prefix *ever*! Azaleas began blooming in February, larger than in Europe, but even the word *spring* didn't make much sense in this climate. The evergreen oaks behaved like cautious rentiers: they never lost all their leaves even for an instant, they renewed them systematically, new leaves grew beneath the previous year's leaves and after a moment mercilessly pushed the old ones out—the battle of the generations crystallized in pure, clinical, horrifying form—so that the trees were never naked. The semester began at the end of January, but the temperature called to mind May or June in my parts. I didn't have a car during my first visit—in the spring of 1988—so I got to know small fragments of the sprawling city on foot and on a bike borrowed from Karl Kilian. One of the students usually drove me to class. Edward Hirsch quickly became one of my best friends. We were both a little ill at ease at first, but soon grew comfortable with each other. I liked his marvelous sense of humor, his love for poetry. I also discovered the Rice University campus, located near my apartment, and above all its wonderful library, in which I spent blissful hours, hours borrowed from life when I forgot about Texas; only after leaving did I rediscover the old oaks' arabesques and remember where I was. Rice University is better known for engineering than the humanities, it's true, but its library has splendid holdings in the European literatures. Long shelves brim with books of largely forgotten authors, who labored their whole lives. In vain, since the dusty tomes of their poetry and prose now shivered hopelessly in the library's air-conditioned halls? But occasionally someone still got read, still lived. And from the moment I landed in Texas I started to miss Europe and its art. I chiefly read the French and the Germans—there wasn't much Polish literature. Still, I found many books that I hadn't been able to get in Parisian libraries. American libraries are far better than their European counterparts, perhaps because memory infiltrates the structure of European cities, urban development, even rural fields and meadows, are shaped by archaic models, layers of memory shape the light, under naked skies, laid open to the rain and wind, they're inscribed in the layout of streets, in the architectural details of old houses, whereas in the United States memory is preserved chiefly in libraries and museums, since the cities mostly suffer from amnesia, old buildings are laid waste and gleaming new buildings take their place every couple of decades.

I spent a great deal of time in the comfortable, nearly empty library at Rice, I always carried one of my little yellow French notebooks, and sometimes, while reading some poet or philosopher, I managed to jot down a few words, a line of poetry, a thought, an observation headed for one of my essays. I used to meet that great publisher and gentleman of letters Roger Straus— he's no longer living—every so often in New York, and whenever I mentioned Houston, he'd smile ironically and announce that he'd never been to Texas and never meant to go. Then he'd ask jokingly if we were certain that Texas was in fact part of the United States of North America. On the East Coast they see Houston as a kind of black hole, antimatter. My East Coast friends treated me with sympathy—I had to return to the Southern jungles. Susan Sontag was among them; she adored New York and couldn't imagine life in the American provinces (although, or perhaps because, she grew up in Tucson, Arizona). I gradually met more people, many of them warm and friendly in a distinctly Southern way. So the Rice library was no longer my only consolation. I also discovered other places, for example, the Menil gallery and its surroundings. The slim, beautiful Mrs. de Menil, a child of the Schlumberger family, wealthy French Protestants, was still living then, although she was very old. She founded the museum, whose design, by Renzo Piano, is a wonder of modern architecture. It's a variation on the old Southern style, a distant imitation of colonial mansions, though it holds not masters and slaves, but great works of art.

The University of Houston campus wasn't nearly so attractive, but its library slowly took the place of the one I'd discovered at the beginning of the semester. Edward burst out laughing when he asked me what I'd shown M. on her first visit to Houston, and I said, you know, the library at Rice University. M.'s visit overlapped with that of Joseph Brodsky, fresh from his Nobel Prize, who'd been invited to Rice for a reading. Michael Maas, a history professor at Rice, a specialist in late antiquity, had gotten to know Brodsky when they were both in Rome, at the American Academy; he told me about his conversation with the dean when he first suggested inviting the famous poet. When he said he knew Brodsky quite well, the dean responded with disbelief, even disdain: "*You* know *him?*" Michael and I went to pick up Joseph at the airport in short-sleeved shirts, which startled our guest, arriving from chilly New York. I remember he was wearing a woolen tie dotted with moth holes. I liked that. Moths spare no one. Brodsky was no dandy. Once he gave me a splendid cashmere jacket that was a little small for him; I wear it to this day. Joseph wanted us to take him to NASA. I remember that day, the day of our trip to NASA—its imposing buildings with cast-off rockets carelessly strewn between them, rockets scorched by the air rushing past as they sped homeward—as one of my best moments, a moment of carefree friendship. As if it had given us an instant of weightlessness, the state that past astronauts had experienced first during their long training and then in orbit, in their cosmic flights.

•

During one of my semester-long pilgrimages to Houston, I lived right next to the Menil gallery, in one of the old wooden houses surrounding the cream-colored museum. Unfortunately, the rooms on the other side of my paper-thin walls held exceptionally noisy young neighbors, barbarians eager to crank up their speakers full blast in the middle of the night as they listened to the music of the zeitgeist, i.e., electric guitars and percussion. I was saved by the museum's director, who heard me complaining and invited me to use the empty house that served, luckily not too often, as a guesthouse. He requested only that I use the guesthouse as a studio, that I didn't move in completely. The contrast between the first house, where the zeitgeist might explode at any moment—not just terrifyingly loud music, but also sudden invasions of my neighbors' friends, who would turn up after midnight from bars and clubs to demonstrate loudly how much fun they were having (since having fun is predicated on making sure everyone else knows you're having fun)—and the ideal quiet of my new studio was remarkable. The two houses were divided only by a small field, which I often crossed in one direction or the other, day or night. In some sense this arrangement of space ideally reflected the topography of any intensive intellectual efforts, our residence in two realities, one nervous and noisy, the other filled with peace—or music, but music that we choose. The arrival of one or another of Mrs. de Menil's guests, often Buddhists, Tibetan monks—since the beautiful older lady developed spiritual interests late in life, religious, not aesthetic, concerns came to predominate—sometimes deprived me of my workroom, my ideal quiet, my music for a few days, and this would drive me to genuine despair, since I was homeless once more, subject to the whims of my idiotic neighbors. It was no consolation that the guest, indulging his Eastern practices in *my room*, had no notion that his Asiatic contemplation had been taken from me, torn from me, had been ripped from the fabric of my Western solitude. The joy was all the greater when I could finally return to the little house and once again enjoy the quiet, the freedom, the occasional moment of revelation.

•

But once more on Tadzio—that is, on someone who borrowed several traits from our acquaintance Wladyslaw Moes, that unfortunate baron—the hero of *Death in Venice*, a novella that still radically divides its readers into two camps, the ardent admirers and passionate opponents of Thomas Mann. The story's style may be a bit baroque at times (the rhythm of the hexameter surfaces in the German original, alongside allusions to Plato . . .). But what it presents, the history of a famous writer who falls deliriously in love with a slender boy, so deeply in love that the refined intellectual abandons his art, his all-engrossing literary and spiritual labors, his lifelong quest for truth and form, only to perish in poverty, to die as a homeless pauper, a nameless beggar, might, to die like a pet cast off by its owners, like a worm— it could happen anytime, anyplace, to anyone (almost anyone). Gustav von Aschenbach, the renowned author, a specialist in the human heart, in European history, who clearly feels most at home in the silence of his study, someone who lovingly caresses his books, who is intoxicated by ideas, his own and others', who lives by thinking, by writing, writing rocks him, bears him through the decades as the ocean carries a sailing ship, suddenly, from the moment he sees that beautiful boy, he loses his mind completely, and the capacious world of intellectual discipline that had hitherto offered him daily refuge and inspiration loses all its charm. In the space of a few days this seemingly weighty edifice of education and creation, intellect and inspiration, risk and dignity, vanishes, sinks into oblivion; its place is taken by chasing Tadzio, watching him from a safe distance, observing his routines, his walks, his runs along the beach, his games with other boys, the impatient waiting until he appears again, first in the hotel restaurant, surrounded by family, then later on the sands of the Lido, where the famous author sits in his cozy, shaded beach chair, trying to write, all the while keeping an eye out for the boy, for Tadzio, he *has* to watch him, and gradually losing interest in what he tries to write. Aschenbach meets with great misfortune: he falls in love. He falls hopelessly in love with a young creature, a creature possessing the charm of youth, a boy whose life he cannot share in any respectable fashion, and he thus goes insane and dies shortly thereafter. And what becomes of the countless virtues and pleasures of intellectual labor, the careful, fruitful reading on winter days with the white city drowsing outside the window and logs crackling in the fireplace, jotting down thoughts with a fountain pen on clean sheets of paper, above all, that sweet moment when a new idea appears, when new notions emerge out of nowhere, a new take on a topic you've been contemplating for ages, when it suddenly assumes new shape, generates new energy, a moment of rapture expands, extends to several hours, fuses with a rhythm of smooth but enthusiastic work? No one knows where they go, those moments, where they've vanished, since they've been forgotten, they're ridiculous in comparison with the sole force now governing the fifty-year-old Aschenbach, the wild passion, the pursuit of the beautiful boy even though this boy embodies no ideas, has read next to nothing, doesn't know Plato, couldn't possibly hold his own in a conversation about Greek tragedies or the crisis brought on by scientific progress and the triumph of positivism in the last part of the nineteenth century, or the attempts to surmount this crisis mustered by Bergson and other thinkers and artists driven to despair by the barren world of science. One smile from this ephebe holds more meaning than all of Rembrandt's paintings,

Keats's poems, Rilke's *Duino Elegies*, Mozart's piano concertos, Shakespeare's plays, Goya's *Caprichos*. When he runs along the beach, only this matters, that he runs along the beach, with his slim, sunbathed body bent so as to form a right angle with the earth's surface, and only this is precious, splendid, both fragile and final, unique. This slim body is more important that libraries and museums, concerts in which pianists labor so mightily to stir the impressionable souls of their listeners. And why must Aschenbach, honored and esteemed not just in his native land, but throughout Europe, laden with so many awards and honors— but where are they now, those honors and awards?—why must he perish, perish like the homeless of great cities, swiftly buried in anonymous graves so as not to disrupt the pleasures of the self-satisfied bourgeois? He, who has over the years made his name a synonym for great intelligence, a symbol of wisdom, sees this name erode gradually, day by day, it contracts, diminishes, and vanishes in the same abyss into which all his awards, his glowing reviews, congratulatory letters, and honorary degrees had already tumbled with a gentle splash. And he knows—or rather senses, since he doesn't know much anymore—that he must die, there's no other choice, since nothing ties him to that boy, not the slightest hope, and yet he can't live without Tadzio, without seeing him. Moreover, the Polish family fears the epidemic that everyone is talking about, they're leaving, taking the lovely boy with them (he'll vaguely remember some older gentlemen gazing at him intently), so the great writer has only one way out, if you can call it that, to perish, vanish, die. And thus his great misfortune draws to a close, his disaster evaporates like the shallow puddle left by a brief shower on a sultry day, his pain dissipates; his name will be resurrected briefly to ornament a few European papers, the news of the literary titan's death will shock readers (shock them, but also, truth be told, rather please them, a diverting story to accompany their morning coffee, they'll feel a bit better, at least something's happened, sad, of course, but interesting, too). But then his name will be like a dead butterfly, dried in the sun, a blind moth, like a fly lying supine on a windowsill, its tiny legs folded as if in prayer.

•

On the other hand, the story's author, Mann himself, experienced the same thing—or not precisely the same thing, but close—as Aschenbach and emerged from this crisis unscathed, he kept his head. He suffered, to be sure, but unlike the writer who became the novella's hero and martyr, he had an extraordinarily strong sense of *decorum*, he could never have fallen as low as his hero. Moreover, he was staying in that elegant hotel with his wife, not alone, so he could watch his ephebe only surreptitiously, on the sly, he had to act out a comedy, keeping secrets from his wife. But something else really saved him; he was saved by writing, that odd activity that sometimes turns pain into pleasure, a chemical process that takes suffering and transforms it into black marks on a page.

•

Let's return for a moment to the Central Laboratory—the nickname that Jerzy Stempowski happily gave Paris, the capital of the avant-garde, of aesthetic innovation; *Le laboratoire central*, the title Max Jacob used for a book of poems he published in 1921, was doubtless the source of Stempowski's metaphor. Max Jacob was Jewish, and his fate might serve as a parabola for the history of the European avant-garde. Jacob, as we know, was one of its most active representatives; he was friends with Apollinaire, Picasso, he knew everyone and inspired many. In 1921 he took up residence in the Romanesque abbey of Saint-Benoît-sur-Loire. He'd undergone a conversion a few years earlier. He still went to Paris, visited his friends, but he always returned to the abbey, set above the broad-spread Loire. Someone must have denounced him as a Jew—his conversion meant nothing to the

Nazis, who had no interest in spiritual life. On February 24, 1944, Max Jacob was arrested and sent to the transit camp in Drancy, outside Paris. Transports left from Drancy for Auschwitz and other extermination camps. But Max Jacob died before they could transport him, of pneumonia on March 5 in Drancy. It's said that his close friends Picasso and Cocteau—especially Picasso, since Cocteau did mount an effort to rescue him—didn't do everything they could to save him: they both had influential friends among the Germans. So ended the Central Laboratory, not in flames, but through neglect, indifference, hard-heartedness.

•

Unlike the passengers of the Paris metro, clutching their thick novels, I liked small, slim books that fit easily into my pocket. I had no taste for tomes the size of collected works, stout as peasant women in their winter sheepskins, but I also didn't care for the excessively elegant volumes of the French Pléiade, whose Bible paper strove to imbue lay writers with the authority and aura of the prophets Jeremiah or Samuel. Since you can't take the ponderous volumes of someone's collected works out with you for a stroll . . . And books should be as portable as thoughts. But I admired that splendid invention, the *livre de poche*, the pocketbook. Slim volumes—unlike lengthy novels—don't cast bridges between one day and the next, they scarcely require bookmarks. (Where's the doctoral student who'll do a comprehensive dissertation on the bookmark? The metro passengers had remarkably interesting bookmarks, whose life span almost always exceeded that of their books; a novel once read instantly lost its value, whereas the bookmark triumphantly proceeded to the next volume, like an organ grafted to a new body.) Small, narrow volumes were reader friendly, more than friendly, at times they revealed new images to the reader, cast a lantern light on new environs, but they also gave him only isolated moments, they weren't true bridges, just light footbridges suspended over alpine streams. Marcel Proust's great novel holds an exceptional place here, it unfolds a carefully considered narrative that could satisfy both metro riders and voyagers on the Trans-Siberian Railway, but when we get to the end of the line, after traversing a thousand kilometers, when we reach *Time Regained*, the final pages, we discover that the epic's true hero is the moment, the instant of vision, the moment of memory restored, of clarity, joy, mystical rapture. The story's vast machinery exists to praise the moment! Proust must be acknowledged by serious scholars of the literary epic; those who rely on urban and international transportation, though, those who read in airplanes and doctors' waiting rooms consider him a traitor; he passed the entire arsenal of narration to enemy hands, to those who opposed endless stories, who sided with the moment, the flame, the revelation, all short-lived by definition. So many volumes, so many fates, and all culminate in a hymn to the instant . . . Readers with epic inclinations must have been outraged. They expected a bittersweet avalanche of generations, cradles with black stars above them, they looked for despair and consolation, and got a moment. But Proust wasn't the only one to mislead his readers. From *War and Peace* we best recall the extraordinary moments, when in the midst of battle Prince Andrei contemplates the sky, the clouds, thus neglecting the battle, the war, the Russians and the French . . . In my chaotic library I kept a special place for those little books, portable volumes holding poems, aphorisms, observations, brief essays, diarists' notes. For example, the miniature edition of the poems of Gottfried Benn, that short, stocky man whose temperament— combining impracticality (he wasn't the greatest dermatologist, he lost a hospital job once because of his unreliability, he was also an unsystematic reader of the Berlin Nationalbibliothek and a frequenter of cheap beer halls) with occasional, but remarkably persuasive, bursts of genius—made him a splendid companion on long strolls. There was no narration here, just attention to the moment, professions of faith in intense, transient experience, explosions, violent or calm (if calm explosions exist), as in the poem "Asters," for example. Ideal for Parisian boulevards and streets, but well suited to other cities, too, including Krakow. I also carried volumes of Eugenio Montale on my walks. His poems are always a little hurried, I liked—and still like—their pace, which makes itself felt even in his first book, *Ossi di seppia*, their impatience, their inventive metaphors, the magic of names (Dora Markus), invented names that sometimes belonged to real people, I liked the images forcing their way into poems—such as the unexpected jackals led on a leash in one poem from the cycle *Mottetti*. Literary scholars tell us that Montale rebelled against the hyperbole of D'Annunzio's poetry. But Montale himself later came under attack for his discretion; in a review of his volume *Satura*, Pier Paolo Pasolini accused Montale of opposing fascism too obliquely. An absurd charge, but it gave the appearance of serious criticism. Absurd, since someone who writes splendidly elliptical poetry will never stand in the first ranks of those doing battle with a tyrant. Elliptical poets can't attack tyrants in the stanzas of their poems. Which is a shame: we'd like to have artists who both made beautiful objects and risked their lives at the same time. If they died, though, those beautiful objects wouldn't exist, you'd have to pick, substance, not thought, would determine the choice. Pasolini's reproach must have wounded the poet deeply. He took revenge by writing what was for him an unusually brutal poem, "Letter to Malvolio," which holds the following lines: "No, you're not wrong, Malvolio, the science of the heart / hasn't yet been born; each invents it as he likes" (translation by William Arrowsmith). But these aren't the brutal lines, I can't bring myself to quote Montale's malice, however apt, given Pasolini's tragic death. Another book for walks: the excerpts from Jozef Czapski's *Diary* published in a Polish underground edition. The print was blurry, sometimes scarcely legible, but what a joy to read the notes of Czapski, that wonderful observer and artist, a man of great intelligence and absolute truthfulness, frail, like all people, but unashamed of his frailty. And this was one of the greats of our emigration—as a rule, the great ones of our emigration couldn't admit weakness, they were serious activists with political aspirations. Czapski was not a serious activist, he had, fortunately, no political ambitions, he didn't pretend to be a titan; just the opposite, he routinely lamented his various shortcomings and sins. He was his own worst critic in his *Diary*, he laid himself bare, he refused to exploit the privileges of *aristocracy*, of being *a great emigrant*. He struck a note that must be called *absolute simplicity* among the Parisian émigés. Since Czapski never pretended, he openly admitted his ignorance. He loved ignorance, like many exceptionally well-educated people. He possessed a mystical nature tempered by sincere interest in others, curiosity about the world. The excerpts from his diary hold notes from his Parisian strolls, observations on the images, colors, and grayness of the city through the years—and I would read them during my own Parisian strolls; amid the grayness and colors of my hour, his diary would overspread the real city like the carbon copy of an image. Another favorite companion on these walks was Antonio Machado, the great Spanish poet, unfortunately little known in Poland. I read him in translations, chiefly French and English, I later found a little Polish volume published in the yellow "cellophane" series. Don Paterson's *The Eyes*, his collection of Machado "imitations" published by Faber and Faber Limited, lent itself splendidly to my purposes:

> So is this magic place to die with us?
> I mean that world where memory still holds
> the breath of your early life:
> the white shadow of first love,
> the voice that rose and fell
> with your own heart
> the hand you'd dreamed of closing in your own . . .

all those beloved burning things
that dawned on us,
lit up the inner sky?
Is this the whole world to vanish when we die,
this life that we made new in our own fashion?
Have the crucibles and anvils of the soul
been working for the dust and the wind?

("Nothing," translated by Don Paterson)

But I can't list all my pocketbooks, those gatherings of great moments. How those great moments fit into such tiny books, we don't know. Also—another time—A.J.A. Symons's *The Quest for Corvo*, a delightful book recommended to my generation by an older generation of writers, Konstanty Jelenski and Gustav Herling-Grudzinski. It's the story of uncovering the biographical traces of Frederick Rolfe, an author and eccentric enamored of Venice; he lived in poverty for years in that strange and beautiful city built on stilts and held every kind of job imaginable (and unimaginable), but he was a genuine writer nonetheless, with sentences of great power. One fault of Symons's book: you can't return to it ad infinitum, as you often can with poems, aphorisms, some journal entries. Since here, following both Corvo's adventures and those of his biographer Symons, we come close to narrative, and we can accept and experience narrative only once—we're not talking about Homer or Tolstoy—before it starts to bore us, weary us; the more sensational the narrative, the more wearisome it gets on the second reading, to say nothing of the third or fourth. One can imagine a sophisticated system of incarceration in which the punishment would consist of reading the same novels seven, eight, nine times—under the supervision of specially trained guards armed with glasses of tremendous optical strength. This difficulty might also cast a shadow on the notion of reincarnation (wouldn't the soul get tired of living over and over? And reading the same novels for the second, third, fourth time—in a different body, true, but you'd still have to proceed through the same indispensable stages of life). In the 1990s, Ryszard Przybylski published his translation of Osip Mandelstam's tremendous *The Noise of Time* in the Nike series; here the narration continuously stops short, splits into moments, so there's no danger of repetition, and the density of remarkable thoughts is truly astonishing. No, these aren't bibliographic guidelines, I can't suggest a long list of little books. The poems of André Frénaud come to mind here; the poet spent a year in Lvov right before the Great War, teaching French. Although that's not what drew me, that he spent some time in Lvov, although his stay in the city intrigued me; after all, he might have sat in some Lvov café right next to my grandfather, my parents, my aunt who studied the piano. His poems, in a perfectly sized pocket edition, were translated by two poets, Artur Miedzyrzecki and Zbigniew Herbert. I never met André Frénaud, although he was still alive during my Parisian years, I even know that he lived on the rue de Bourgogne; he came from Burgundy and lived on a Burgundian street at number 7.

•

The end of June, a crisis of nature—spring, which has galloped through several months, suddenly stops short, silence takes its place, a cease-fire that will last for a couple of months before it is broken by the autumn winds. The blackbirds and other birds gradually fall still, the city becomes as dull as a provincial railroad station, only primitive music blaring from the occasional car enlivens the space of the orphaned streets. In the evening carefully made-up girls teeter toward discos on extremely high-heeled shoes. Bored ducks fly awkwardly from spot to spot for no apparent reason. Only swifts and swallows still refuse to yield, they circle through the warm air at great speed, as if wishing to demonstrate to lazier creatures that life goes on just the same. Grain stands, patiently waiting for combines in fields just outside of town, summer's great quiet commences. The quiet of heavy August days, when nature, like a plump Turkish lady in the sultan's harem, lies on a sofa (an ottoman) and sighs, remembering her youth. Yellow fields, ripe. Sometimes a violent storm approaches, the wind lifts the sand from country paths and hurls it against the gardens' stone walls. The boredom of summer. Of satiety.

•

At one point in his *Notebooks* Cioran comments on the tremendous impression made on him by Mozart's Piano Concerto no. 17 in G Major, KV. 453. We don't know whose version he heard (I'm listening to a recording with the pianist Murray Perahia). He spends a few days under the concerto's spell, he keeps coming back to it, to its melancholy. At last—and here we see how his exceptional intellect operates—he proposes a definition of melancholy. He says that melancholy is typical of "spiritual souls who cannot believe" in God. But that's not all. A few days pass (or so we suppose, since the notes in the *Notebooks* usually go undated), and he adds another note: "We find in Mozart the recollection of *another world*, something our memory hasn't managed to register." He clearly found his definition wanting—or perhaps he simply dislikes definitions generally, formulas that trap reality inside conceptual cages. But what's to be done, given his phenomenal talent for definition? So he can't resist jotting down definitions only to annihilate them later . . . And then other subjects come up, other thoughts, other definitions, other annihilations.

•

A little while ago I discovered the following fact: Doctor P., who'd been my ethics teacher when I was studying philosophy, admitted that he'd actively collaborated with the political police, he'd been what we now call an SI. The initials might signify Superior Intellect, Safety Inspector, Servant of Ishtar, but unfortunately they don't, they mean Secret Informant. For some time now a group of fanatics has been—and continues to be—active in Poland; their sole purpose seems to be unmasking as many Secret Informants as possible in every walk of life. I never joined them, I never trusted them, I found their narrow, hateful passion as repulsive as a dogcatcher's lasso. But the news about Doctor P. was different, it bothered me. He taught us ethics, after all. None of his students considered him a stellar professor. His lectures were completely unlike those of his other colleagues in philosophy. He deployed a full arsenal of outlines, index cards, a homegrown system of files and folders holding notes written in different colors of ink (you could see them). In short, we got the impression that he read and cited chiefly himself—from various rough drafts. But he rarely mentioned the great philosophical authorities, he seldom quoted Kant or Plato, instead he acted as if he himself had invented all the categories and concepts that he presented, and that we obediently transcribed in our notebooks—although not without some ironic commentary after class. He wasn't liked, but he wasn't hated either. In the great army of philosophers, marching cautiously and awkwardly (since you can't reasonably expect athletic ability from ontologists) through the forests and fields of various continents, he had clearly only reached the rank of noncommissioned officer, something like a sergeant of ethics. We went along with it, we didn't have much choice. Doctor P. seemed to recognize his limitations, since he apparently tried to offset them by his behavior, which was meant to suggest that deep down he was just like us, one of the guys, he didn't set himself above his students; he preferred the confiding tone employed by soccer and volleyball coaches in dealing with college-bound high school boys or university students. His bespectacled face would twist into a smile intended to say, We're all the same, we're equals, I don't set myself above you. In some fantastical anthropological classification he would fall under the category of Sly Fox, fundamentally self-satisfied. But he was after all a professor of ethics, he was in some sense, or, rather, should have been, an emissary of the Good. He should have shown us the border between good and evil, how to recognize it, to name it. And he deceived us. The Secret Informant taught us ethics. Our Smiling Companion jotted down his observations and reports—and told us how to live.

•

Let me return once more to my private bibliography of volumes lending themselves to long walks. For a long while I kept a volume of the Czech poet Vladimir Holan, *The Crying of Symbols*, in my pocket. I was struck by those poems, sharp at times, with their startling, sometimes even vulgar metaphors. Holan moved me on two levels—he was a religious poet drawn, just the same, to the realm of plebeian language, like a parish priest who ministers both to distinguished professors and to carrot and onion peddlers, to notaries sipping white wine as well as to cart drivers drinking beer, only beer, yellow beer. The introduction spoke of the fifteen years in which Holan never left his apartment. Later I understood that this was meant to be read metaphorically, that fifteen years indicated the period in which the poet could not be published in Czechoslovakia, but I preferred to take this literally, that the poet never left his home, that he watched the four seasons only out his window, the snow and rain, the streaks of sunshine in April. Much later I read that Holan had been an anti-Semite, which grieved me, but I kept on reading his poetry. And since we've landed on *H*: another small book, selections from the diaries of Friedrich Hebbel. Karol Irzykowski translated extended passages from these diaries. Here is one of his aphorisms: "Though it grows in the furthest depths, a tree cannot complain. The whole earth belongs to it." And a volume of Boris Pasternak's poetry. And a small selection of Blake ("Mock on, mock on / Voltaire, Rousseau"). And Emil Cioran, whose aphorisms finally can't compare to the works of the greatest poets. Cioran's aphorims are always bracing, always witty, always bring us down to earth, the Parisian earth, the gravel paths of the Luxembourg Gardens on which the Romanian poet used to take his evening strolls. But to be brought down to earth, you must first be somewhere higher up, soaring in the air. Cioran lived in a cynical city, its very center (rue de l'Odéon), and perhaps he shielded himself from its cynicism through his irony. "I threw myself into cynicism as others might throw themselves into debauchery or asceticism," he says in his *Notebooks*. But he sought other things: "Once again about that Mozart concerto. It's remarkable how melancholy can *cheer* us. Nothing else matters in its presence." I admired Cioran's brilliance, but sometimes I preferred a single poem by Georg Trakl, for example (I carried a little selection of his on occasion), or Emily Dickinson or Jozef Czechowicz (who wrote the wonderful poem "Grief") to Cioran's intelligent malice; I didn't need to be brought to earth, I didn't lack for sobriety, skepticism, I needed to escape my own irony, I sought light vehicles in poetry that might lift me for a moment, I sought inspiration, elation, I had plenty of earth and gravel. I looked for rapture, even though if anyone had asked what that was, and why I preferred even amorphous rapture to sardonic wit, I would have had no answer. Mozart's melancholy cheered me, too, like the melancholy of Schubert. At times I preferred a single line of Montale to the aphorisms of Cioran, our modern-day La Rochefoucauld. Poetry is defenseless against ironists, aphorisms are like sharp scissors, they can't function without points. Poems don't want points, they don't want to wound anyone, they don't need sharpening, which is why young poets don't know what to do with their hands when seated next to famous satirists. On the other hand, though, when Osip Mandelstam, my beloved Mandelstam, says, "The age like a wolfhound throws itself at my shoulders, / But I'm not a wolf by my blood / Shove me instead, like a cap, in a sleeve / Of the hot fur coat of Siberian steppes," the ironists tiptoe out of the room smiling apologetically. My little books were meant to elevate me. But I also tried Cioran, Cioran, who always disagreed with himself and was also capable of writing the following sentence: "There's something of Antigone in Simone Weil, which shielded her from skepticism and brought her close to holiness." Which reminds me, Simone Weil also took long walks with me, I read her either in Czeslaw Milosz's Polish translation or else in French; the selection of her thoughts edited by Gustave Thibon, *La pesanteur et la grâce*, fulfilled the conditions for a walking book, a pocketbook. If I happened to stop by the Luxembourg Gardens—as often happened, it has wonderful metal armchairs that lend themselves to reading and meditation, you just have to shift them to some quiet, shady spot—that great mystic, almost comically awkward in empirical life, came home again in some sense, since she had lived right next to this elegant garden before the war, in a massive stone building on rue Auguste Comte. Once she scolded Trotsky there; a young girl, she went after "the great leader of the revolution" for the terror used in suppressing the Kronstadt rebellion. Simone Weil wrote the following in her *Notebooks* (since she also kept notebooks—comparing them to Cioran's notes would reveal a great deal about the modern mind): "A poem's beauty tells us precisely if and how our attention during its writing was directed to the ineffable." It's one of the most important things ever written about poetry. Weil's comments in the *Notebooks* aren't witty; they often have no clear point. She was a great stylist, but her style seldom makes itself known in obvious, coquettish ways, we never laugh out loud while reading her. The comments in the *Notebooks* often have a working, provisional character. They enter into our lives, even though they're not constructed on formulas, even though they frequently seem more like whispers than finished aphorisms. Cioran's *Notebooks* also function in principle as workbooks, drafts, but the power of style, of formulas, invades them, as the author himself knew perfectly well. Simone Weil kept the ineffable in mind while writing her *Notebooks*. Hence the absence of sharp points. A well-turned aphorism can't lead to the ineffable. Whatever tends in that direction must be a little hazy, leave something unsaid. Those lost in thought don't seek for points. Cioran is a great master of the expressible. Weil reigns in the realm of the ineffable.

•

The graffiti on an old building in Krakow (where a ruthless war between two soccer clubs, the Vistula and the Cracovia, has long been fought): "I'd rather have a sister in a whorehouse than a brother in Cracovia."

•

Much nobler sentiments also turn up in the graffiti, such as the inscription my friend Alissa noticed once, fading, but still legible, on a wall by the Planty Gardens not far from Wawel Castle: "We'll honor Herbert's testament."

•

One of Krakow's beautiful trees also grows in the Planty Gardens: an enormous red beech (a beech of the red-leaved variety, as the botanists say). Its crown grows in every direction since it's not impeded by other trees. It's attained an almost perfectly circular shape. The earth under the beech's crown looks scorched, a barren circle stretches beneath it.

•

Speaking of Cioran—I recently read a book by Alexandra Laignel-Lavastine, *Cioran, Eliade, Ionesco: On Forgetting Fascism*. The author collects and synthesizes fragments of scattered historical information on Eliade's and Cioran's links to the Romanian Iron Guard (since Ionesco's position was completely different), that hideous, virulently anti-Semitic, radically fascist organization.

Much of this was already known, but the French scholar's research presents an appalling image of Eliade's and Cioran's engagement in the rhetoric of hate. It was an extreme instance of the treason of the intellectuals. Anyone who reads this work will never forget the sentences pronounced by these sophisticated intellectuals in the thirties and forties and also won't forget the systematic cunning (vileness) with which Eliade in particular hedged and lied in his efforts to erase the traces of his inglorious past. Cioran chose silence instead, the enigmatic remarks of his *Notebooks*, and the despair of a brilliant nihilist.

For all that, both later wrote important works, both were genuine intellectuals, not superficial party hacks; it wasn't simply a matter of feigning interest in essential questions and predicaments, no, they ardently, authentically experienced these great problems. It's more complex in Eliade's case, since his love for "archaism," for the "Balkan village" and pre-Christian religion, persisted throughout his industrious life, and this can be seen as a thread tying his later work to the aberration of his younger years.

•

This Silesian city, which possessed its own history reaching back to the early Middle Ages, which once had defensive walls and old churches, was forced at a certain moment to accept displaced newcomers from Lvov and its environs (the defensive walls could not mount an effective resistance)—but it also had to dislodge, eject, expel its German population, it had to erase German grammar, German cooking (if such a thing exists), German postcards and textbooks. Fine, but this was years ago. And now? What happened afterward? There are two answers, one simple and the other complex. The first goes as follows: The older generation of newcomers passed away. More precisely, at least two generations died, perished, passed away. Younger generations also grew older and will likewise, perhaps in some distant future, pass away.

The younger generations don't want to know anything about this. Nothing. Caught up in their own business, they're glued to computer screens, they listen to music with American words in American accents. This is a simple answer, very simple. The difficult one is very difficult. Invisible. Some rituals must be observed. Someone prayed, someone cried, someone wrote poems. Someone mourned for times gone by, someone else killed those times with alcohol. How do you live walking along an abyss? Since they lived over an abyss. They hovered over an abyss. They had nothing here. In the beginning there was nothing, just the black hole of war, which had just now ended, and streets with strange names. Rituals had to be created. Symbolic gestures were required. My grandmother, my father's mother, brought a few pots and dishes from the City, along with a certain frying pan that I thought was magical: potatoes fried in it had a special taste. Other frying pans took its place, but something was missing, they lacked what the French call that je ne sais quoi. Other frying pans were ordinary. My grandmother must have loved my enthusiasm. I loved eating dinner at my grandparents'—only they had a magic frying pan. Aunt Wisia, my grandmother's unmarried sister, who would have a long life, brought an enormous quantity of elegant small objects from long ago: tiny scissors, little knives used for embroidery, pocket mirrors in pretty frames, silver pencils. I imagine she must have spent her free time sitting at her desk with her hands plunged in these treasures. I think she must have closed her eyes while her hands swam in little things, bibelots, metal, ivory. I suspect that she could sit like that for hours. She also brought a great quantity of small change from other times, tiny copper coins, but also a few silver pieces adorned with sailing ships and other elegant emblems. Perhaps that currency, which had long since ceased to circulate and had been replaced by plebeian aluminum coins stamped in Communist mints and lacking the dignity of earlier means of payment, was meant to be used—in unforeseen circumstances, in the event of a sudden change in the international situation—to pay for return passage to the City, including bribes for guards and railwaymen . . . The silver sailing ship would take Wisia on board and transport her to Lvov. So she waited. Each person had a separate plan for survival (and for returning to the City).

•

A certain lady, an acquaintance of my parents, composed musical works, which she then sent to eminent personages, to the pope, the queen of England, the president of the United States, the president of France. The works were never performed, but all these distinguished individuals, with their vast staffs of secretaries and assistants, thanked Mrs. L. for her compositions. And Mrs. L. would read these thank-you letters to her friends and acquaintances, letters from the pope, the queen of England, the president of the United States. True, the letters were signed by the secretaries of these eminences and not by the eminences themselves; still, they were written on letterhead so beautiful that its very appearance in a modest Silesian town was a great event. It's enough to recall the shoddy paper for sale at the local stationery store, the ugly paper on which my father wrote his memoirs . . . That the answers acknowledging receipt of Mrs. L.'s composition and thanking her for them were written on paper so unusual that it revealed mysterious watermarks when held to the light, marks guaranteeing their authenticity, that the signature was ordinarily accompanied by a round seal, like a nest holding an eagle, an owl, or a hawk, proud heraldic animals, mythical, in no way resembling their poor cousins dwelling in the real world, an ordinary forest, this very fact turned defeat into victory. Defeat? Why defeat? Mrs. L. desired nothing more. She had her thank-you letters eminating from the offices of the high and mighty. Her works were never performed, but they had their virtues; no critic could attack them. She stood beyond criticism. She was independent. She corresponded exclusively with the world's great ones; that whole comic subspecies of critics, reviewers, spiteful ordinary people, failed artists, journalists consumed by envy, didn't dare to touch her work. She towered above them. She moved in a different sphere. The pope and presidents. Perhaps the UN secretary-general. This was her public. She had attained artistic fulfillment, even though her compositions went unplayed. She discovered a new way of existing in art—a leap from completed but unplayed work to public acclaim. Mrs. L. practiced conceptual art. The intermediate step (all those rehearsals, concerts, ovations, hisses) proved unnecessary. When she received guests, persons of quality, acquainted with the hierarchy of that world, she would take these letters from a special drawer and read them out loud. Her guests were moved, thanks to these ornate, solemn letters, they suddenly, temporarily entered a higher sphere, the highest sphere. They lived, after all, in a provincial town, which had never achieved any kind of renown—it was remembered, if at all, only because the Second World War had begun here in some sense, with the so-called Gleiwitz incident, but this was a rather ambiguous claim to fame. Ill-prepared SS operatives dressed in Polish uniforms had conducted an unsuccessful attack on the local German radio station, they couldn't even carry out their commanders' instructions—they didn't know that the station only transmitted a program originating in Wroclaw, that is, Breslau, so they couldn't even broadcast the communiqué about the purported Polish attack—no, that wasn't serious. Mrs. L. was displaced, one of the displaced, but she had achieved success: she received letters from truly distinguished individuals. From the secretaries of truly distinguished individuals. Let the critics sharpen their talons on other composers, ordinary composers, those who didn't know her secret: how to create without exposing oneself to the music critics and their vulgar observations.

When I think of her today, I smile, I'm amused by the humor of that situation. Back then, though—if memory serves—

Mrs. L.'s accomplishments impressed me, at least up to a point, although I knew of the letters, their solemn recitation, only through my parents, I was too young, just a child, I wasn't invited to Mrs. L.'s dinners. My parents described these performances humorously, but their amusement was clearly mixed with respect. Did Mrs. L.'s method arise in some way from her situation, the situation of a displaced person? I don't know. I only know that back then we—if I may permit myself to speak for the great *Pluralis* of the displaced, newcomers from the East—had been cut off from the past. Our graves stayed in the East, our past remained in the East. No one knew where the future lay. And if it existed. We were guests in reality, in German walls, in solid German apartment houses. We had nothing at first, nothing to rival the solidity of those Prussian bricks. First we had to get working on our own buildings, our own projects, our own bricks. Mrs. L. was, in a manner of speaking, our artist. In her we could see the first attempt to create something of our own. Unfortunately her works were never completed. It was conceptual art, but I doubt that she opted for such art on purpose. Her compositions may have been exceptional. Or maybe not.

The displaced needed something to root them in the new soil. Their dubious ally was time; time decimated their ranks, but at the same time each passing year affirmed their right to be there. The displaced needed something more: a symbolic gesture. They needed art, invisible symbolic nets cast over trees and church steeples. Mrs. L. answered this need, albeit rather cartoonishly. She had only letters from the secretaries and assistants of distinguished individuals. My father described Mrs. L.'s successes ironically. He was different, completely different. He was in some sense her perfect geometric opposite. Shy, self-effacing, he usually sought to diminish his accomplishments. Even if he had written music, he would never have dreamed of sending his compositions to the pope, the president of the United States, the queen of England.

But he didn't write music, he didn't write poems; the only literary genre he mastered was postcards, sometimes with pictures, sometimes without. My father was an aphorist. When, at my request, much later, he wrote his memoirs—he never actually said it, but reading the memoirs was proof enough—he must have felt like a first-class sprinter who'd been ordered to run a marathon. It wasn't his distance. The limited space of a postcard suited him; he especially like adding some ironic (though never mocking) comment on whatever my mother had already written. So he wasn't simply a laconic writer, he also enjoyed the role of commentator, he liked reacting to another, preexisting text, providing it with a comic gloss. In her correspondence Mother artlessly transmitted information—about the weather, the illnesses of friends and family, the visits of acquaintances and relations; her letters and cards were classic family bulletins. And beneath her delicate, old-fashioned script there usually appeared a note from my aphorist father, always brief ("Mr. Skierka was nasty . . ."). My father's handwriting was contemporary somehow, the Bauhaus creators must have written that way, with their love for the simplest, most functional structures. My father gladly employed stenography, which he'd learned at his father's urging, and his nonstenographic handwriting seemed to retain some of the geometric transparency of stenographic notation. After my mother's death he continued to send postcards (more rarely letters), so he didn't absolutely require a primary text (my mother's bulletins) for his ironist's task, deriving as it does from a parasitical relationship to positive affirmations . . .

•

In Gustaw Herling-Grudzinski's diaries I found a quote from Huizinga describing his admiration for Vermeer: "In everything that Vermeer paints, we sense at the same time the atmosphere of childhood recollections, the calm of dreams, complete stillness and an elegiac clarity too subtle to be called melancholy.

Vermeer's realism is far removed from the vulgar, naked reality of everyday life."

Huizinga's comment captures splendidly the trait we find in certain great artists, and in some great poets as well: they see the world simultaneously through a child's eyes and the eyes of an adult, their vision is both drowsing, dreaming, and maximally sober, at once melancholy and joyful. That's impossible, the rationalist says. Of course it is, but it happens just the same. In certain works of art a person achieves unity, summoning childhood, sleep and reason, sorrow and exaltation, movement and stillness, to his aid. Thus he becomes—for a moment—a whole being, happy and sad at the same time.

·

But I shouldn't forget my first months in Paris, just after I arrived, months of intoxication—with the city, with strangeness. I lived, true enough, in a ghastly hole in Levallois, in a building that must once have been a cheap hotel, but now housed a mass of microscopic apartments. Their occupants were chiefly young and poor. The scent of poverty carried everywhere; a thin film of grime coated the stairwell and corridors. Fearless cockroaches often made an appearance in my room. So I bought a bug bomb and sprayed the walls. The cockroaches' response was immediate—this is how every empire should react when troubled by neighbors who fail to recognize its might: suddenly, on the ceiling, the walls, a vast army appeared simultaneously. The cockroaches swarmed in every direction, like Roman legions. My maneuver had annoyed them, but their might was too great for one modest bomb full of insecticide to cause even the slightest harm. I understood then that I would never win this war and confined myself henceforth to minor skirmishes with the repulsive insects. I often left the house, fled the house; fortunately, spring was slowly growing closer, the weather permitted ever-longer strolls. M. couldn't come with me, she had her work, her office right next to the neoclassical Madeleine Church. This church, not particularly attractive, was first intended to celebrate a secular holiday, it commemorated the soldiers of Napoleon's Grande Armée, and only after the little emperor's fall, during the Restoration, was it given over to the French Catholics. Still it had its own history, three thousand mourners gathered there just after Chopin's death to listen to the funeral mass, Mozart's *Requiem*. I wandered through Paris, fled my apartment and traced circles around the city, I visited the Luxembourg Garden, and I also discovered—then, or perhaps a bit later—the garden hidden within the Palais-Royal, a quiet little garden, idyllic, a gravel-strewn square amid the buildings where Colette once lived, where Cocteau once lived—and it struck me as the ideal spot for an apartment, with a view of the square, with the peace that this district offered because of its distance from the busy avenue de l'Opéra. I would walk along the boulevards, then return to the Seine, I'd gaze at the plane trees, the branches with damp buds just now opening to reveal the architecture of the five-pointed palmate leaves so carefully prepared during long winter nights. I was slightly homeless (since losing the war with the cockroaches), I didn't belong to that city, I didn't have an office, I didn't have money (or not much), but I had moments of happiness nonetheless. I was free. It seemed to me that I, a dispossessed tourist, was the true owner of the city that spread before me not like a real place of work, a great metropolis with its centers of finance and politics, but as if it were purely a painting, a fresco, as if it concerned itself only with spring, and the slow growth of plane tree leaves, and my watchful eyes. Paris belonged to me, not to the bureaucrats shut in their offices. Only someone who knew its streets and squares could truly own the city. It was as if that rich city with its vast history would willingly reveal itself only to its most marginal occupant; fed up with dignitaries, ministers who rarely abandoned their black limousines, it decided in my favor. True, the antique shops on the rue Bonaparte, shops with dark,

enigmatic interiors, brimming with old furniture and gilded stat-
ues, repeated emphatically, We have all we need, even the German
occupation couldn't rob us of the treasures we'd accumulated
through the centuries, it didn't get the heavy bureaus holding
the family silver, the Chinese vases, the candelabra, our angels
and putti taken from altars before which no one prays these days.
But this changed nothing: the antique dealers were helpless before my freedom, my mobility. It came as no surprise that these
dealers chose the rue Bonaparte as their home: it was Bonaparte,
after all, who transported so many treasures to Paris! But I was
at the time in life when nothing is for certain. I remember back to
1981 when I spent three months in the MacDowell Colony in
New Hampshire. Someone asked about my personal and professional plans in regard to what Americans, who, unlike the
French, have no tradition of literary moralists, so gladly term a
career; in light of the obvious impracticality of my situation, my
lack of prospects (as my interlocutor quite rightly thought), he
called me a "desperado." I should have been even more of a desperado here, on these prosperous Parisian streets, but no, just the
opposite, the moments of happiness, March in Paris, and then
April, and the evening meetings with M., these turned me into
a kind of *esperado* instead.

•

Almost all the displaced settlers belonged to what might be
called a category of individuals with suppressed political temperaments. Since Communism perfectly understood only one thing,
how to stifle human multiplicity, how to conceal a multicolored
reality beneath a protective coat of gray paint. People who had
once professed the most varied views imaginable, sometimes wild
or fantastic, now held their tongues, they didn't permit themselves
to express their former convictions. Fear functioned as the ideal
Occam's razor. As every student of philosophy is taught, Occam
thought that one should be parsimonious in ontology, in the

science of entities, that one shouldn't carelessly "create new entities." Fear played a similar role now: people who had once said
all kinds of things now committed themselves to the highest degree of methodological simplicity. They disavowed their earlier
convictions. Perhaps they spoke out only in the smallest circle of
their closest friends. Perhaps not. Caution was the chief virtue of
this historical moment. We seemed—superficially at least—to
live in a completely apolitical age, no one held any opinions, life
was monotonous, tidy, dull, aseptic. It may have been poor (it
was certainly poor), but it had been purged of all that had so
pained Dickens and other writers (as I thought). One no longer
encountered the cruel, rapacious merchants with ugly faces
whom I knew from illustrated Dickens novels and who might
haunt the dreams of anyone who spent long hours reading Dickens (I spent long hours reading Dickens). Purged, or so it seemed.
So it might seem to the very young, at any rate, since that's what
life had been arranged to suggest: certain terrible things from
the past would never again appear, certain rapacious types, certain faces consumed by hatred, with avarice inscribed in their
family crests. After a while I came to understand that this carefully planned purgation had amputated not just Dickens's mon-
sters; it likewise deprived us of many beautiful, splendid things.
Not to mention that we no longer had a choice between ugliness
and beauty. After a while I began—like others—to yearn for
what had been purged, cast off, for the raw reality that preceded
this great, ruthless operation. But not everything in this colorful
past world, painted over by the Communists, in the world for
which we had begun to yearn, would have made us happy. To
give one example—for reasons that are both obvious and unclear to me, I must say something here about my grandmother,
my mother's mother, an unpleasant woman, even her own family
didn't particularly like her. She held strong political views, first
and foremost her abhorrence of the Jews, which the Holocaust
hadn't mitigated in the least. I loathed the mentality of the ND,

the far-right National Democratic Party, from before the war, even though I'd never heard of the National Democrats back then. But thanks to the living, rather aggressive presence of my grandmother, who, unlike others, never held her tongue, was never "suppressed," who gladly shared her aversions with others, I came to know that mentality in the flesh long before I'd learned the acronym that suggested it in shorthand. My grandmother doubtless thought that she was beyond harm, a weak old woman hiding in a private existence, dividing her time between her son in Rzeszow and her daughter in Silesia; she could display her political passions with impunity, since these passions weren't linked to any social institutions and were thus in some sense disinterested.

•

The ND mentality consisted chiefly of distastes and hatreds culminating in anti-Semitism. I couldn't understand one thing: after the Holocaust, after every suppressed National Democrat had seen the suffering of the Jews up close, all political prejudices should have vanished in the face of their anguish, a pain so intimate, so immediate that ideological filters could not, I thought, be used to contain it, to escape its emanations. But let's take a better look. My family had an acquaintance we'll call Mr. D. My mother—as I recall—knew Mr. D. from her university days. He'd studied law, he worked as a legal consultant in some business after the war, at least that was his official title (why anyone would need a legal consultant in a purged and repressed society is totally beyond me). Anyhow. Anyhow Mr. D. was—in my eyes—a self-satisfied, aging man, one of those men whose faces often betray an almost imperceptible smirk of self-satisfaction, a faint glow of complacency. He liked making ironic proclamations, convinced of their significance. He had faith in his own wit. He was one of the displaced, he met all the criteria, he came to Silesia from Lvov, he had to start from scratch in

Gliwice. He turned up, along with his wife, in my parents' apartment a few times a year, chiefly, although not exclusively, for name days, especially my father's name day in October, when everyone had returned from vacation—my mother's name day came in August, when most of our friends had not yet exchanged their blissful holiday diaspora for the familiar gray city walls. Mr. D. underwent a certain unpleasant change sometime around 1968. After years of imposed fasting, the newspapers were suddenly permitted to ingest carefully measured doses of anti-Semitic rhetoric—permitted, or even commanded, by the highest authorities in the land. Mr. D. doubtlessly read all the papers. The vocabulary of his elegant conversations changed abruptly, words such as *kike* began to turn up in his talk. I gazed at him in astonishment. I'd never heard such an ugly word from his lips before, a word belonging, as far as I was concerned, to a banished past. I considered it shameful. But the witty Mr. D. clearly felt no shame. The self-suppression had ceased to function. Mr. D. was no longer displaced. Or so I saw it. Since the fate, the dignity of the displaced, which they shared with all the world's exiles, held not just suffering, I thought, but also a kind of glory. Modest, perhaps, but incontrovertible.

•

I'd like to imagine the kind of ardent reader who could spend his life between two books, between the *Notebooks* (*Cahiers*) of Simone Weil and the *Notebooks* (*Cahiers*) of Emil Cioran, by turns mocking and admiring first one, then the other (but never both at the same time), avoiding them, evading them, and always coming back, but never to both at once. Poets should be required to study Cioran's *Notebooks*, which hold nothing sacred, except for the music of Bach, Handel, and Mozart. Poets like to enhance, to expand. Even the most genuine inspiration can veer toward exaltation. And it's difficult to take up residence in some serene, balanced, moderate, objective middle ground.

There is only Cioran or Simone Weil, mockery or sanctity and prayer. Poets are drawn to hyperbole, not litotes. Cioran cultivates a geometry of sharp angles, caustic, cutting, horizontal. You need Simone Weil for verticality.

•

Cathedrals were passé. Prayer was passé. Only the writings of the Methodologists stayed in fashion, along with a few films, a few books and ideas. But I still loved cathedrals. This wasn't because of some theory. I admired French cathedrals with their enormous stained-glass windows. And the little rural churches that grace nearly every village in the Île-de-France. So tiny sometimes that they look like a cathedral's puppies. The Parisian Notre Dame came closest to these rural churches, but its rough edges had been softened by that nineteenth-century genius and maniacal conservationist Viollet-le-Duc. Eugène Viollet-le-Duc added an attractive, previously nonexistent tower and threw in a few sculptures to make Notre Dame *pretty*. He gave her a becoming makeover. He made her attractive so that she might grace the very heart of Paris. Notre Dame is lovely, there's no denying it, but she's been a bit too tidied up, too well-groomed, so as not to offend the sensibilities of the capital of European fashion; dark medieval humors could not be allowed to disturb complacent ladies and gentlemen of fashion, dim-witted, spiteful chimeras could not be permitted to cast shadows on smiling passengers in cabriolets dashing along the Seine. The cathedral in Chartres is an entirely different matter, slightly neglected, even a little wild. Chartres is a provincial town with no claims to fashion. Fashion doesn't reach this far. Paris isn't distant, it's true, but I suspect that the hairdressers and hatmakers of Chartres must use the word *Paris* on their signs to lure customers. The city of Chartres doesn't have much to say, in any case; only the cathedral speaks. Blades of grass or small weeds sometimes sprout from its stone roof. This would be unthinkable in Paris. Fortunately

Viollet-le-Duc didn't make it as far as Chartres, he didn't tidy up the cathedral, didn't give it a new spire. M. and I occasionally visited Chartres, usually by car, sometimes by train; the cathedral's towers began rising on the horizon just a dozen kilometers outside the city. The closer we drew, the more the dark towers grew, expanded. And the city diminished. The cathedral dominates the little city, which practices its small trades, sets up its market stands, displays its melons, artichokes, tomatoes, fish, and cheeses beneath the cathedral's shadow. Living in Chartres means living in the cathedral's shadow. Waking up in Chartres means waking in the cathedral's neighborhood. A notary in Chartres will always be a notary near the cathedral. A tailor will be a tailor near the cathedral. The cathedral is a great antediluvian creature. Its stones are weighty and moss laden. The town lies beneath it submissively like a pillow beneath a signet. The great signet of the cathedral rises on a hilltop. A dusky blue dominates within. Everything depends on the weather, if it's sunny or cloudy. On gray, dreary days the stained-glass windows, which have plenty of time, after all, they never hurry, they don't have to glow daily, they pay no heed to the quantity of enraptured spectators, they withdraw, grow introverted, fall still, wait patiently. The windows must likewise have kept quiet— even more quiet—during the last war, when they were taken from their giant frames and removed from Chartres for safekeeping. It must have been hard on them, the darkness, the neglect, parting with the old walls. But when the sun shines, the windows revive, they radiate blue light. The windows are vast and peaceful. They're giants. They're sleeping, or so it seems, until you look closer, then you see that they're beset by work, workers clear away grape vines, construct chapels and churches, the candles aren't idle either, they heal the sick, the Jesse Tree grows slowly, but surely, whatever the season, prophets make their wrathful proclamations, the generations listen halfheartedly and take their places in the niches of the world's long history, in rooms reserved in history's motel. Thomas à Becket disembarks from a ship that has reached the English shores. Saint Eustace spies a stag with an image of Christ in its antlers. The Good Samaritan saves the wounded man. Peasants keep to their plows, bricklayers to their buildings, priests to their castles, saints to their biographies. The tourists who crowd the cathedral on weekends are the real idlers. The windows labor without a moment's rest. Weavers at their spindles, farmers in the fields. The small silhouettes of medieval women and men are occupied either with work or piety; piety seems to spring from their daily routines. But the Mother of God is much larger than the other saints. You need to observe the windows closely, it's easy to assume that they're asleep. Nothing could be further from the truth. The tourists photograph the windows nonstop without noticing that the figures within their lead-rimmed panes are preoccupied with handiwork or prophecy or healing. The cathedral is as open to people as a railroad station, one of those oversize, gigantic stations constructed at a time when railroad connections were crucial for the economy; now they're as anachronistic as hurdy-gurdies or droshkies. Chartres's inhabitants often take shortcuts; instead of circling the cathedral's great mass, they walk through it, moving from south to north or north to south, they pass the transept, cut across the main nave, sometimes acknowledging the Blessed Sacrament, sometimes not—they're caught up in their own business, and this is not lèse-majesté, just the opposite, it's a positive good, since they bring with them the rain or fine weather, the winter or summer. They import their lives, their bustle, their inattention, and it's not improper, just the opposite, it's a shame that other churches don't offer shortcuts to the inhabitants of other cities—since they aren't quite so vast, they don't block the road, they aren't benign giants, they don't reside in the city's very heart. The population crossing through the cathedral keeps it up-to-date, it learns the latest news about the world, about the century that lies outside its walls, always changing. But they, the residents of Chartres, pay no attention to what the cathedral is thinking, after all, they didn't raise its walls, they didn't hew its stones, they didn't tumble from its scaffolds. They received the cathedral as a gift, an inheritance, they fear it, love and hate it, forget about it, use it as a huge hall to be crossed while hurrying elsewhere.

And visitors, how should they treat the cathedral? Here's what I think: You need to take your time in Chartres Cathedral, you can't hurry, like the tourist groups; you should take a seat, study the windows, then stand up and stroll around, forget that you're in a cathedral, then remember again, and after a while you'll sense something undescribed in any guidebook, a kind of strong longing or desire that isn't contained within the cathedral's walls or its windows, it's in the air, in its very lungs. After some time, after you've circled the cathedral several times, crossing its zones of light and shade, purely visual impressions recede while this ever-growing desire comes into focus. We don't know why the cathedral inspires such longing. Why its dark interior gives rise to longing.

•

What do poets actually know? And what did Mozart know?

•

It sometimes happens—particularly when I come across a review by one of the cynical poets (this week I read a piece about a certain well-known New York poet)—that I experience a moment of painful disillusionment, an instant of vertigo, of profound disorientation. There aren't too many cynical poets—the classic twentieth-century example is Philip Larkin, a genuinely great poet—but they do turn up, and their existence poses a problem. They mock humanity (not that there's anything wrong with that), they sing the praises of the easy life, convenient, comfortable, sensual, they completely reject what's usually called political correctness, compassion for others, the fraternal instinct, they scoff at vertical yearnings. Such things don't exist, quit pretending, the cynical poets seem to say. They apparently direct their remarks not to some classic version of the reader, but to their fellow writers, the uncynical poets. For a moment I suspect they may be right, that all the poets who follow a more circuitous route, laboriously ascending the tall peak of truth in search of light, struggling to reach the hidden sense of life, recognizing the religious impulse, acknowledging mystery, may just be fools, or worse, hypocrites, who act as if they're preparing to brave a dangerous mountain stream while willfully ignoring the convenient footbridge that would take them safely across in half a minute with dry feet. When they might live comfortably, pleasantly, rarely leaving their fine restaurants, mocking the unenlightened, occasionally jotting down clever lines on their napkins, smiling scornfully as they drift off to sleep, perhaps chuckling quietly even as they die . . .

•

A scrap of conversation caught on Karmelicka Street: one young woman says to another, "When I write her back, I'll be polite, but brutal." Another time, a different girl to her friend: "And you know, I got the audience award there."

•

July in Krakow. Weekends in the city center are noisy, but in more distant neighborhoods sparrows bathe peacefully in puddles left by a brief but violent storm.

•

May and June are the loveliest months. But in September dreams run level with reality.

•

In the Massolit bookstore, where you can also buy coffee or wine, I overheard a conversation between two young American students. The girl told the boy, You know, I've just about had it with Krakow. I sent a letter home today, and you know, they don't have self-stick stamps, you've got to lick them, it's disgusting.

•

Paul Claudel is largely forgotten today, even in France. Admirers of his sister Camille remember him and sometimes blame her brother for his supposed persecution of the unfortunate sculptress. Occasionally someone will stage one of his plays. But his work as a whole, the deep breath of his poetry, the strength of his intellect, his essays, don't stir much interest these days, they probably seem too solid, too monumental, they lack fear and doubt, they're anachronistic. The certainty of his convictions seems compromising, old-fashioned. In his famous elegy for Yeats—Claudel probably makes an appearance just for the sake of the rhyme *Claudel* and *well*—Auden admits that the French poet was a good writer, but suggests that he must first be forgiven (presumably for some political transgression, probably his support, purely theoretical, of Franco in the Spanish Civil War) before we can actually enjoy his work. During the Second World War, Claudel, by then a retired ambassador living in the Castle of Brangues—briefly sided with Pétain and even wrote an ode in his honor (a small ode, as opposed to his five great odes), but Claudel soon grew disillusioned with the Vichy regime. Shocked by the tragedy of the Jews, he sent a courageous letter to the chief rabbi of France in December 1941, in which he stood up for the oppressed. It's true that he had another, less attractive side, the hateful Claudel, the inquisitor—though he never actually performed such a function—who thought that all Protestants would roast in hell simply because they were Protestants. He didn't like Germans, the sight of that country's citizens consuming grilled sausages and drinking beer filled him with true Gallic loathing. But he counted himself among the admirers of

Poland, Catholic Poland. He doesn't seem to have been personally appealing; Iwaszkiewicz valued and translated his work, but on their first meeting, he was struck by Claudel's artificiality. Iwaszkiewicz uses the French word *facticité* (Paul Valéry gave him the same impression). None of this helps us to gain entry into the writing. Claudel's nature: He was quick to damn, to reject, and to despise; he despised Eliot, despised Rilke, and also, bearing in mind his many aversions, he seems almost physically repulsive as seen in photos, too bulky, no neck, a short, stocky man hewn from a single block of wood, a perpetually unsmiling bourgeois clad in an ambassador's uniform embroidered with braids. After the Second World War, this humorless playwright and poet was crammed, doubtless with some difficulty, into a different uniform, that of a French Academician, likewise embroidered and accompanied by a sword, purely symbolic in principle, but in the case of this choleric Academician, one might theoretically imagine it landing actual blows—on Protestants, for example. However, anyone who looks through his great odes, *Cinq grandes odes*, without prejudice, or excerpts from the plays, for example the scene on ship deck in *Partage de midi*, will instantly fall under the spell of the poetic enchanter who hid in daily life beneath uniforms and braids. Claudel's diary, the *Journal* in the two-volume Pléiade edition, is also marvelous, a great prose poem where over several hundred necessarily uneven pages, dull quotations from Latin theological texts alternate with radiant poetic observations, fruits of the purest inspiration.

•

In the Berlin Pergamon Museum: a bronze Apollo found in the sea. His life under the water, his conversations with Poseidon, the long wait for a return to dry land.

•

Which books get left behind in a vacation rental? I took notes two years ago in Rapallo, in an apartment that apparently once belonged to a German nun and was now rented out by her heir: Edmund Gosse, *Father and Son*; Paul Rohrbach, *Der deutsche Gedanke* (a book from 1911; German thought concludes that Germany wants and needs colonies); Wilhelm Michel (author of a good biography of Hölderlin); *Das Leiden am Ich* (1930 edition, meditations on the links between life and spirituality); Ferdinand Gregorovius, *Römische Tagebücher*, engaging remarks drawn from the diary of a recognized historian and lover of Italy, mainly on Italy's political situation in the nineteenth century, the struggle to create a modern Italian nation; Kazimierz Wierzynski's biography of Chopin in Italian translation; and finally Malwida von Meysenbug, *Memoirs of an Idealist* (*Memoiren einer Idealistin*), the two first volumes—her arrival in London, her acquaintance with Herzen, Ogarev, and finally the move to Rome. And many other volumes in that library, in Rapallo, the place where Nietzsche, during his strolls in the nearby hills, would meet his superman (he had already met Mme Meysenbug, far realer than any superman).

•

Joanna Ronikier, who published a wonderful book, *In the Garden of Memory*, a history of her extensive family (they were Jewish) before the war and during the Holocaust, once told us that for a long while she never went back to her memories of that period (she was hidden by nuns in a convent near Warsaw). This is how she explained it: She was so closely tied to the cabaret Cellar Under the Rams, she was so close to those performers, the cabaret was so much her home, that laughter banished memory. This intrigued me: Does laughter really hold such power? Could you really survive nearly all of Poland's Communist years beneath the shelter of that liberating laughter? Even for someone who—as a child, it's true—had felt the threat of death daily, laughter could drive off memory's terrors, could distract her from the chief experience of those early years. Only after Communism had ended and the cabaret's energy had dissipated did Joanna return to those early memories and write her compelling book.

•

I spent many hours in Rapallo with Massimo Bacigalupo, an Italian American professor (and a charming person) at the University of Genoa. Ezra Pound's poetry is his passion. Massimo's father had been Pound's doctor, so Massimo, as a boy and young man, had known the poet extremely well. Once when he took us out sailing, he pointed to a spot in the boat and said, Ezra used to sit there. He also showed us the little beach where Ezra used to swim. And the house where he'd lived. And the house where Olga Rudge had lived. But when I asked him what they used to talk about, he looked at me in astonishment and said, Ezra didn't talk. He was shrouded in silence. I tried to imagine it: the silent old poet and the young Massimo. If I could only learn to like Pound's poetry. If just to please Massimo, who—as the concept behind his name suggests—labors with all his might to draw new friends to Pound's writing. I try, but I can't manage it, and not just for political reasons.

•

The modest returns of the dead: Helmut Kajzar died in 1982 from cancer, after a brief, impassioned battle with the disease. He was forty years old. He was a dramaturge and director, interested in new developments in European theater, he followed German literature particularly. He'd had some success both as an author and a director. His name was recognized during his lifetime, but now it's forgotten, as so often happens. Almost forgotten. His friends remember him, and his family. I got to know him through Jerzy Kronhold. He came from a Protestant family near Cieszyn. He died in the summer. When I told my father about his death, he asked me if Kajzar was young. I was a few years younger than Kajzar, I wasn't sure how my father saw it, I hesitated and said, He was forty, pretty young, I guess. Sometimes he returns in my thoughts, tiptoes in quietly. We sometimes argued while he was alive. That was when the opposition was starting up in Poland, and I identified with it almost completely, this was the period of my ardent oppositional orthodoxy. That is to say, whenever I was around anyone indifferent or hostile to the movement, I was a committed dissident, while among my friends within the opposition, I was often critical (as usual, I was never 100 percent sure I was on the right track). Helmut, on the other hand, openly sided with the contrarians, he preferred to play the "artist" in every situation, as if he lived inside art, not in a Poland ruled by men with square heads. He became friends with Tadeusz Rozewicz, who also viewed the rebellious intellectuals and students suspiciously, as we know. Helmut treated my stories of "underground" lectures and readings—events held in private apartments or churches (Catholic!)—a bit skeptically. I rarely played a leading role in those meetings, I liked staying in the audience, I didn't often read my own poems, since I didn't write much then, didn't get much finished. My passion didn't run deep, or rather I should say that my political ardor didn't mix well with my passion for poetry. I wasn't entirely convinced that poetry should serve as propaganda, even for the noblest of political causes. Still, this movement had something quite splendid about it. I got to know extraordinary people, experienced unforgettable moments, learned many things. But it seemed to me that poetry shouldn't simply cling to this new political direction, this social protest, like a lizard on a sun-warmed boulder. It doesn't mean anything now. I no longer argue with Helmut when he enters my thoughts. Now he stands among the dead, and the dead have cast off all irony, all perversity. The dead wear dark suits and are exceedingly serious. I also see what was different about him now. In a Catholic country every Protestant is a little different. Something about Helmut was fascinating, something even in the way he spoke, distinctive, elegant, considered. One time we went for a walk in Berlin, in the direction of the Olympic Stadium where Hitler had once congratulated victorious German athletes. Helmut demonstrated various elements of contemporary theatrical training for me, for example, exercises based on unnaturally slow walking, on decelerating every motion. It couldn't occur to me at the time, but it came to me later: this must be how the dead walk. They have more time than we do, they never hurry. They take tiny steps, placing one foot in front of the other. They walk attentively, slowly, watching the ground.

•

Dave Brubeck—listening to *Jazz at Oberlin*. It's the CD version of the old vinyl album by the same name, which was recorded, as the notes scrupulously inform us, in 1953. Listening to Brubeck's and Paul Desmond's insane improvisations, I relive a great shiver of joy and liberation from years past—this was one of my finest jazz albums, a gem in my little collection back in my high school days—that is to say, I felt this shiver some ten years after the concert was recorded at Oberlin College in Ohio. Those improvisations, those wild blocks of sound, blocks Brubeck created, so it seems, by scaling piano chords up the highest mountain, haven't aged a bit. The audience, the students' emotional reaction. Today those students must be comfortably retired, bored, living in Florida.

•

I remember again my father's comic essay on the characters from *Balladyna*: Skierka was a hard worker, while Chochlik was spiteful. I'm writing a whole book on the same subject . . . Gravity is our Skierka, our Chochlik is irony. We need them both.

•

We all know the formula of good versus evil that shapes most
Hollywood movies as well as, more recently, electronic games,
where the classic conflict continues to play out, sometimes in
rather aesthetically unappealing form. Intellectuals of various
countries generally deplore this primitive argument and expend
great energy in developing theories that hold no place for either
good or evil. But doesn't a similar battle rage in each of us?—
although you'd need far subtler concepts to do it justice.

•

My father has been ill for many years, he's growing weaker,
leaving; for all practical purposes he's been in another world for
a year or more. He's slowly dying, although all the chief organs
of his inexhaustible organism—he's ninety-seven—are in good
shape. But he's completely lost his memory, he doesn't get out of
bed. He doesn't recognize anyone. He has to be fed and bathed.
I think of what he used to be, that kind, witty, obliging man. I
don't know why, but the answer he gave a journalist some ten
years back comes to mind. The journalist was doing an interview that later appeared in the monthly magazine *Silesia*. Recollections of the transfer (deportation) from Lvov were the main
subject, both my father's memories and those of other employees
of the institute, all of whom had to abandon the baroque city of
hills and churches, Orthodox and Catholic alike, for the Prussian brick walls of Gliwice or Wroclaw. Even then my father
was one of the last surviving veterans of that great, unwelcome
migration, the journey of resettlement. But at the moment when
the journey began, he ranked among the youngest—tenured
professors, full professors, were among the resettled, while he
was just beginning his academic career. The correspondent from
Silesia magazine must also have known my books, since at one
point he asked my father what he thought of one passage from

my essay "Two Cities." The journalist cited a few sentences from my text—about how people are divided into three camps, the settled, the emigrants, and the homeless, and some like painting, while others prefer music, the most metaphorical of the arts. (Literally: "Music was created for the homeless because, of all the arts, it is least connected with place . . . Painting is the art of settled people who enjoy contemplating their native haunts. Portraits confirm the settled in their conviction that they are really alive.") My father never liked language sprinkled with metaphors. He was—I use the past tense since his mind is already gone—an engineer, he understood the world empirically, he doubtlessly endorsed the principles of positivist philosophy, the stern dictates of the Vienna Circle, everything you discuss should be strictly quantifiable. He was a no-nonsense engineer—he liked reading history books, he also liked paintings. Paintings made him happy, he loved them (though he himself wouldn't have used the word, he couldn't ever even tell his children that he loved them), impressionist paintings covered with blooming meadows and quiet Parisian suburbs. My passion for writing poems and essays full of poetic tropes must have worried him since he, like most of the human race, suspected that rich language, saturated in metaphors, was often the language of liars, or at least tended in that direction. Anyone who filled language with figures of speech, who revealed emotion, who introduced elements born of invention, improvisation, who shook language as one might shake a tree, came perilously close to falsehood. He was honesty personified—that's also how they thought of him at the Gliwice Polytechnic Institute, that's how his countless students remember him. He read a great deal, mainly memoirs— mountains of memoirs, the memoirs of generals and engineers, bankers and ministers—but also countless history books and a fair number of novels. But I'm convinced that he simply skipped the pages of which the authors were proudest, the poetic pages swarming with hyperboles and comparisons, synecdoches and litotes, pages containing the novelist's most ardent professions of faith; he skimmed them, waiting for the author to settle down and get back to more normal forms of narration. I can only imagine how the journalist's question, citing as it did an essay written by his son, must have embarrassed him. Since he couldn't simply dismiss words written by his own son. He knew that whatever he said would be written down, would appear in print at some later date. We were on the best of terms; my being among the ranks of those who—occasionally—employed metaphors didn't ordinarily bother him in the least. I even think that in his own peculiar way, that is to say, discreetly, he enjoyed it. But his son's "social situation" was a completely different matter, as was the opinion he was expected to pronounce. I'm sure that he fell silent, there was a pause while the journalist politely waited for my father to formulate his response, he may even have turned off his tape recorder for a moment, perhaps he lost hope that any answer was forthcoming. Finally my father said, probably in the slightly husky voice he always had when he was embarrassed, That's a slight exaggeration. A slight exaggeration. I burst out laughing when I read that, it expressed his views on poetry so perfectly, so completely, really, his views on the whole strange world that had swallowed up his son. A slight exaggeration. That's what engineers think of poetry. There's nothing inherently wrong with it, the engineers think, it doesn't necessarily lead to falsehood, effeteness, aestheticism, it's guilty, above all, of exaggeration. A slight exaggeration. It's an exaggeration, it unnecessarily confuses the boundaries and lines of reality, which grows feverish and dances.

•

A slight exaggeration—it's actually a good definition of poetry. An excellent definition for poetry on cool and misty days, days when the morning rises late, falsely promising sunshine. It's a slight exaggeration, until we make ourselves at home in it. Then it becomes the truth. But when we leave it again—since permanent residence is impossible—it becomes once more a slight exaggeration.

•

My father had a rather skeptical attitude toward poetry, but when he'd been much younger, he'd read Galczynski, as witnessed by the volumes on his shelf, books by that splendid poet who readily admitted in his poems to his lack of character ("too much wind for my wool"). But something shocking happened in the 1980s. I found out about it only many years later: my father copied out my poem "To Go to Lvov" for his friends and acquaintances. I wrote a poem about it:

Not Thinking About Aesthetics

When, in the eighties, my father copied out
my poem "To Go to Lvov" for friends
(he told me about it much later,
with some embarrassment), I doubt he was thinking
    about aesthetics,
metaphors, stresses, deeper meanings,
only about the city he'd loved and lost, the city
where his early years, his epiphanies, his meetings with
    the world,
had been detained, like hostages,
and he must have struck the keyboard of his faithful old
typewriter with such force that if we
better understood the conservation of energy
we might perhaps regenerate
on this basis at least one street
of his first rapture.

I still don't know what exactly my father, this practical, slightly ironic man, felt as he copied out this poem, with its copious metaphors and metonymies. He might have justified himself in part by saying that these were conspiratorial times, he was participating in the great process of disseminating underground writing. But he was thinking first and foremost about Lvov, which he knew far better than I did. When I showed him photos I'd taken just after returning from a trip there in 2001, he knew the spot, the street or square, instantly, just like that, as if he'd seen it the day before, but more than half a century had passed since he'd left the city. I understood then that he'd never really left Lvov, although he'd led such an active life since the war, he'd even forged a professional career of sorts. After he'd already started to lose his memory, he once told Mrs. L., who looked after him, You know, I'll be seeing my wife soon, I'm going to Lvov. My mother was no longer living.

•

"There is no merry music"—these words are ascribed to Franz Schubert. You may not agree, but you must bear in mind that the words were spoken by a great master, who must have known what he was saying.

•

We live between hyperbole and litotes (litotes is the opposite of hyperbole, it means to diminish something, not to enhance it). These are the names of rhetorical figures, but their meaning extends beyond academic handbooks. Since we must always enlarge or diminish what we see, what we encounter, what wounds or gladdens us. How difficult it is to find the space between hyperbole and litotes in which our experience takes place.

•

All those who've received the gift of poetry, whether in writing or in reading, must take it as their foundation, but at the same time, they must serve it cautiously, so as not to stifle other powers drowsing in it, to permit this gift to engage in free conversation with the most varied realms of life. Generally speaking, I think we should pay close attention to trees: they know how to grow—not just through one central core, but also sideways, through their branches, through the complex harmony and equilibrium between them. More than one old ash tree has taken a lyre's shape, old linden trees may likewise develop an economy supported by a mighty trunk divided in two at the start. Only tall poplars, like anorexic teenagers, neglect their side branches, they grow straight up. While on the other hand, their cousins, the silver and black poplars, are less frivolous, as if they'd guessed that upward thrusts must be accompanied by horizontal growth—a candle's flame doesn't live long.

•

A slight exaggeration—if you follow my father's line of thought, achieving the ideal balance between a language unashamed of metaphors and completely nonfigurative, declarative (though not necessarily dry) speech might seem nearly impossible. Since sooner or later purely factual language inevitably begins to yearn, so to speak, for livelier rhetorical gestures, for images, apt comparisons, metonymies, in short, for slight exaggerations. But if the exaggerations grow too powerful, if the language grows too baroque, we begin to miss precision, the modest, prosaic articulation preferred by engineers, who form after all a substantial part of our species. In Robert Musil's lovely essay on Rilke—given as a lecture on the first anniversary of the poet's death—there's a paragraph in which he analyzes the peculiarities of the imagination and takes the opportunity to make a general observation: "There's something tragicomic, after all, in this human proclivity for comparisons . . . The comparisons we make create the impression that we can't just sit still in whatever place we actually happen to be." What a wonderful remark: we can't just sit still in whatever place we actually happen to be! We continually seek out metaphors, as if we can't simply agree on a definition that might describe us too precisely, too unequivocally. As when we visit the doctor (and some doctors are, after all, just engineers in white jackets!), the doctor asks our age, then commands us to stand on the scales, and places us beneath the little guillotine that takes our height; we dislike being reduced in a few minutes to three numerals. We instantly start questioning the absence of nouns and adjectives. We look to escape dull definitions (and doctors' offices); in life, that vast, actual life that courses and flows past doctors' receptionists and dentists' waiting rooms, elegant ladies always on the watch for new gowns, new stoles and cloaks, but men and women alike, whether they worry about their outfits or disregard fashion's latest dictates, keep on the lookout for new comparisons, as if they suspect that "something else" exists, we're surrounded by a thick cloud of invisibility that can't be satisfied with hackneyed epithets, it requires constant invention, new definitions.

•

Malraux says people die only for something that doesn't exist.

•

I think I've already mentioned this somewhere: in Chinese the sign for "music" is also the sign for "joy." We'll have to ask Franz Schubert what he thinks of this.

•

Only the Jews were truly *displaced*—they never returned. They were displaced right off the planet, they were incinerated, they were shot en masse at the edge of mass graves. They were displaced into smoke, into oblivion. Just as the Polish officers were *displaced*, career and reserve officers alike, officers who were doctors, mathematicians, artists, and lawyers, who were killed in Katyn, in Kharkiv, and in other cities, where they were executed by a shot to the back of the head, a shot in the nexus of human intelligence. All the others, my aunts, my uncles, my parent, Poles, Germans, all those who somehow reached their designated destination—it took a week by freight train for my parents to cross the four hundred kilometers separating Lvov from Silesia—who entered their unpromised land, only these were resettled. Only resettled. And a few died, of resettlement.

•

My *Defense of Ardor* came out in France as *Éloge de la ferveur*, in Laurence Dyèvre's translation. I mention this only because some nice young Frenchman, whom I met in December 2008 in Toulouse, gave me a little book written by François Jullien. Its title: *Éloge de la fadeur*. It's difficult to translate *fadeur* into English. *Fade* in French means "drab" or "bland," "flavorless." So it's a defense, or praise, of "blandness." Jullien is a distinguished sinologist, his book addresses Chinese culture, in which, as he describes it, a taste for blandness predominates, it avoids strong accents, sharp tones, it dislikes passion, ardor—everything in good measure.

•

I remember once in Holland—I think it was a poetry festival in Rotterdam—I took the train to Delft, not a long trip, and I found the spot from which Vermeer had viewed his city while painting his famous *View of Delft*. Three concrete benches stand there now. Two retired people sat on one, the other two were empty.

•

And Pavel Florensky once said, Beauty is the heart of faith.

•

A sudden change in the weather. Yesterday was sultry, over ninety degrees, no breeze, then clouds and rain in the evening, the temperature dropped to sixty-five degrees. Swimming yesterday in a pond outside of Krakow. The pond must have risen on a spot where they used to quarry sand; the water is pure, green, transparent. A tall rock rises on one side, the other side is flat, overgrown with grass. The locals use it for grilling, the weekenders' new passion. The smoke mixes with the third-rate pop music blaring from one of the cars parked at the water's edge. You can't even really call it music—a pounding, primitive beat pours from the red car, so powerful that the car seems about to disintegrate . . .

•

I'm listening to Johannes Brahms, the Rhapsody for Alto, Male Chorus, and Orchestra, op. 53, in the archival performance of Kathleen Ferrier, the legendary English singer (accompanied by an orchestra and chorus), and I remember William Styron's book on melancholy, *Darkness Visible* (it's Milton's phrase, he uses it to describe hell). Styron suffered from severe depression, and he recreates one of the worst bouts of the disease; after a long, sleepless night, he's considering suicide, then turns on the radio and suddenly hears Brahms's rhapsody. And something extraordinary happens—the crisis passes, the music, that very rhapsody, opus 53, heals him, cures him, saves him from suicide, permits him to endure the worst. The new day will begin, the light will return, the first bakeries will open, and the fresh scent of bread will fill the narrow streets of old cities.

It's hard to imagine a greater tribute to the music. Brahms's rhapsody is intimate, hushed, and yet intensely dramatic. I read that he composed it, to Goethe's words, as a wedding present for Robert and Clara Schumann's daughter Julie (what a wonderful gift!). The melody rises above the orchestra's delicate accompaniment, drifts over it as lightly as a dragonfly floats above a May meadow, but it's powerful, dramatic nonetheless. The woman's voice gives the listeners strength, perhaps because the rhapsody's drama, both powerful and calm, Brahmsian, differs from the violent, even hysterical outbursts of Wagnerian melody—it's distributed, dispersed in time, in melody. The drama continues in the music, it undergoes modulations, changes—it's sustained, set out in many moments, subject to repetitions, and is thus didactic, in the noblest sense of that usually pedantic word. It may give us courage, may even, as we've seen, save someone's life. Brahms must have understood how the tragedy of a single moment, a single day or even week, stands in relation to the epic duration of life: he must have known that we live longer than the lovely, blithe, but foolish dragonfly flitting over a dark pond, we live a long time, we labor and endure in the intervals between intense moments of the greatest sorrow. We live in ecstatic moments, but epic pauses stretch between them. Life consists chiefly of such intervals, intervals that, longing perhaps for the next epiphany, dreading the next defeat, extend between those great, rare moments like a gentle plateau in high mountains. While we occupy this plateau, we never know what's coming next, what life's next great blow will bring. At times we think that nothing will ever happen, the sadness will never end. But we're usually mistaken—the next shock always comes, sometimes also the next rapture. The next chapter always follows (though we may think we've finished the book), bringing hidden treasures. It must have been this wisdom, inscribed into Brahms's music, that healed William Styron, opened him to the future, saved him. It restored his sense of the epic. It reminded him that we live, by necessity, in two registers, not just in one, we live both in the moment and in duration. It unexpectedly revealed this expanse with its bright irony, its inexhaustible message: "You've seen this much, you'll see something more." Since duration can be, often is, good-naturedly ironic, like the beloved old aunt who smiles as we confide our most recent heartbreak—and suddenly this tragedy no longer seems so monstrous. Endurance has experience, a sense of humor. Whereas depression destroys our capacity to anticipate the future, depression is a moment that doesn't realize how many siblings it has, other moments and long periods of limbo, expectation, preparation. The Rhapsody, opus 53, is a wonderful gift for those who invest too much in the moment, but also for those who love only duration.

•

In the late 1990s I used to take up residence in Houston every spring just as Czeslaw Milosz, who divided his life then between Krakow and California, was returning to Berkeley, to the small, bright house high in the hills on Grizzly Peak Boulevard (how many people made pilgrimages to that house, took photos, boasted of their visits to the poet). We'd talk every so often over the phone. One day Milosz called me. I heard sorrow, deep melancholy in his voice. We began talking and I realized after a moment that he was at the end of his rope, he needed my help. Finally he asked me, Adam (he used the formal, as we always did), please tell me honestly, have I ever in my life written a single good poem?

•

When I listened to Brahms's Rhapsody, opus 53, once again, this time with friends, I understood something new: the composition is structured so that initially we hear only the woman's voice, the alto, and the orchestra. Only gradually do we discern the growing voices of the chorus interweaving with that of the soloist. At first they engage cautiously, like strangers walking side by side, mistrustful, but they slowly grow more familiar until the alto nearly fuses with the choral voice, although it retains a hint of individuality up to the end. I also realized that the union of the soloist and the chorus is a gift to the listener. We don't need to perceive it "theoretically," we simply experience a

kind of unconscious relief or consolation; the alto's tragic solitude doesn't last to the work's end, the chorus's delicate voices
join it sympathetically to build a frail but genuine solidarity—
with suffering, with loneliness. This progression—from the alto's
isolation to its union with the chorus—also fits the dramatic
essence of the Goethe poem on which Brahms based his
composition.

•

I keep thinking about my "polemics" with my father—although
it's difficult to speak of polemics when one side of the discussion
has gone missing. My father is already in a different world, in a
different space, oblivious, unconscious, helpless, dependent on
others. His joke about the "slight exaggeration"—made in far
better times, when he hadn't yet lost his autonomy (old people are
like nations that can no longer defend themselves, like eighteenth-
century Poland, weak, ailing, without memory)—still bothers
me, I feel compelled to address the worldview of the "engineers."
Robert Musil comes to my assistance once again; I've recently
gone back to his essays. He says the following about art in one
essay: "It doesn't create anything that can survive without enthusiasm." This is the word I was looking for—*enthusiasm*. This
notion, seldom articulated, was treated quite skeptically by Enlightenment thinkers, who feared religious fanaticism. Still, it is
the key to understanding art. With its help, we can discern the
subtle but unmistakable difference between a purely reportorial
tone and the language that records a moment of rapture ... The
history of the word *enthusiasm* is significant: as we know, it originally designated a state when a person experienced something
like a divine invasion. Apollo or Dionysus entered a human soul.
We still like using the term, but we're all too happy to forget the
divine element etymologically contained within it—the Enlightenment thinkers didn't labor in vain, they successfully stripped
the concept of its insolent thorns. *Enthusiasm* today may be used

to describe soccer matches, a new kind of laptop, political events. Under the Soviet regime the word *enthusiasm* was recruited into the party; you'd regularly hear phrases like "youth marched enthusiastically in the May Day Parade"—or so the radio broadcasters assured us. But we truly require enthusiasm in art, on both sides: both the creators of art and its audience would be helpless without it.

•

In my old notes, I found the following comment: "The great, mysterious individuals that we are, reduced to miniature dimensions." Is this really so? Yes, it is. People meeting each other, conducting what we innocently call a social life, generally can't express themselves even minimally, they shrink, they stoop. I remember a—grotesque—passage from Gombrowicz's diaries, a description of his visit to the great avant-garde artist and writer Witkacy, who, needless to say, couldn't do anything the way that other people did. He opened the door while hunched over to dwarfish proportions and only gradually straightened up, returned to his natural height. We meet others and shrink before them (though not exactly like Witkacy). The tortures of introverts, even those with a rich inner life, when they come into contact with others. Silent introverts—it's not that they're guarding their treasures from outsiders, they're just paralyzed by shyness. They may appear to be arrogant, but it's an illusion, an error, they're shy. What are they so afraid of? We don't know. Some force keeps them from speaking. They're perfectionists in a certain sense: they're afraid that whatever they say will simply caricature their ideas. They have plenty of experience, they've embarrassed themselves so many times, committed some gaffe, expressed themselves badly, and suffered for it later. That's why they prefer silence— it's actually a form of respect for others, for whomever they're meeting. But that person often sees it very differently . . .

•

Listening to Mahler. I've listened to Gustav Mahler's work less frequently in recent months, although I still think his *Song of the Earth*, like the Ninth Symphony, is an extraordinary work. As are the other symphonies, other song cycles (Krzysztof Meyer's story about Shostakovich: when he asked the composer which of Mahler's symphonies he liked best, Shostakovich hesitated, then listed one after the other). I think I've already mentioned my conversation with the German writer Hartmut Lange. We both love *Song of the Earth*, but he goes further, he even sees this work as *God*. Literally. The theologians would be appalled. I can't agree with Hartmut. I rarely listen to *Song of the Earth*—but not from lack of interest, no, just the opposite, I'm afraid that my musical memory will record it too precisely, that I'll feel boredom, not joy, I'll know it by heart . . .

•

Among my childhood memories is the despair I felt when my father left for military exercises. He must have taken an early train; in any case, he was already gone when I got up. And I knew he'd be gone for a long time, many weeks. And he didn't say goodbye to me . . . I remember sobbing. Military exercises were a grim business back then, almost like the war that was hanging over our heads (the generation of the displaced, preoccupied with the loss of their city, longed obsessively for the next war . . .). It was morning, and I cried, since my father had left without saying goodbye.

•

Schopenhauer loved music above all else—the authors of books on the philosopher note with some irritation that his favorite composer was Gioacchino Rossini, now largely dismissed as a

composer of light music . . . These were the arias that the Frank-
furt recluse used to whistle.

•

I found a document dated October 26, 1988, among my old papers.
The document, composed in the language of Racine, bears the
title "Attestation à remettre à la préfecture de police," and it
attests—after giving my name and address—"qu'il est possible,
en raison des antécédents que l'intéressé nous a fait connâitre,
que soit mentionné sur les documents officiels le concernant,
l'activité d'écrivain." Meaning: "whereas it is possible in light of
the proofs presented to us by the interested party that his literary
activity is indicated in the documents concerning him." This is
followed by the seal and signature of the responsible committee,
which bears the title Commission de la professionalité. This certificate was essential if you wished to obtain an extension of the
residence permit issued by the prefecture of police, in my case
the prefecture in Nanterre, the capital of the department of
Hauts-de-Seine. The Commission of "Professionality" was located in the very heart of Paris, on the rue Saint-Dominique; it
occupied an apartment on the ground floor of an ordinary
Haussmann-style building. In the little waiting room you might
meet Japanese artists with large portfolios likely holding fashion
designs (haute couture) or perhaps sketches for theatrical costumes,
Americans lugging cello or bass cases, Czechs and Hungarians
with sheaves of reproduced paintings or perhaps photographs of
sculptures, since this commission existed so that freelancing foreigners could present certificates, later endorsed by the police,
confirming that they were not panhandlers, freeloaders, but had
some kind of employment, they paid their way without employment in any French institute or industry. And thanks to these
certificates, they could count on their residence permits being
renewed. It always struck me that this commission bore the hall-
marks of a civilization that combined a high degree of bureau-

cracy, on a par with the Middle Kingdom during the Ming dynasty, with respect for art and individualism. So every year— since the residence permit had to be renewed yearly—I carried my handful of books to the rue Saint-Dominique, a few steps from the splendid boulevard Saint-Germain, which was and remains one of the greatest streets created by Western culture, to confirm that I was in fact a writer. I presented the same books every year, occasionally enhanced by some freshly printed collection of poems or essays, in translation or in my native tongue, and when I returned to collect my document, the tomes, or rather slim volumes, were handed back to me. So I was a writer with a yearly expiration, like some medications, or canned food with a date stamped on its tin bottom. Every year, at the end of September or the start of October, I began to have doubts—was I still a writer? I accepted the commission's decision with relief, I could rest easy for another year. But had the commission chief studied my books at home? Had he liked my poems and essays? Such questions remained unanswered, the certificate was couched in maximally dry, efficient prose, it drew no evaluative conclusions, it spoke only of "literary activity." A minimalist review, so to speak. Not much different from most ordinary reviews, at least from the laconic reports on recent publications that appear in the daily papers. I stopped carrying my books to the rue Saint-Dominique long ago, but I'm seized each autumn by a certain anxiety—am I still a writer? Who will provide confirmation? . . .

•

A year ago, as I was working on an essay about Rilke, I cut a short passage in which I'd juxtaposed the famous, powerful opening of the *Duino*'s "First Elegy"—"Who, if I cried out, would hear me among the angel's / hierarchies? and even if one of them pressed me / suddenly against his heart: I would be consumed in that overwhelming existence. / For beauty is nothing but the beginning of terror, which we still are just able to endure,

/ and we are so awed because it serenely disdains to annihilate us," in Stephen Mitchell's translation—with the equally powerful and famous first bars of Johannes Brahms's Piano Concerto no. 1. The two works are difficult to compare: they arose over fifty years apart; they belong to different modes of art and were composed in two dissimilar languages; yet the force of their opening outbursts suggests a kind of kinship.

•

I visited my father a few days ago. Although *visit* isn't quite the right word, since he's not present mentally. Not only does he not recognize me; I always come away with the impression that his gaze no longer retains concrete images, it doesn't focus on any single object. My father lies in bed and sleeps for days on end. He's still in his apartment, in his room, he's well cared for. These visits are so sad. And once I fell into despair because he left without saying goodbye.

•

Cioran reports that Dylan Thomas was seized by convulsions and threw himself on the floor when someone once tried to interpret one of his poems in the poet's presence.

•

Papa Bruckner, a composer who heeded others' suggestions, altered his symphonies, agreed to cuts . . . Papa Bruckner, pious and humble: I read in a concert program that once, while lecturing on musical composition, he fell to his knees because he heard a church choir singing somewhere nearby. Biographers confirm that he was in fact too yielding; as a young man, for example, he accepted a position that made no allowances for his creative work; only at forty could he dedicate himself to composition. The scoring of his works was completed only many years after his death. One of his greatest compositions, the Ninth Sympony, was supposedly edited and cut so extensively that it shrank to the dimensions of a harmless serenade to be squeezed in between opera arias. Fortunately, the artist's original concept was later restored, and the Ninth is what it was once more, a monumental work, a bona fide rock-and-roll symphony.

Yesterday I was seated in the hall of the CSO, the Chicago Symphony Orchestra, in the section called the terrace. These are the seats behind the orchestra— behind and alongside it. You can see the conductor's face and the musicians' shoulders—you can't see the full wind and percussion sections—and also the sea of listeners in the enormous balcony and below, in the orchestra. The faces are a little blurred, you can't tell at this distance if they betray boredom or rapture. But you can follow the conductor's expressions perfectly. Yesterday Bernard Haitink conducted the entire great and splendid orchestra: to play Bruckner you need the full fleet, you must gather a vast number of husky trumpets and tragically deep trombones, you need oboes to smooth the transition from bows to brass, you require humble bassoons, plaintive clarinets, English horns (like hunting dogs), and you can't manage without the preoccupied, always melancholy cellos and mournful violins, and also the drums, on whom all subtleties are lost. Haitink is in his eighties; sparing in his movements, absorbed in the musical organism of the orchestra, he keeps no distance from the instrumentalists. His gestures are minimal, but each of them, as though by means of some unseen apparatus, releases vast energies within the orchestra's sprawling body. I remember that some British writer once remarked that the two things in the world he found most astonishing were parliamentary democracy and the symphony orchestra. It's true, no assemblage of people and objects is more extraordinary than a great orchestra: all these people, so different from one another, ordinary, some perhaps sleep deprived, others doubtless aggrieved (that they hadn't made greater careers, become famous soloists), and yet, in that single, unifying moment when they appear onstage, all dressed alike, the men in black tie, the women in black evening gowns, they forget about themselves and become the ideal parts of a greater whole, obedient to the conductor's motions. I won't speak of parliamentary democracy here; still, the image of general elections—when, on the contrary, no one worries about uniforms, each freely wears his own individuality—is also immensely moving.

It's hard to imagine Bruckner's Ninth—an unfinished symphony—in the shape of a brief serenade. Yesterday we heard the entire work, fortunately, though we were also fortunate to be spared the less than successful fourth movement, apparently reconstructed from Bruckner's posthumous papers. I was happy, the second movement with its marvelous rhythm, its spectacular gallop (which goes unnamed, we're not forced, luckily, to imagine stout Walkyries) moved me to my core, gave me an instant of true joy. A couple sat beside me, on my left: he was tall, well dressed, obviously from the world of business or banking, handsome, around fifty, and she, a blonde, young, but not too young, her features already slackening, although she was still dressed like a girl in a short pink (I think) dress. Or maybe yellow. This was apparently her first time at the symphony, but he seemed to be a music lover, he told her in whispers about Bruckner's Ninth Symphony, how he loved the final, slow third movement, he explained, briefly, hurriedly, between the movements, who Bruckner was. She received the information with a slight smile, passively, a bit dismissively, as if to say, "But my world deserves attention, too." When the music sounded, though, and they couldn't speak, he once or twice put his hand on her knee, her bare (beneath its stocking) knee.

•

And one day, in my car, driving back from Jerzy and Grazyna's summerhouse, I was listening to the radio, the classical station. It was Sunday evening, the show featuring contemporary music.

The star was the Argentine composer Osvaldo Golijov (pronounced Golikhof, accent on the second syllable).

•

In some houses in Pompeii you can still trace faded election slogans. Such as "Vote for aedile Gaius Julius Polybius. He provides good bread" (Panem bonum fert).

•

Reading Cioran: Cioran thought that true happiness would be a completely unhistorical life. If this were so, the peoples who found themselves beneath the Turkish yoke, under the Ottoman domination that divided them from a Western Europe convulsed by one feverish enthusiasm after another, with all the crises attending an energetic, expansive history, should have been extremely happy. But there's not one shred of evidence to suggest this. Not a single thing.

•

If you're going to make friends with anyone, it should be with painters. Why? Of all artists, painters strike me as the friendliest. Poets—of course I have poet friends, close friends, I've also had to tolerate myself for many years—are as a rule absorbed in a boundless introversion, bordering at times on autism. I remember that back in the early seventies I got to know the painters of the Straight Ahead group, Zbylut Grzywacz, Leszek Sobocki, and Jacek Waltos (since Maciej Bieniasz, the fourth member, rarely left Katowice); they made a tremendous impression. The lives of these young artists seemed immeasurably more interesting than the monotonous existence of poets—almost regal. The young poets had thousands of books at their disposal, they were free to seek the fire of ancient and recent poetry and philosophy in them, but these books didn't hold a clue about how to get along with others in the visible, practical world, how to maneuver among persons and objects. Young poets began rather modestly, familiarizing themselves with a few streets, taking a break to chat with peers, then scurrying back to their solitary reading and reflection. They usually holed up in sublet rooms, in attics, in basements; they held long discussions during spring nights, they met occasionally in cafés, sometimes at the hall of the Writers' Union on Krupnicza Street, after which they would disappear for days on end. (*Signum temporis*: the same hall that once eavesdropped on dramatic debates involving Czeslaw Milosz, Kazimierz Wyka, Stefan Kisielewski, or Andrzej Kijowski, now houses a calm vegetarian café!)

Young poets, it seemed, did not know how to live. As if poetry, whether dealing with a genuine poetic calling or the painstaking labors of some future hack journalist, placed the same excruciating task before all its acolytes, saying brusquely, Maybe someday, after years, after decades, I'll tell you how to live, but meanwhile you'll stumble blindly between joy and despair, profound doubt and ecstasy, blissful, festive, but never convinced of its right to exist, its lasting place in the economy of human affairs. I give you only strict but vague directives. I promise nothing.

While beside us strode the painters, fortune's true favorites (so I thought), smiling and free, painters, who knew how to make friends, who managed to criticize each other without giving offense, who treated each other to bona fide Renaissance feasts— these were in fact modest meals modeled on Italian cuisine, but back then, when restaurants and cafeterias specialized in tough, tasteless steaks and prefabricated cod fillets, they seemed truly extraordinary . . . Painters traveled, painters had access to models, painters knew how to dress, their clothes revealed that you were dealing with a genuine artist, but without fin de siècle affectation; capes were no longer in fashion. Painters kept their eyes open, they existed in the external world. Painters, even young ones, knew perfectly well who they were, they knew their rights, they knew that for the time being they might be absorbed in practice, solving technical problems, but they realized that humanity needed them, that thousands of walls in thousands of apartments awaited their works, that in the end, when their talent stabilized, when they were recognized, no one would question their activity. Young poets were another matter—compared to their artist contemporaries, they were mere shadows. Their realm was language, and language then was like air, like water, it belonged to everyone and no one, party lecturers rinsed their lips with it, television announcers exploited it, as did priests, awkwardly gesturing through their humdrum Sunday sermons. Young artists seemed to be striving toward the light, no, they were already awash in light, while poets crept from the world's dark corners, from provinces, pale courtyards where a single rickety poplar rose. One of these young artists was Zbylut Grzywacz, who later became my friend.

•

Suppose that one day an invitation to a conference comes from the University of Padua, and its subject will be the Veneto, a region of Italy. Your knowledge of the Veneto is slight: you'd have to study a map, some books, give it some thought . . . An inner voice tells you to refuse, you're not qualified, you'll make a fool of yourself. But you love southern Europe, and your personal principle says otherwise: invitations to Italy, Spain, or Greece must not be rejected.

•

So here is the text I prepared for the conference in Padua:
Before me lies a map of the Veneto: the region extends from Verona through Cortina d'Ampezzo, from Vicenza to Venice. Among the tourists headed to Italy by car, train, yacht, and jet, doubtless only a few know the names of Italy's regions. For the average contemporary European, Italy is a handful of great cities with legendary names—Rome, Florence, Genoa, Naples,

Bologna, Milan, and of course Venice. And also smaller cities whose names are no less picturesque: Siena, Mantua, Ferrara, Ravenna, Lucca, Parma, Arezzo, Orvieto, Pavia, and also Padua. This is the same Padua where so many Polish writers studied in the past—in the sixteenth century, for example, there was Jan Kochanowski; at this very university he met, among others, the humanist Francesco Robortello (called *Canis grammaticus,* "a dog for grammar," thank heavens he wasn't my professor). His colleagues here were Lukasz Gornicki, Andrzej Trzecieski, and Andrzej Patrycy Nidecki.

On my map of the Veneto I spy not only Verona, Bassano, Treviso, Vittorio Veneto, but also the city, or rather town, of Rovigo. Some fifteen years ago I had no idea where it was, or that such a place even existed. Even the famous green Michelin guidebook we use while traveling doesn't offer much: in the alphabetical list, between La Rotonda and Ruvo di Puglia, there's no trace of Rovigo. But in 1992 a book of poetry came out bearing that very name: *Rovigo.* The author was Zbigniew Herbert, a great poet and seasoned traveler, a connoisseur of Italian cities and towns who described Siena and other Tuscan marvels in his book *Barbarian in the Garden.* But why Rovigo? Let's listen to the title poem:

Rovigo

Rovigo station. Vague associations. A Goethe play
or something from Byron. I passed through Rovigo
so many times and just now for the umpteenth time
I understood in my inner geography it is a singular
place though it is certainly no match for Florence.
I never put a living foot down there. Rovigo was
always coming closer or receding into the distance.

I lived then in the throes of a passion for Altichiero
of the San Giorgio Oratorium in Padua and also

for Ferrara which I loved because it reminded me
of the plundered city of my fathers. I lived torn
between the past and the present moment
crucified many times by time and by place

But nonetheless happy with a powerful faith
that the sacrifice would not be made in vain

Rovigo was not marked by anything in particular
it was a masterpiece of averageness straight roads
ugly houses but—depending on the train's direction
just before or just after the city a mountain suddenly
rose up from a plain cut across by a red stone quarry
like a holiday cut of meat draped in sprigs of parsley
apart from that nothing to please hurt catch the eye

But it was after all a city of blood and stone like others
a city where a man died yesterday someone went mad
someone coughed hopelessly all night

AMID WHAT BELLS DO YOU APPEAR ROVIGO

Reduced to its station to a comma a crossed-out letter
nothing just the station—*arrivi*—*partenze*

and that is why I think of you Rovigo Rovigo

(translated by Alissa Valles)

I've read and admired Herbert's poetry for many years; still,
I didn't pay much attention to this poem at first, it even seemed
weaker than the rest. Its hidden sense came to me only gradually, and though it still doesn't rank among my favorite ten or
twenty Herbert poems, its purpose grew clearer to me, took on
greater weight.

It's one of Herbert's late poems. It comes from the penultimate volume in his bibliography; only *Epilogue to a Storm* will follow.

So why Rovigo? The poem explains everything. Rovigo is a place that the poet has seen from a train (Herbert never learned to drive; he almost always traveled by train, especially in Italy). And every time he traveled south, he passed a railroad station called Rovigo. Likewise every time he went north, to Venice, or homeward, heading toward Vienna or Warsaw.

The poem opens with a joke. "A Goethe play"—Herbert was surely thinking of the play *Clavigo*, which is linked to Rovigo only by a similar-sounding name. *Clavigo*, an early Goethe play, involves an episode in the life of Pierre Beaumarchais— Mr. Clavigo, a man of letters, has jilted his fiancée, the sister of the famous playwright, who goes to Spain in hopes of avenging his sister's honor. Why Byron? I don't know. I read it as an internal debate. After all, we don't go to Italy to look at ugly houses, to think about a man who "died yesterday" or "coughed hopelessly all night"—we're only interested in those who died five hundred years ago. We don't come here to be reminded about life's trivial side, we don't want to think about Berlusconi, the endless troubles of the Italian government, or the reform of national health care; we've got the same problems back home. We come to Italy for beauty alone. For its heroes, who continue to amaze educated travelers centuries later.

And here in the poem "Rovigo," Herbert—the aesthete, the same Herbert who "lived then in the throes of a passion for Altichiero" and for Ferrara, which he loved because it reminded him of "the plundered city of my fathers" (that is, he saw a resemblance between Ferrara and his native Lvov), so someone who would ordinarily never notice drab Rovigo, that "masterpiece of averageness"—suddenly undergoes a transformation. In the poem's second part, this unprepossessing spot suddenly changes its color. Literally: the poem turns red. The red mountain seen from the train, sliced like an Easter ham, reveals something far removed from the typical aesthetic pleasures of the traditional grand tour. An apocalyptic note appears in the poem. The mountain's red is the red of the Apocalypse. The mountain is sliced open to reveal a gaping wound in its side—a quarry (like a butcher's marble counter). But since Herbert is a discreet poet, an elliptical poet, he doesn't alter his artistic language (his register), he doesn't blow apocalyptic trumpets. He drops hints only at the poem's close, in Italian: *arrivi—partenze*. And one line is printed in *upper case*: a rarity in Herbert's poetry. The bells are in *capitals*.

Rovigo, a station not worth leaving the train for, hints at the end of the human journey. Rovigo, a place no one wants to visit, a city not worth even a few hours of our precious time, an ugly spot (most likely, since I've never been there either), a spot "not meriting a side trip," to use the language of our green Michelin, is the apogee of dullness, and as such is the opposite of beauty, the opposite of *bellezza italiana*; but its triviality unexpectedly assumes metaphysical dimensions for the poet. Still, this city becomes an existential sign for him only through its proximity to Venice, a universally acknowledged apogee of beauty. Since it's difficult to imagine Herbert writing a poem in praise of, say, Bytom (perhaps the ugliest spot in the industrial region of Upper Silesia), the area's other cities can't serve as an adequate counterweight. Even Gliwice, celebrated in Silesia for its medieval city center, couldn't play this role.

So what finally happens in this poem? We witness an aesthete's defeat. The author of "Rovigo" starts thinking about the ending of all those cries of rapture and enthusiasm inspired by various churches and museums. He sees not just the end of the aesthete's stance but the end of everything else as well. "Rovigo" is a poem about death.

Is this the Veneto's true message? A warning, as part of the region's ambiguous charm? Let's recall Thomas Mann's *Death in Venice*, Joseph Brodsky's *Watermark* (a variation on the theme of death in Venice, in this case, though, the forces of destruction are countered by the poet's insight, an unequal duel). Let's call to mind the countless other novels and poems that feature Venice in a leading role. Rovigo grows even poorer in this company. Very poor. As poor as disappointment. Wretched as an hourglass. Here "a man died yesterday someone went mad / someone coughed hopelessly all night."

And here, on a very personal note, memories return of Joseph Brodsky's funeral on the island of San Michele. It was his second funeral; his body was transferred to Venice from New York a year and five months after the poet's death.

The day after the funeral we (my wife and I) went to Vicenza, where we spent the night in a little hotel in the city's center. We got up early and went into town, struck by the moment's loveliness. The day—the morning—was otherworldly. An early hour in late June; a cloudless sky, deep azure, as in a utopian novel. Swallows sliced the air on every side, emitting the shrill whistles that I love. Maybe you know, or perhaps you've only guessed, that swallows traditionally symbolize the promise of eternal life: it was once believed that they spent their winters buried in the earth, from which they reemerged each spring, revivified, in their gleaming, elegant attire; swift, joyous, intelligent, splendid, dancing.

And suddenly the Veneto (more precisely, Vicenza) became a lens, but not a sad, sober lens transmitting apocalyptic hints—as in Herbert's "Rovigo"—no, just the opposite, this was the lens of ecstasy. Perhaps this happened because I'd come to Vicenza steeped in melancholy, in fresh mourning (thinking about Joseph Brodsky, his dazzling intellect and early death, but also about Krzysztof Kieslowski, who died, like Brodsky, in the winter of 1996), and that morning, which was like the first morning of creation, unexpectedly fused deep sorrow with unfettered joy. The Japanese wear white for mourning; the brilliant clarity of that June day brought me both despair and rapture. Grief was followed by a sense of happiness whose sources lay concealed (the azure sky and shrill swallows can only explain so much).

My first encounter with the Veneto came much earlier. In 1975 I received an émigré literary award for young writers, the so-called Koscielski Award (it's still being given today). Back then the unwritten tradition was that the recipients should use their award money for a trip to Italy—a rather extravagant gesture for a young *scrittore* from a Communist country, a country that possessed in principle no currency at all, just something along the lines of Monopoly money. The award money—please don't go imagining millions, the sum probably equaled the monthly income for a Swiss cabbie, and a novice cabbie at that—could have been spent more rationally in Poland, for example as a partial down payment on an apartment. But I frivolously opted for tradition and set off for Italy. Venice held first place on my list, and so I stopped there (following the lead of so many writers from the north).

It was late August; Venice was swarming with tourists— girls in miniskirts (this was the moment when girls' legs were displayed for appraisal like wares before an auction), young and not-so-young men in jeans—and the city teemed with the typical, chaotic crowds of tourists, people who'd fled their offices, their histories, their dignity, their cares—but not their sex. Venice was emblematic and enigmatic: the canals' cloudy waters reflected palaces, and they also seemed to reflect all the poems ever written about that city. Rilke and Aleksandr Blok drifted through the dark water. Chateaubriand passed nearby. Hofmannsthal observed churches, museums, human beings, with astonishment. Goethe wrote his letters to Mrs. Stein (but not to Gertrude). Baron Corvo was hungry and hunted for an Englishman whom he could drag to dinner. Henry James sat, artifically erect, upon a bench. I understood then (or maybe it only seems so now, many years later) that this was one of those mythic cities that defied familiarity, comprehension. One of those cities swathed in a haze of fame, one of those cities where symbols overlap reality, where the waters of memory carry greater weight than the droplet of the present, than today's teardrop. A city where current dramas count for nothing, hold no meaning, since the mighty burden of the past overshadows them, mocks them.

Unlike Rovigo, where "a man died yesterday somone went mad," here, in this sprawling, splendid city, this city of death, death loses its weight—at least momentarily.

I'm not saying I don't like Venice, it intrigues me, but I don't quite understand its hold on me. Beauty, of course: an extraordinary concentration of beauty, nothing but beauty, extravagant palaces, theatrical *piazze*, friendly cats. I liked Venice, but not entirely. The city's fever infected me; I grew impatient, I tried to penetrate its secrets. I'd been stricken with "Stendhal syndrome" (he fell victim to this illness in Florence, not in Venice). Our ancestors thought that the earth rested on a turtle's back; water carries Venice. Our ancestors thought the earth was flat; Venice is flat (though countless towers rise from it). The bricks of Venice have a warm, pleasant hue, though you can't exactly say that its inhabitants are pleasant; they're either invisible or they've been reduced to pragmatic functions in the tourist industry, exchanging smiles for tips. Venice (I started thinking about this much later) has no base, no foundation, it has no Greek *arché*; water isn't suited to this purpose. Water, capricious as a child; wind, its ubiquitous trainer and teacher, is helpless; it can neither rouse it to rebellion nor lull it to sleep. Even later I realized that if I had to choose my place, my home in Italy, it would be Rome (forgive me, Veneto), Rome, with the wealth of its past, but also with its solid base, its stable *arché*, its Aurelian Walls.

While admiring the famed Villa Rotonda near Vicenza, I understood that Veneto is a magnifying glass: it allows us to perceive the secret links between beauty and destruction. In Venice you see through one end of this peculiar telescope, in Rovigo through the other. Is this a ridiculous hypothesis?

We don't know the details of the clandestine economy governing our planet. We know of course why the Arctic climate is frigid while Africa's is hot, we've fathomed, more or less, how volcanoes operate. But do we know why in certain peaceful, prosperous nations the percentage of suicides is so high? Do we know why—at least in recent eras closer to our own times—the mild light of Paris proved so advantageous to painters? And why lemmings throw themselves into the sea?

Perhaps the world's inscrutable economy assigned the Veneto a special task: to serve as the glass that magnifies our lives. In Vicenza, speeding swallows disrupt Andrea Palladio's classic geometry. I'm certain that Rovigo possesses its own equally frenzied swallows. We head for Venice to meditate on the end of everything through the lens of beauty; we pass through Rovigo and what can we contemplate then? Another limit, but viewed this time through the prism of the quotidian—through an ordinary, trivial town, where people experience just as much as in a splendid metropolis, that is, they experience the two most important, perhaps the only, things: they arrive and depart. *Arrivi e partenze, partenze e arrivi.*

•

Anyone who writes is beset by all kinds of dangers. The list is extensive, it's not difficult to guess what traps it holds. The intellectual dangers are particularly unpleasant, though. Very briefly speaking, the writer cannot not think, he can't help but participate in the intellectual life of his age to some degree. He cannot, he must not, take refuge in absolute, childish innocence, since with time this becomes stupidity. But what's to be done, since an abundance of theories, beliefs, and even, in relatively recent times, ideologies proliferates on all fronts? Absolutely accepting any single theory means losing all freedom of thought. The greatest misfortune is—was—embracing some fashionable or dominant ideology. But we can't escape at least partial asphyxiation, the era poisons us all. Poisons and redeems, since we can't live out-side time.

•

A poetry festival in Krakow, some ten years ago, the final evening in the Old Theater. Perhaps six or seven poets on the stage. An enthusiastic public fills the hall. At the end all the poets rise and bow—not as gracefully as actors, they've had no practice, they don't know how. The audience likewise rises to its feet: a stand-ing ovation. The happy poets bow and bow again. The applause continues, it goes on endlessly . . . The poets are blissful, such happiness rarely befalls them, perhaps never. Later, I found out that the stage manager had complained about those inexperi-enced poets: they stood in the wrong spot, too far forward, where the curtain was supposed to drop, so the curtain had to stay up for the longest time . . .

•

Two, or maybe even three languages. We apparently speak and write not just in one language, there are more—and I'm not thinking of ethnic languages. There's one language that has its start in radiance, in great dreams. This language is rarely used today, but it's not extinct. Another language is rooted in despair. This is the language of direct statement, naturalism, pointed observations, astute critical remarks, a language that takes no prisoners, leaves no stone unturned in our world's composition, a language that annihilates illusions. This second language is fre-quently encountered. And finally there's a third dialect: the lan-guage of irony. This is the language employed by those writers and orators who can't decide between the first two, so for the time being they reach provisionally for irony. And sometimes stick with it to the end.

•

In Chicago. Yesterday I presided over an evening of film; I was asked to pick a film that I'd like to show the students and professors of the Committee on Social Thought at the University of Chicago. At first I wanted to refuse the invitation; I don't often go to the movies and I don't like theorizing after watching a good film (the principle here being that a discussion must follow the showing). But I remembered one especially beautiful film that I'd seen long ago in Paris with M.—on checking the production date, it turned out to have been twenty-five years ago. The film is called *Kaos* (yes, *Kaos*, not *Chaos*) and it was made in 1984 by the Taviani brothers, who based it on several Pirandello short stories. I wasn't sure if the film would still speak to me so many years later. But it exceeded my expectations. It's marvelous. In this Sicilian landscape serious matters play out against the backdrop of ancient walls and baroque churches. The protagonists of this film, which runs for two and a half hours, are villagers, poor Sicilian peasants, but its real hero is the delicately drawn battle between cruelty and kindness. The first scene, the prologue, shows a group of peasants catching a crow, which they release after tying a little bell to its neck, and then the crow rises over Sicily, over hills, the ruins of an Ionian temple, the seashore, and we hear the voice of the little bell; and precisely this bizarre juxtaposition, the black bird and the bell's delicate music, holds the key to one of the film's chief meanings. There's also an epilogue, totally different in tone. Here not the villagers but Pirandello himself is the protagonist; no longer young, worn by life and work, the writer returns to the region of his childhood (Pirandello was born in Agrigento, Sicily) in search of renewal. As if he wished to fathom the mysterious place that shaped his life. The film concludes with a remarkably beautiful scene; in this retrospective fragment a cluster of children, including the young Pirandello, descend to the azure sea from a sandy cliff, and for an instant, sliding over the bright sand, they seem freed from the force of gravity, dropping to the sea in the gleam of a sunlit day like birds.

•

We live in times of great indifference; only terrorists seem to take ideas seriously.

•

Back in Krakow. I read—for the first time—D. H. Lawrence's letters; they enthrall me. From what I recall of his novels, it's clear that he had his "ideology." But the letters are different: he's clearly an extraordinary individual who radiates some charismatic power (nearly everyone he met commented on this). The letters confirm this while revealing the great difficulties he encountered in formulating his credo. The correspondence projects the image of a man at once both weak and forceful, exceptionally sensitive, absolutely, at times brutally, forthright, consumed by a passion for travel; he couldn't stay in the same place, the same country, for more than six months, he grew restless, even in southern Italy, in Taormina, which he loved so much, after a while he couldn't bear it, he had to leave. He takes off for Ceylon, and after a couple of weeks—and his first raptures—he can't stand Ceylon. So he travels on—always with Frieda, the famous Frieda, at his side—to Australia. He really likes it, but has to leave almost immediately. He finally makes it to the United States, to San Francisco, and then on to New Mexico, to a place he made famous, Taos. Raptures once more, but then he *can't take it anymore* and moves on to Mexico, Old Mexico, as he says. The impatience of the traveler—and settler, since Lawrence travels and settles everywhere, samples settled, permanent existence, if only temporarily, since the last thing on earth he wants to be is a tourist—is also a sign, a splendid metaphor for something far deeper, something that intrigued me. So, the impatience of the traveler/settler mirrors the thinker's anxiety: Lawrence knows that he's fundamentally different, he suspects that he lives more intensely than others, that he'll never simply be a man of letters, a writer like other writers, content with their daily grind, the fixed hours spent behind a massive oak desk, carefully tracking the fluctuations of an invisible literary stock exchange, discussing reviews and prizes with unconcealed envy, celebrating their triumphs, major and minor. It's true, he must live by his writing, he has to consider money, which holds a regular place in his correspondence, but still he's different. Lawrence comes from a race of prophets, witnesses and agents of spiritual regeneration—or at least the dreamers who seek such renewal. Lawrence can't simply blacken pages—although blackened pages are unavoidable—he dispatches his apostles across the globe, that is to say, his writings, his poetry, his novels, his traveler's notes, his essays. I'm not a expert (I've read too little of his work), but I think the letters best reveal his doubts, he doesn't know, he'll never know, exactly what shape his prophetic mission should take. He doesn't know what to call his calling. He's a prophet who always hesitates. Advice to friends proliferates in some letters, but it can't be assembled into a clear message, a coherent whole. Lawrence knows only that he can't live like his contemporaries, locked in the cramped cage of their success (or failure), harnessed to the treadmill in the West's great cities, or in Mexican villages, doomed to the hypocrisies of social rituals. He often stresses the significance of eroticism, sex, but elsewhere he objects violently, this wasn't meant to be taken seriously. Everyone irritates him, acquaintances publishing literary journals, friends from school, past loves, other writers, artists, but also ordinary bourgeois, politicians amuse him, he hates the military (the First World War was his most trying period, not least because he couldn't travel for several years, he was confined to his loved and hated England). He seems to have been bothered by anything finished, defined, small, self-interested, practical, good-natured. He seeks munificence, magnanimity. He has, or wants to have, the limitless, the infinite—but not in a religious sense—in his camp. Rejecting the life he knows comes easily to him. Nothing could be simpler. One gesture is enough to erase what is, what manages to exist only with such difficulty. But what should he call the force that appears to him in moments of illumination, how does he define the better life that speaks to him during his solitary walks, that he cautiously transfers later to his poems, what should he call that other tone in his experiences, in his dreams, in those brief moments of ecstasy, what's the name for the light that must have shone in his eyes, the light that drew friends, men, women, to him? He himself doesn't know. We don't either. But while reading Lawrence's letters, gentle and violent by turns, we understand his yearning for another life, for a pure, intense existence, although we're more cautious than he, since we've now seen—even experienced—so many false faiths and prophecies. We tell ourselves, no one can deceive us now. But the yearning for something better endures in us, it's survived all disappointments and defeats. If we could only find a name for that yearning . . . Let's give it one more try.

•

The paradox of surrealism: In a fascinating volume of conversations with Jerzy Nowosielski, the painter and sage, we find the artist's confession—he owes so much to surrealism, and not he alone, but the entire twentieth century (Zbigniew Podgorzec, a specialist in Russian culture, conducted these conversations in the 1980s). Nowosielski sees surrealism as a great religious movement that radically renewed our sensitivities, opened our eyes, taught us to comprehend the *sacrum* of other faiths, allowed us to understand Orthodox icons and appreciate African fetishes, to comprehend the gods of completely different civilizations. But if this is so, then why are the standard products of surrealism, in poetry and perhaps especially in painting, so pedestrian, even pedantic—always the same neckties, apples, irons, trains exiting from the wall above the fireplace, umbrellas . . . A notary's after-dinner dreaming.

•

We gladly speak of the "past century" today, although only a few
years have passed since the last century ended and a new one
began. But it's not a bad trick—the monstrous twentieth century,
one of the worst in the entire history of our solar system, floats
away from us like a floe drifting along a river, it turns into history, into books and movies. While we stand safely upon a new
scrap of time.

•

But maybe D. H. Lawrence opened us to something new, something we hadn't known before, or perhaps knew but couldn't
fully express—I'm still thinking more of the poems and letters
than the programmatic fiction. This prophet, who didn't know
what his prophecies should hold, who spent his whole life ardently seeking for their content, seeking and discarding, may
have something profoundly important to tell all of us who have
rejected ideology, who repudiate any utopia, any binding social
belief—but who also refuse nihilism, fear, nullity, reject, so it
seems, the purely skeptical, pragmatic stance that leads us to
plan only a week in advance, since even imagining what coming
months might bring is taken for bombast these days . . . At least
in his letters (which are a key part of his work), Lawrence never
found a name for his faith, never simply pasted labels on his
longings, he demonstrates perhaps an alternative to a seemingly
hopeless dilemma, the choice between ideological fervor and the
bleak silence of resignation. Resignation, which might also be
called despair, even when it is a still, calm, even idyllic despair, like
a carefully tended garden seen at sunset. Lawrence never lost his
ardor, never allowed his passionate quest to cool down, but he
likewise never accepted a single, concrete "belief" or "idea."
    I'm not proposing that we could or should imitate this writer's
life, far from it; it would be foolish, even ridiculous, to throw

ourselves into a torrent of travel, to set out restlessly, as he did, in hopes of spanning the globe. That's not the point. We do have something to learn from him, though. Discarding ideologies, refusing utopias, casting commonly held expectations into doubt, doesn't necessarily lead to apathy, to the glum worldview of the technicians who build bridges and houses without knowing what they're doing. We can learn through D. H. Lawrence to tolerate a constant, permanent willingness or readiness to affirm strong beliefs—I'm not thinking here of religion, which grows ever more personal, more private, I'm more concerned with what links individuals of varying temperaments, the power that can make a crowd a crowd, endowing it with the kind of cohesion we see in an athlete's muscles. We can learn endurance from him, the great persistance required to remain ready at all times for enthusiasm, passion. And we can also learn to discard the routine, the trivial, the mundane, the pragmatic, the dreariness of a merely correct existence.

We know, after all, the examples of those thinkers who burned early on with great political passions, but when the scales fell from their eyes, they turned into hardened skeptics, scoffers.

In his correspondence—sometimes it deals only with money, with complex but ultimately trivial matters of publishing, but there are also letters of extraordinary beauty, genuine poetic masterworks—D. H. Lawrence reveals an alternative, we don't need to give up utopias entirely, as long as we maintain a corresponding restraint and don't burn with the desire to name them . . .

•

In one letter, D. H. Lawrence disparages Proust's great novel, back in the twenties when it was conquering readers across Europe and the world (it captivated Rilke, for example): "water-jelly," Lawrence calls it. I just returned to its final volume, *Time Regained*, to that remarkable scene in the library of the

Guermantes mansion, where the narrator reckons his spiritual accounts while waiting for a concert to resume. This comes after a series of small but marvelous discoveries, beginning with the famous "uneven paving stones" in the courtyard, which unexpectedly release great imaginative energies in Marcel. Unfortunately, the discoveries of Proust's narrator have already entered literary textbooks and encyclopedias—the mechanism of association always takes pride of place—in the shape of the famous madeleine. These marvels are reduced to a rather uninteresting psychological phenomenon: stimulus and reaction, as in the dreariest associative psychology of Wilhelm Wundt or some other forgotten, bewhiskered professor. But in Proust there's so much more. Above all there's the joy of brushing up against the magical, the miraculous, the joy that reveals so much more than all the labors of associative psychology . . .

•

And once we were taking the night train back from Florence after a full week of industrious exploration, examination, epiphanies, and moments of exhaustion. We had berths in the sleeping car, and in the morning, when the sky was already light, still far from Paris—the flat green fields of the French provinces flashed by the window—we struck up a conversation with our fellow travelers, who were surfacing, like ourselves, from the imperfect sleep of railroads. These were two friends, Frenchmen; both were singers, countertenors. This wasn't some great revelation; still it doesn't happen every day that two countertenors turn up in your sleeping compartment. I don't remember the details of our talk, but we were both curious about their young world, the world of countertenors, who had recently come back into fashion after many years of neglect—suddenly there was public demand, multitudes of young singers were finding their calling once more. So we didn't learn anything earth-shattering, we just discovered a new field, or rather patch, of human ambition. These young men told us a little about the competitions and concerts awaiting them. They talked as though this were common knowledge, not just some narrow sliver of reality. I know that we even planned to go to one of the concerts they'd mentioned, enthused by the sudden spark of a new friendship, which, as always, faded after a few days. We never went to the concert and we lost all contact with the two singers. I only remember that morning in the speeding train, when countless images of Florence, paintings we'd seen in museums (sculptures, especially in the Bargello, Donatello's *David*), and also just fragments of streets, bridges, and restaurants, still engulfed us. And also the two nice countertenors, discussing their problems, other countertenors, some they liked, they *hated* others.

•

January 27. Very cold, snow. Winter now reveals all its vulgar, predictable tricks; the city's life grows slower, pedestrians flounder in superfluous snowdrifts. Intellectual life also decelerates. Winter is a provincial prestidigitator who's only really mastered one trick: transforming water into ice and snow, and then turning it back into dirty water again. For some time now—ever since I recognized the potent symbols the date contains—this day has fascinated me, combining as it does two dimensions of our historical moment. January 27 marks the anniversary of what is called the "liberation" of Auschwitz, and thus it is Holocaust Remembrance Day. It's also Mozart's birthday. There's no mistake here. And no coincidence. Wolfgang Amadeus Mozart was born on January 27, 1756, in Salzburg, and the Russians entered Auschwitz on January 27, 1945. The soldiers of the Sixtieth Army of the First Ukrainian Front, as the press release wrote, "opened the gates of KL Auschwitz," where only seven thousand prisoners remained. I prefer the phrase "opened the gates": *liberation* suggests energy, the meeting of two forces, but there, within the barbed wire, only sick, utterly depleted, dying inmates could be found. As we know, the SS forces had driven more than fifteen thousand prisoners out of the camp, condemning most of them to death from exhaustion. Which is why it's called the death march. Among the prisoners who trudged across Silesia's snow-covered roads (it's difficult to speak of a march, it was a death crawl), one was missing: a timid Italian chemist, Primo Levi, who fell ill and stayed behind in the camp infirmary. This miraculously saved his life; as we know, he survived and later wrote his superb books. It's hard to imagine a day more deeply divided, more complex, more ambivalent, a day that reveals the nature of our reality more completely.

Every year on January 27, a gathering converges on the grounds of the former camp: warmly dressed politicians, news crews wrapped in thick sheepskin coats, and an ever-dwindling number of old people who survived the Holocaust. When the anniversary falls in a new decade, the cameras and political leaders of various nations proliferate. In more modest years, the list of renowned political leaders contracts, journalists find other stories, famous newscasters head elsewhere. The same holds true, conversely, of Mozart. In the years when the anniversary isn't round, the number of articles on the great composer drops sharply, while television forgets him completely or gives him only a quick mention. When a more noteworthy anniversary approaches, is upon us, Mozart once again becomes the genius we adore. But I shouldn't joke, January 27 is exceptionally serious, it poses a crucial question every year. How is it possible to remember Auschwitz's horror each year, not just to remember it, but to integrate it into our worldview, our perception of reality, so deeply that—as the philosophers and theologians say—we're prepared to admit that human history falls into two periods, before and after Auschwitz, and still, on that same day, find the time and peace of mind to celebrate Mozart's splendid music?

This music combines rococo elements, sometimes almost frivolous, comic, cheerful, full of fireworks and fantasy, with deeply tragic moments, as in, to give just a couple of examples, the somber, tragic finale of *Don Giovanni* or the uncannily beautiful *Requiem*. I can't compile a list—even a purely subjective one—of Mozart's works, this isn't the place for it, I don't have room, and that's not the point in any case. I only recently discovered the "Andantino" from the relatively early Piano Concerto no. 10, K. 271, with Murray Perahia. I've long loved the Eighth Piano Sonata, K. 310, written in Paris in the spring of 1778, while his mother lay sick and dying, melancholy in the "Andante cantabile con espressione," but opening with such swagger and glee that it might be some March of the Visionaries (if we could imagine such a thing; in fact, it's a psychological impossibility, since visionaries don't march, they most likely run, in any case they don't march in military formation, but if we were to imagine it, it would be the "Allegro maestoso" from the Eighth Sonata). I listen to Dinu Lipatti's rendition, to the famous recording from the Romanian pianist's last concert—he was already ill, near death—in Besançon. Whereas in the *Requiem*, especially in the movement called "Lacrimosa," the music's beauty and sorrow are almost beyond bearing. The whole world seems to weep in the "Lacrimosa" (in our more sentimental moments, we think it weeps for us, but we are of course grossly mistaken). The whole world sobs in the "Lacrimosa," and its grief isn't maudlin. Mozart is a tragic composer, great, one of the few artists about whom we don't fear to use the now spurned word *beauty*.

Whereas when we speak, or even think, of Auschwitz, we forget music completely, we suddenly find ourselves in a different register, in a black-and-white film. Numerous specialists on the Holocaust are among us, historians, writers, survivors, nonsurvivors, filmmakers, journalists, activists, and archivists. I may be mistaken, but I suspect that *Mozart* is an empty word for them, just like the word *beauty*. I may be wrong. But in principle this should be true: *Auschwitz* and *beauty* are terms that shouldn't turn up in the same company. We also have scholars among us

who specialize in Mozart, professors who know all there is to
know about eighteenth-century music, who understand the language of forms created in eighteenth-century art. And some
of them certainly don't want to think about Auschwitz; their
subject—as they would no doubt say—is far more interesting.
They resurrect people in powdered wigs, courtiers in splendidly
embroidered silk attire, and they resurrect Mozart's extraordinary story, his final years, for example, when his music fell from
favor with the Viennese public, while he grew ill and composed the *Requiem*, which, as we know, he never finished (you
can't complete your own *Requiem*, after all). So how can this
be—since Auschwitz closed something in human history, shut a
certain chapter, cut us off from certain levels of sensitivity, we
shouldn't be celebrating the birth of any composer on that day.
Especially Mozart's birthday, with his rococo, his indescribable
grace. But these elements, these layers, refuse to admit defeat,
they have no intention of vanishing, they have no desire to curl
up like a piece of paper tossed into the fire. Mozart was born
on January 27. On January 27, Russian soldiers entered KL
Auschwitz. And we're living now, in January, but also in May
and June, in September and November; we're living, endowed
with memory, we remember both Mozart and Auschwitz.

We're alive, we listen to music, and sometimes, not always,
we're able to concentrate, to open ourselves, we experience it
deeply and painfully, we feel its beauty, which links despair and
joy, and this presentiment, so rare, and yet so real, this presentiment of something that far exceeds us, belongs to a higher order
that we might call *divine*, if such words didn't embarrass us. And
we don't forget about Auschwitz, this experience doesn't distance
us from this horror, sometimes we even manage to experience
rapture and recollect horror simultaneously, but afterward, when
we've come down to earth, we try to incorporate this experience
into the entirety of our worldview, and we conclude that those
who insist that Auschwitz has ended something forever, has shut

the gates to certain regions, are mistaken, they don't know what they're talking about, or perhaps they've fallen into rhetorical exaggeration, guided by noble impulses, wishing, quite rightly, to underscore the enormity of this crime, its incomprehensible extremity. The world after Auschwitz will always be different, after Auschwitz and all the crimes that accompanied it. The world has been shattered and mended like a Chinese porcelain vase. But Mozart was born in Salzburg on January 27 just the same, and his music lives, sings in the great pianists, conductors, cellists, and violinists, who enter it as one enters a river in July or August, who submerge themselves completely, up to the neck. It also lives in us, the dilettantes, who can't produce a single note, but also—now and then—we permit it to dwell in us, we offer it shelter, we sustain it for a bit, we take it in—after which we quickly discover that it has in fact received us instead, the situation's suddenly reversed, music is our host and we are its guests. To cut off these levels of being, these branches, these regions, to decree that they've ceased to exist, that there can be no *beauty*— this means declaring, not directly, but by way of an almost Aristotelian syllogism, that they carried the day, those relentless organizers of the death camps, the KL, Hitler, and the Nazis were victorious, they succeeded in reducing our humanity, in making us consider only them, we've exaggerated the obligations of memory. This is why January 27, a day containing two dates, demands so much thought, it holds the elements of which we're made, both the lowest and the highest, and hence our winter calendar is not nearly so accidental, so aleatory as it might appear to visitors from another planet—or another continent. The winter calendar is severe, demanding, but it knows what it's about, it orders us to consider what we are and why we must live in doubleness, in difficult, impossible doubleness.

.

Since everything is divided into brief moments of certainty and the endless, systematic plateaus of persistence, into poems and prose, preludes and symphonies, laughter and tears, we've long searched for the theoretician who could, with an ideal prestidigitator's smile, tell us how to live between these two forces, how and where to hide—or just the opposite, where and how to break ranks and boldly raise our voices.

The instant, brimming with happiness, the instant of the great promise, the moment of illumination, of poetry, of faith, and the slow river of narration that winds between them, the sequence of days and nights, days, industrious or lazy, dark or radiant with expectation—when will the world pronounce its next word?—and nights, when strange, impassioned dreams blossom, dreams that we can't understand. And so we live, torn between brief explosions of meaning and patient wandering through the plains of ordinary days. Will these two parts of life ever fuse? I liked thinking about this. I liked thinking about people reading books in the Paris metro, since they are underground, in the earth's dark shadow, in the artificial light of electric bulbs, with the mute, graffiti-covered walls of corridors and tunnels rushing by their windows. I also liked traveling on the Paris metro during the hours when the intense rush of morning crowds had subsided and the equally intense thrust homeward had not yet begun, the ebb and flow of this statistical ocean, whose times and dimensions could be predicted as precisely as the sea's motions.

Above us, in the airplanes, someone is also reading a book—most often one with shiny covers, devoid of mystery, constructed on simple premises and the sincere desire for abundant royalties, but it may also be that someone up in those expanses is studying a Sufi epic or Dante and will experience illumination. And if this reader looks out the little window, he or she will see not black walls, as in the metro's labyrinths, but the white gleam of clouds, a splendid, perpetually sunlit landscape, and below the threads of rivers quivering like children's thermometers, strips of highways streaked by cars like nervous insects, the yellow strips of sand along the sea, the dark smears of forests, sometimes snow-topped mountains, profoundly motionless, self-absorbed, autistic, and also cities chattering in different languages, resisting sleep, glowing even at midnight with feverish neon lights. Above the earth and below the earth, in metro cars and airplanes, someone is always reading books.

Conservatives have condemned our times, saying that they're soulless, dead, but they've forgotten the people reading Dante or Milosz in planes or the cars of the Paris metro. Conservatives have praised past centuries, venerating chivalrous Europe, Gothic cathedrals, and the long, quiet naves of Romanesque churches filled with the whispers of monks. The conservatives weren't wrong to love these old churches, but they were wrong to condemn our age; they didn't want to see that everything endures, base and splendid things alike, they live on. Their proportions and names may change, their shadows may grow and diminish, but they still exist, though they demand our unceasing vigilance; each generation must recognize them anew, divide them, endure them, and finally die from them, since they first waken us to life and then they kill us—for among them, among these things great and wonderful, grim and tawdry, we also find their inseparable companion, time. Time walks alongside them, just as back in the Communist days, every delegation of artists or scholars was assigned a silent attendant representing the regime, which was mentioned only in whispers. The point here isn't some theory, some professorial argument; this concerns our life's sources and its murderers. It's difficult to discuss, no one claims that these are simple perceptions, easy observations. Conservatives measure new times with a well-worn silver ruler. They pace the city with an elegant cane topped by a silver ball shaped like a dolphin's head. I understand them, since I have conservative days and weeks, it's hard to keep them at bay when faced by the constant, permanent, shameless incursions of time, which often behaves like Genghis Khan. But I usually wake from these conservative naps to watch the endless, exhilarating battle of base and splendid things, dreary and inspiring things. A battle in which I, too, took part, although I didn't know it. A patient battle, a war without cease-fires or truces.

In Berlin, where the subway bears the rather dark, Germanic name U-Bahn, akin to the word *U-boat*, and linked associatively with the little prefix *ur-*, that is, archaic, prehistoric, my attention was directed elsewhere. (I spent two years in Berlin and so could study the city's anthropology up to a point; up to a point just because you can't entirely trust an introvert when it comes to learning the terrain.) In Berlin, the loveliest moment was always that moment of absolute silence and deliberation when the stationmaster's voice issued from the speakers on the U-Bahn platform, saying, *"Zurückbleiben,"* that is, loosely translated (since a word pronounced underground is fundamentally untranslatable), "Move back" or "Remain on the platform"—without the mitigating word *bitte*, "please," no, it was almost a military command. *"Zurückbleiben!"* This moment always filled me with delight: a silence would fall (Berliners are well disciplined and don't try to storm the train doors as Parisians do), and only two or three seconds later would the doors slam shut and the train begin to move. It set off, and life returned to normal, the passengers took their seats, reached for a newspaper or book, the wheels struck their regular beat, the lights set at equal distances in the tunnel flashed past, someone chatted on the phone, someone might cry a bit, a pair of lovers argued, a child shrieked, someone removed the cellophane from a thick tuna sandwich. But first those two or three seconds of silence! Two or three seconds when nothing happened, a moment of suspension. The beauty of that silence! That lull. That pause, when nothing happened. Absolutely nothing. *"Zurückbleiben,"* emanating from a different throat at every station, here a woman's, there a man's, with slight variations in stress, sometimes placed on *zurück*, sometimes on *bleiben*: the word was magical, narcotic. After *Zurückbleiben* everything came to a halt, stopped short, the history of the world paused momentarily.

We know that the Germans had splendid mystics long ago, in Rhineland, in Silesia—we also know that they don't have them now, but something must have lingered after them, it couldn't have vanished completely, it still persists in its lazy, peaceful, passive way deep below the earth's surface, in the corridors of the U-Bahn. Those two, or three, or even four seconds after *Zurückbleiben* were priceless, a momentary pause, *Gelassenheit*, inherited from Meister Eckhart and Jacob Boehme. A momentary void. A motionless moment. The world held still for a few seconds. This would be impossible in Paris, a city of the Enlightenment. Nothing like this ever happens, could happen, in Paris, in Paris you catch only a laconic, scientific signal, such as a short siren or whistle, the doors shut, and the blue-and-white train vanishes into the darkness—on some lines it seems to glide on the deluxe tires of prewar limousines, on others it rumbles like a mundane motorcycle. There was no *Zurückbleiben* in Paris. *Zurückbleiben* means literally "Please don't board," "Please move back," "Please stay put"—although without the *please*, as I've said—at least that's how it was intended, and no doubt the earnest employees of the Berlin U-Bahn, the conscientious, punctual subway workers, have never realized that they're taking part in a ritual that exceeds them, that their lips utter a magic formula with vast implications. Sometimes the word's utterance was entirely superfluous, it lost its pragmatic sense: late evenings or at night, when the platform was virtually empty, hence there was no one to urge away from the train doors, but the word was broadcast just the same. Even when the platform literally didn't hold a living soul. And so it is, so it will always remain. *Zurückbleiben* will always sound forth; even when there are no passengers, no driver, no stationmaster, that magic word will reverberate and silence will fall.

I also liked the smell of the Berlin metro, which remains unchanged to this very day; I got to know other subways later, in London, Barcelona, Rome, and other metropolises, but I've never encountered the precise, sober smell of the Berlin metro—like brown coal. There's something mineralogical in the smell of the Berlin metro, like the scent of Novalis's writings. The Parisian metro is no doubt more attractive, elegant, and only in a few stations—for example, Saint-Michel, far underground—do you catch a whiff of burnt paper, and it's precisely in Saint-Michel that rats with short, military fur turn up from time to time on the tracks, seeking easy loot, like Roman legionnaires. Only do the Berlin U-Bahn stations greet you with a raw aroma, as if Germanic geological strata had been unearthed when the metro was constructed. Few thought to delight in this subterranean world—for most people, after all, it was chiefly a key component in so-called urban transportation, not the site of enigmatic investigations; people fell to work, desperate to get the yellow trains up and running, they didn't notice their extraordinary location, a place demanding veneration, a moment of reflection, meditation.

•

In Berlin, the U-Bahn with its *Zurückbleiben* and its mineralogy delighted me, but I was also struck by the many canals crisscrossing the city. The city was festive in spring and summer; enormous trees basked in the velvety air, their leaves breathing serenely, and birds, hidden in their thick branches, conducted their leisurely family life in good bourgeois fashion. Berlin may be the blackbird capital of Europe, who knows? They also sing in other great cities, but their conditions are better in Berlin. Blackbirds are apolitical, but they took full advantage of the city's long-standing division, a division that produced many ownerless zones quickly overtaken by bushes, brush, and vines. Berlin's

canals are like its metro; the same story once more, not as elegant
as French canals, which, though constructed some two hundred
years ago, seemed instantly to have been created for the im-
pressionists, with their light, cheerful brushes, their variegated
imaginations. For example, the Canal Saint-Martin, in the
heart of Paris: lyrical, delicate, it might have grown from one of
Jacques Prévert's poems; green like a young chardonnay with a
rich but not excessively broad bouquet, with a raspberry palate
and a slightly tart fugue. Oh, no, Berlin canals were an entirely
different matter, Gothic, static, black. They even seemed a little
vexed, as if remembering something.

•

Zofia Nalkowska writes in *Medallions* that we're never given
reality in its entirety, it reaches us only in "fragments of events,"
and this alone permits us to bear periods of historical catastrophes. But isn't it just the opposite? We manage to survive great
misfortunes, times of terror, only because we receive an excess of
reality. Of course, tyrants waste no time, but a bird is still singing somewhere, a tram bell rings, rain begins falling, a neighbor
asks to borrow a pinch of sugar, I hear my heart beating, stars
burn at night as they always do. Someone plays cards in the suburbs, a bottle of rotgut stands in the grass, green tomatoes ripen
in the sun (the landscape of Milosz's wartime poems). The old masters knew this well (as did their gifted student W. H. Auden—in
his famous "Musée des Beaux Arts"): Icarus falls into the sea,
he'll vanish in the water any moment now, and all the while the
stalwart, neatly dressed plowman takes advantage of the lovely
weather to march ahead as his plow cuts exceptionally precise
geometric furrows in the black earth. The shepherd gazes upward, but in the opposite direction, not where poor Icarus has
fallen. Another of Brueghel's paintings (the artist, with his
philosophical turn of mind, evidently liked to consider how
terrifying events coincided with completely innocent, everyday

occurrences), *The Procession to Calvary*, is no less didactic, asking, Did anyone even notice Christ being hounded to his execution? A merry crowd is caught up in a thousand things: the
atmosphere is like that of a festive May picnic, who'd stop to
notice a bearded young Jew stooped beneath his heavy cross
who's clearly fallen out with the local police? Piero della Fran-
cesca's *Flagellation of Christ*, in a small museum in Urbino, likewise gives a splendid picture of the world's indifference. In the
background the torturers torment Christ, while in the fore-
ground three impeccably dressed philosophers (academicians,
no doubt, not like Kierkegaard or Shestov, these must be full
professors) conduct a theoretical discussion whose subject we
will never know. Paintings are mute, but if you were to attach a
sound recording, we'd hear, in Brueghel, the carefree clamor of
a great throng of people drowning out the victim's moans. Or, in
Piero, the theoretical discussions of three self-satisfied thinkers,
debates perhaps on the nature of suffering, like those being held
at scores of universities after a good lunch and before an even
better dinner. A little like the serene conferences at which scholars discuss the problems of the Holocaust. The same thing
happens whenever we attempt, incredulously, to peer into the
past, asking ourselves what it must have been like to live through
World War Two, the Holocaust, or during Stalin's purges, the
years of the greatest terror, and it seems impossible, inconceiv-
able, to survive even an hour in such a nightmare—but for those
who weren't *that day's* direct victims of persecution, there was
always more reality, always some kind of weather, they were
either hungry or well fed, a dog was barking somewhere, a plane
flew overhead, Mother was making pierogi in the kitchen, you
had to think about buying winter boots, making the soup . . .
They went for walks in the park, they *forgot* for a moment. They
were in love, happily or otherwise, they read *Madame Bovary* or
some other nineteenth-century novel, the radio played a Schubert
sonata. Anyone who spent his or her childhood in Stalin's Poland

will remember the scent of the first spring pussy willows and the stammering priest who taught catechism in a cramped parish hall smelling of floor polish better than the gigantic portraits of leaders floating awkwardly, flapping over the May Day Parade. Even the fear that paralyzed so many in its time evaporates as the years pass, becomes difficult to imagine. Especially fear, fear, which is like a migraine—it disappears and leaves no trace. Although it may leave scars upon the soul. And the fear wasn't ubiquitous even then; the boys playing soccer on school playgrounds had other problems. When I was ten, I spent a few days in a hospital in Zabrze; they took out my tonsils under anesthesia. I remember the moment when I lost consciousness to this day. I seemed to be strolling across an earthly globe the size of a tennis ball. But I also recall the conversations, as I was recovering, between much older political prisoners, probably former Home Army soldiers, recuperating in the same hospital. This was the beginning of the Thaw, they weren't monitored as closely as before. They must have been longing for conversation after years in prison, they liked impressing me—me, a ten-year-old boy, who still didn't know—with their stories about the Nazi occupation, their love affairs, their exploits, about unexpected visits to aristocratic manors, the young ladies, wrapped in shawls and blankets, who made them supper. It was spring, the smells and voices of reality wafted through the open window. As always, there was too much reality; there's more of it during a thaw than there is under winter's stern dominion. But we also know that during the French Revolution, large crowds would gather beneath the guillotine, seeking sensations, and within these crowds, the so-called *tricoteuses* stood out particularly, women who didn't want to waste time and knitted as they stood; every so often they must have looked down from the enthralling spectacle so as not to drop a stitch . . .

•

In the journal *Akzente* I found a series of notes written by an author I didn't know, Walter Kappacher, who lives in Salzburg. I instantly sensed a kindred spirit in him, someone I could really talk to. For example, when he says, "I would give all the rock concerts, race cars, soccer matches, and so on for the first blackbird's song of spring." I read those words at the end of February, just as a freezing spell gave way to a few warm, sunny days, and the blackbirds did in fact make themselves known for the first time that year.

•

Walter Kappacher quotes a witty remark from Ernst Jünger: "Why do so many people complain that they're not appreciated? It would be much worse, after all, if the situation were reversed."

•

He also quotes Javier Marías, who describes Joyce as follows: "In the company of others he was so quiet that many people avoided sitting by him, since they knew that he'd probably utter one word at most, 'yes' or 'no.'"

•

If we're still looking at the transition from novels to poetry, from long duration, painstaking continuity, to the sudden flash, the poem, then it seems—you can't be entirely sure in advance— that death, which we so fear, belongs to this second category, that it happens like a poem, not a novel. Whereas our fear takes place in duration, in "the novel."

•

Leo Tolstoy tells a story somewhere about a preacher who, when the congregation interrupted his sermon with applause, turned to them and said, Did I say something stupid?

•

Yet another moment of happiness (which occurred in an otherwise depressing, dreary month): I was returning from Athens to Krakow and changed planes in Vienna, I had three empty hours. I was sad, I had good reasons. I read, not for the first time, Nicola Chiaromonte's splendid book *The Paradox of History*, the chapter on Tolstoy, whose *War and Peace* I'd recently reread. And I suddenly sensed (not thought, precisely sensed), in the instant that I laid the book down to think about something, that I have an immortal soul. I can't call it anything else, I can't explain, though I can only imagine how pretentious this must sound. But that's what I felt: I have an immortal soul. And my melancholy vanished. I felt joy, great joy, a wave of joy. It was as if, after many weeks of silence, emptiness, I suddenly recalled something crucial: I have an immortal soul.

•

Zbigniew Herbert, who had been living with his wife, Katarzyna, in Paris since 1986, where we'd often met, fell seriously ill in 1991. One time I visited him in a hospital in a distant suburb of Paris (on the eastern side of the city, toward Val-de-Marne). The hospital was called Maison Blanche and was principally a psychiatric facility. But Herbert had been placed in the general-medicine building (they transferred him shortly thereafter to a completely different hospital, since his illness required intensive therapy that had nothing to do with psychiatry). This was during the summer, in June or July, the day was hot. Maison Blanche consisted of light wooden buildings scattered through a large park; they were painted green and called to mind the prerevolutionary Russia of Chekhov or early Gorky. Herbert shared his room with a boxer named Albert, who suffered from severe Parkinson's. I wrote then in my notebooks, which I've just now discovered, that Albert was a tall, handsome man who'd been completely destroyed

by his long-term illness. He gave the impression of someone who
no longer understood the world (I'm speaking as if everyone else
understands it). Both patients were lightly dressed, just in their
undershirts. They were both pale, as happens in the summer with
seriously ill people whose skin no longer absorbs sunlight. Zbyszek
told me with satisfaction, perhaps even pride, that he still remembered Albert's fame in the early 1950s, he'd been the European champion. He said, You know, I followed his career, I read
about him, about his successes, and now see, we've met. But this
situation—a great poet, very ill, living in a foreign country, where
almost no one knew him, was sharing a room with a boxer, a
former European champion who no longer had his full wits,
whose brain had been destroyed by his opponents' blows—was
shocking, for me at any rate, since Herbert saw it as completely
normal, maybe even a kind of distinction . . . Now, when I turn in
thought to that moment, I'm not horrified as I was back then; the
atmosphere in the hospital room shared by a poet and a boxer was
actually quite friendly. It was summer . . . I worried more at the
next hospital, the hospital Saint-Louis, which is in the tenth arrondissement of Paris, near the passage Hébrard (this was the
Herberts' address at the time) and the picturesque Canal Saint-
Martin (so many saints in this agnostic city). The heat wave hadn't
let up: this time Herbert was in a large, collective room and I
thought his condition had grown worse.

•

Athens, the Acropolis Museum—a mother with her son, perhaps ten years old. The boy yawns just as his mother points to a
sculpture and says, Look, it's the god Eros. You won't be yawn-
ing in a couple of years, I thought.

•

George Seferis, the modern Greek poet, came from a family of
displaced persons. His family had lived for many generations in

Smyrna and had to leave their city in 1923, in accordance with the treaty concluded when the Greeks lost the Greco-Turkish War. He wrote many great poems, this one among them, which I give in Edmund Keeley and Philip Sherrard's translation.

The King of Asini

> Asinen te . . .
>
> —*Iliad*

All morning long we looked around the citadel
starting from the shaded side there where the sea
green and without lustre—breast of a slain peacock—
received us like time without an opening in it.
Veins of rock dropped down from high above,
twisted vines, naked, many-branched, coming alive
at the water's touch, while the eye following them
struggled to escape the monotonous see-saw motion
growing weaker and weaker.

On the sunny side a long empty beach
and the light striking diamonds on the huge walls.
No living thing, the wild doves gone
and the king of Asini, whom we've been trying to find
    for two years now,
unknown, forgotten by all, even by Homer,
only one word in the *Iliad* and that uncertain,
thrown here like the gold burial mask.
You touched it, remember its sound? Hollow in the light
like a dry jar in dug earth:
the same sound that our oars make in the sea.
The king of Asini a void under the mask
everywhere with us everywhere with us, under a name:
Asinen te . . . Asinen te . . .
                    and his children statues.
and his desires the fluttering of birds, and the wind

in the gaps between his thoughts, and his ships
anchored in a vanished port:
under the mask a void.

Behind the large eyes the curved lips the curls
carved in relief on the gold cover of our existence
a dark spot that you see travelling like a fish
in the dawn calm of the sea:
a void everywhere with us.
And the bird, a wing broken,
that flew away last winter
—tabernacle of life—
and the young woman who left to play
with the dog-teeth of summer
and the soul that sought the lower world gibbering
and the country like a large plane-leaf swept along by
    the torrent of the sun
with the ancient monuments and the contemporary
    sorrow.

And the poet lingers, looking at the stones, and asks
    himself
does there really exist
among these ruined lines, edges, points, hollows and
    curves
does there really exist
here where one meets the path of rain, wind and ruin
does there exist the movement of the face, shape of the
    tenderness
of those who've wanted so strangely in our lives,
those who remained the shadow of waves and thoughts
    with the sea's boundlessness
or perhaps no, nothing is left but the weight
the nostalgia for the weight of a living existence

there where we now remain unsubstantial, bending
like the branches of a terrible willow tree heaped in
    unremitting despair
while the yellow current slowly carries down rushes
    uprooted in the mud
image of a form that the sentence to everlasting
    bitterness has turned to stone:
the poet a voice

Shieldbearer, the sun climbed warring,
and from the depths of the cave a startled bat
hit the light as an arrow hits a shield:
Asinen te . . . Asinen te . . .
                   If only that could be the
                      king of Asini
we've been searching for so carefully on this acropolis
sometimes touching with our fingers his touch upon
    the stones.

Asini, summer '38—Athens, Jan. '40

I'm moved by the sudden shift near the poem's end, the
abrupt appearance—maybe—of the king. Who was this king?
We know the king of Asini only from Homer's single mention,
in one line of the *Iliad*, in Book 2, in the catalog of the ships that
carried the Achaeans to the walls of Troy.

•

Analyzing poems is so awkward! It's a different matter in
university halls, where portraits of long-dead scholars, who never
did anything else, gaze down ironically upon the students. But
here, within a book, where there are no students, within a book
inhabited only by the shadows of people, shadows of heroes,
where the author reigns supreme—here other obligations prevail,

above all, silence. Nonetheless, I hope that the reader senses the tension between the physicality of the present, the green sea and the light kayak, the rather enigmatic female companion, about whom we learn nothing, and, on the other hand, the absent king of Asini. But this absence contains something real just the same; the poem may even give the impression that the absence of Asini's king is more substantial than the ordinariness, the present day, in which the poet moves. Seferis's poem performs a kind of labor, both intellectual and physical: a short poem, an aphorism couldn't manage it. It takes many lines to encompass the poet's gestures and those of his silent companion, the circling and searching, the doubts, the longing, the successive hypotheses, the quasi-archaeological operations of mind and imagination before the king of Asini emerges at the poem's end, as the bat bears the ancient ruler on his nervous wings. Seferis's poem summons the emotion, sometimes powerful, that many people must feel when they find themselves upon historically charged terrain, in Pompeii, in Jerusalem, in some districts of Rome. We want more than just a photograph. We want to touch something authentic. We're so close to what really was, to those people who once really lived, we think, if we just want it badly enough, they'll rise up before us. We think, it's not fair that we can't see this ancient substance. We look dismissively, disdainfully, at those expressive tourists, so easily satisfied with a photograph's quick flash, so eager to leave. We are, we think, completely different. We've earned an epiphany. They should appear to us. The stakes were even higher for Seferis; he wrote this poem in the last years before a great war, knowing that his country, weak, internally riven, couldn't withstand a barbarian invasion. For him, a Greece changed beyond recognition by a century of Turkish occupation, stripped of its past splendors, had to strike up a dialogue with its ancient past, it needed to cast a bridge back to its former greatness, to Homer. Not that this is a nationalistic poem, far from it; any one of us can identify with the voice speaking in the poem. We all seek for substance, be it in archaeology or the present day.

•

It's exceptional for Seferis, though, that the king of Asini does actually appear in the end—just as sometimes, rarely, when we read Homer or Shakespeare attentively, we're struck by something from an earlier world that—especially in Shakespeare and Mickiewicz—oddly reminds us of our own world.

•

It may be that when the angels go about their task of praising God, they play only Bach. I am sure, however, that when they are together *en famille* they play Mozart (Karl Barth).

•

Any new volume of essays written by someone who's not a debutant should begin with the author's admission that he made errors in the earlier book, the conclusions he drew were premature, mistaken, and only now—so he thinks—is he on the right track. Until he gets started on the next book . . .

•

Once when I was on a transatlantic flight they showed two films, one of the *Harry Potter*s and another about Zorro. What infantilization! Two hundred grown passengers staring at tiny screens filled with the shifting images of childhood heroes.

•

One more thing about Seferis's poem: When you think about what the poet is looking for, and what helps him—the gold mask, for example—you're struck by a kind of "granularity," the tough materiality of his imagination. Seferis contradicts the dominant anthropology of our times. Even the acute mind of Robert Musil, who liked playing the role of diagnostician to our ailing civilization, once defined human beings as "colloidal masses" that assume every random form dictated by the prevailing political system, intellectual fashion, or ideology. But things look different in Seferis's poem, in all his poetry. There is no "colloidal mass," it's been replaced by the quest for a powerful, hard shape, such as the gold mask, such as the Greek ships, such as marble shards, the quest for a point of departure more powerful than the lazy caprices of some puddinglike humanity. Seferis doesn't want to end with diagnoses, he doesn't want ethnography. Poetry doesn't diagnose, it simply legislates. It tries to legislate—but it can legislate only what is.

•

Excerpts from Jozef Czapski's diaries encountered once again in the journal *Zeszyty literackie*. As always, a tremendous sense of sincerity and passion. Enthusiasm came easily to Czapski, so did tears in his final years, and perhaps this is why he's so hard on himself, always making sure that he's not just being naive, that he's not moved too easily, he subjects his reactions to a reality check: Can they be sustained? I remember what Karol Irzykowski once said, "Who needs the sincerity of fools?" But in Czapski's case, sincerity reveals a wise, internally complex individual, always striving for spiritual wholeness, for strong vision, for "grace," a necessarily short-lived moment of illumination. Czapski, a reader of classic diaries kept by the great introverts, Amiel or Maine de Biran, records in his notebooks his efforts, constantly renewed, to attain inner wholeness. Someone interested only in the visible, obvious things that can be fully expressed in political or social reality will dismiss such narratives of inner states as useless narcissism. The conflict between Czapski and Jerzy Giedroyc was classic. The editor of the journal *Kultura* was impassioned only by the behavioral language of political action; he even viewed

Milosz's poems chiefly as a key tool in his strategic instrumentarium. The sui generis Machiavelli of helpless emigrants, Giedroyc lacked any real-world power in his role as the editor of a journal read by exiles scattered across the globe. But in his own imagination, he was a great statesman. And in fact he was a statesman; or at least he became one a posteriori, in the memories of younger generations, thanks to his astute assessments of the political situation, and also because he viewed his fellow countrymen so critically. He dismissed Czapski's inner worlds (he once said that he published Simone Weil's writings "for Catholic snobs"). What use is introspection in a brutal reality? This is precisely that world divided between behaviorists and dreamers. Those readers who like the figure of Hans Castorp in *Magic Mountain*, Hans, who called his hours of intensive reading, his moments of rich reflection or just fantasizing, absorbed in real questions, "dominion" (Juliusz Slowacki had a different word for it, he called it "byronization")—it's one of the best definitions of the contours of spiritual life—these readers will understand perfectly what Czapski meant and why his notes are indispensable. True, as we were reading Mann's novel, one of my students in Chicago remarked acidly of Castorp, "So what, he develops spiritually, but what does he do with it?" The crowning moment of his career involves after all collecting records for the sanatorium patients to listen to (or that he dies on the front, one of the anonymous young men sucked into the muck of Verdun). But this was a classic expression of American pragmatism.

Czapski sometimes speaks of himself—but always in terms of the ceaseless battle he wages for clear vision, for full use of his gifts, the battle to imbue his life with maximal meaning. He frequently talks in his diaries with Simone Weil, whom he admired boundlessly and who tormented him with the perfection and extremity of her religious contemplation, and also with her masterly prose. Here's an excerpt of his diary from

1970—including a citation from one of the great mystic's letters
to Maurice Schumann:

> "January 13—Tuesday. And the same thing for heaven
> knows how many times: I wake up muddled and open
> S.W. 'ceaselessly and increasingly torn, both in my intel-
> ligence and in the depth of my heart, through my inability
> to conceive simultaneously and in truth of the affliction of
> men, the perfection of God and the link between the two.
>
> 'I have an inward conviction that if the vision of this
> truth is ever vouchsafed to me it will only be when I
> myself am psychically in affliction, and in one of the ex-
> treme forms of the present affliction.
>
> 'I am afraid that this will not happen. Even when I
> was a child and thought that I was an atheist and a ma-
> terialist, the fear was always present to me that I should
> fail, not over my life but over my death. This fear has
> never ceased to grow in intensity.
>
> 'An unbeliever might say that my desire is egotistical
> because the vision of truth, received at such a moment,
> can no longer be of any use to anyone.
>
> 'But a Christian cannot think in this way. A Christian
> knows that a single thought of love raised to God in truth,
> although mute and without an echo, is more useful, even
> for this world, than the most brilliant action.' "
>
> [*Translation from* Simone Weil as We Knew Her, *Joseph-Marie Perrin*]

How can you be a painter, a writer, in the face of such a vo-
racious longing for God and suffering? How do you give yourself to any meditation that does not race immediately to the
highest goal, that makes do—whether through laziness, cowardice, or tepidity, or perhaps simply because of other aspirations or
abilities—with halfway points, that clings to the outskirts? It's as
if a wanderer spent whole days ambling through alpine foothills

while the highest peaks, with their magnetically white snows, gaze down on him with contempt, even condemnation. Simone Weil tortured Czapski, and she still tortures us. Czapski labored over each canvas, "sawed away" at it, tried to stay true to the initial vision, which faded, grew distant. He painted with difficulty, was rarely satisfied with what he'd done. For him Simone Weil was like a jet pilot compared to a bicyclist. And not just for Czapski. What's to be done? Nothing can be done. You can try, but in principle it can't be done. Perhaps it's like this: In books for the youngest pupils you sometimes find pictures of people on their way somewhere, pedestrians and bicyclists; a hay-rack cart brimming with scented hay rumbles by, a swift auto flashes past, a train runs farther off, through the windows of its sky-blue cars you can see the passengers' smiling, carefree faces, a little airplane flies overhead. They're all in motion, all en route. They're en route, but also motionless. And if you examine the picture carefully day after day, week after week, month after month, even year after year, no one vehicle outpaces the others . . . The plane is still in the same spot, the travelers still scrutinize the spring landscape, the pedestrian still heads unhurriedly for parts unknown, the tall trees still rise unmoved, a stork stands in the meadow.

•

In Seferis's poem the search for the king of Asini means more than simply tracking down the past. The gold mask is what prompts the Greek poet to seek out the mythic figure of the king, true enough, but I think something more important is also at stake, namely, the consciousness that we must discover (or at least must wish to discover) whatever is indestructible within ourselves. The active longing for eternity. The gate inside ourselves that leads us onward.

•

Once, two years ago, on the southern shore of Crete, I was swimming in a little bay beneath a steep mountain cliff. It was already late afternoon, still warm, but the shadows gradually expanded, they seemed to emerge from the sea. Suddenly a kingfisher flew across the water. It flew quickly, shining with blue-red light, in a straight line, as if on a string. It disappeared somewhere on the shore, then after a long moment it returned in the same straight line to its nest on a solitary rock. It was the genuine master of this bay, and not the rather comical heads of swimmers bobbing on the deep blue water.

•

I was listening to Brahms's Rhapsody yet again. I recently read a review of a book on music whose author asserts that Richard Strauss's *Four Last Songs* are the greatest of all musical compositions. It's a little strange, setting up some arbitrary table of outcomes, as in sports. But Strauss's work, considered hopelessly reactionary, decadent by Schoenberg's partisans, is in fact beautiful.

•

Madeleine Santschi, a writer who saw herself as part of the French literary movement shaped by Nathalie Sarraute and Michel Butor, has died in Lausanne. We first met her at the "creative work space" in Bogliasco near Genoa in 2002; she was eighty-six then, the senior member of our little group of writers and artists. Even then she needed help on the longer walks, as for example when she set out on the nearby *passeggiata a mare*, a path stretching for kilometers along the rocky seacoast—you often saw surfers in black wet suits lying on their boards, waiting for a bigger wave, looking like a herd of mournful seals. Madeleine visited us a few years ago in Krakow. She couldn't understand, a dweller in bright Lausanne, whose reflection bathes in Lake Geneva, why so many old stone houses here still have black, unplastered facades, as if all the dirt and nightmares of nineteenth-century history had settled in them. But, to give one example, the Gestapo were quartered in our apartment in the city's center during the Occupation. A Gestapo officer no doubt occupied the room in which I now write. I liked Madeleine's book *Portrait d'Antonio Pizzuto*; Antonio Pizzuto was, the black jacket flap informs us, "the Italian Joyce." He spent his entire life working in the police bureaucracy, peacefully making his way up the ranks regardless of the political system, be it the fascist regime or the postwar liberal government. He was a serene Roman bourgeois, phenomenally erudite, but clearly, as he occupied ever higher positions, first in the prefecture and then in Interpol, he dreamed only of reclaiming his freedom, gaining time for himself (now we know why so many crimes go undetected). He took early retirement and immediately began work on what really interested him: the writing of hermetic prose. Madeleine translated him into French. I don't think Pizzuto's prose would appeal to me, but Madeleine's book on this intriguing eccentric is superb. She was brave while she was dying. We spoke with her often in her last months. She told us one time that they'd discovered tumors in two places. The prognosis was hopeless. She didn't have long. Madeleine spoke almost cheerfully about this, she didn't complain, she understood the situation perfectly. I admired her for that. She wasn't religious, but she acknowledged the world's mysteries. Someone who's built her sensibilities on the *nouveau roman* isn't in principle particularly well equipped to enter the dark corridor of final things. But there are no rules in this field; there is no real *preparation*, and Madeleine endured dying with calm dignity.

•

Emerson: When Plato's thought becomes my own, when the truth that kindled Saint John's soul kindles my own, time stands still.

•

The artistic "I don't know" derives from Keats's principle of "negative capability," and it is indispensable in art. But art and poetry are always, I suspect, created by the artist in the person, and if the artist always inclines toward "I don't know," then the person in the artist will most likely be seeking for "I know."

•

Joseph Brodsky, whom I so admired and liked, even loved (the way you love some friends), was fond of making rather risky pronouncements. In one essay, for example, he says it's a great shame that Christ didn't know the Roman poets: he meant the Roman elegists, Catullus, Propertius, Ovid. Christianity would be subtler if he had . . . But it's somehow difficult to imagine Christ studying Catullus, making marginal notations in Propertius, perhaps even undertaking a doctoral dissertation on Latin versification. With all due respect for those scholars who labor away in college libraries worldwide . . . it seems that God doesn't read poetry.

•

Yesterday marked the two hundredth anniversary of Chopin's birth. Concerts, concerts (not many speeches, luckily). But I listened to my favorite record, with Krystian Zimerman playing all four ballades.

•

I don't know how my fellow poets live, but I know perfectly well that I don't usually believe in my own poems.

•

I happened on a volume of Helmuth James Graf von Moltke's correspondence; he was the main figure in the Kreisau Circle

(Kreisauer Kreis). I'd long known of him, but I'd never read his letters (though I had read Dietrich Bonhoeffer's letters and essays). I liked the volume of letters immensely, their moral purity, their nobility. Moltke's biography makes an even greater impression; his life draws us even more than his writer's gifts. In the monstrous world of the Third Reich, Moltke stands out through his exceptional human quality. This was a righteous man, tossed by fate into the worst of all systems, cast among hyenas and bandits. Moltke wasn't alone, though, he was surrounded by like-minded friends up until his arrest and death (he was sentenced to death by a hostile *Volkstribunal* in January 1945). His wife, Freya, also shared his convictions, she stood by him to the last moment. But my goal here isn't to delve into the history of the German anti-Hitler opposition—historians and commentators of the period abound—I just want to voice my confusion. Since when I compare the letters written by one of my favorite poets, Gottfried Benn, to Moltke's, or Bonhoeffer's, correspondence, the poet doesn't come out particularly well. He's a wonderful writer, and, for example, in the letters to Mr. Oelze, the Bremen merchant, or in the essays, it's difficult to tear yourself from his sometimes inspired prose or his witty correspondence. Moltke had no such talent. But Benn lacked something we find in this scion of an aristocratic Prussian family. Set alongside Moltke and his absolute integrity, Benn sometimes gives the impression of a petty operator whose sole purpose is to survive. To survive the war, unashamed of his conformism, to outwit his superiors, to hold his tongue while others speak, to return home and only there to become himself once more, to endure this monstrous regime (which, as we know, he initially found so appealing). Helmuth James von Moltke did not plan on survival, he only hoped to do battle with an inhuman system, to defend the most vulnerable. I know I'm comparing things—and people—that don't lend themselves to comparison. Gottfried Benn wore, like a snail, the great, troublesome shell of his exceptional talent, he had the right, even the duty, to defend his calling, his reason for being, while Moltke's gift was the acuity of his moral existence, his incorruptibility, his nobility. This nobility wasn't something achieved, reached by theoretical means—although I must mention his strong faith, the Christianity that engaged him so deeply, so consistently. The two men couldn't have met, and even if they had, they would never have understood each other, though they spoke the same German language. The same and yet completely different. For all that, though, I'll always forgive Benn, it's enough to go back to the poems. But that explains nothing, resolves nothing. Since why should great masters of poetry or prose receive preferential treatment for defending their own talents? Why should we agree to let them off easy, so that they can go tottering through life like a tipsy coachman? This casts a shadow, after all, not only over them, but over literature as a whole. Great poets on the pages of their books, but in life so often schemers, complaining, like Galczynski, that there's "too much wind for my wool," opportunists diminished, put to shame by someone such as Moltke, a splendid person, a true Christian. Shouldn't literature be righteousness embodied, inscribed, shouldn't it radiate righteousness? The world is poorly constructed, I thought, while reading Moltke's letters, admiring him and knowing nonetheless that sooner or later I'd go back to my poets, my imperfect poets, that I couldn't remain forever in the crystalline atmosphere of that prose. Hence my confusion, the questions I can't answer. But there are other poets as well, poets such as Osip Mandelstam, such as Zbigniew Herbert—though they wrote in different languages, they would have understood the German count. They strove to link talent and honesty, metaphor and righteousness. What a tricky business. "A tournament of hunchbacks, literature," Milosz writes in one poem. I never liked that line, but it's borne out by the majority of poets and novelists . . .

•

In the argument between the behaviorists and the dreamers, between Giedroyc and Czapski, the first are in the right, they're the ones who change the world. Giedroyc undoubtedly contributed more to the democratic evolution of the Polish mind-set, to my country's independence, than Czapski did. Still I prefer the dreamers. This may indicate a certain immaturity, an uncurable immaturity, but I prefer the dreamers.

•

Returning once more to Moltke's correspondence with his wife—I gathered from the footnote under one letter that Moltke had no use for Carl Schmitt, that brilliant, if less than courageous, philosopher who claims so many followers today. I should add something else here, namely, that the people who participate actively in their historical moment, the people who get written, one way or another, into history, can be divided into two categories: those who are absolutely prepared to dedicate their lives to defending their ideals, their cause (and these aren't, don't even remotely need to be, fundamentalists, fanatics); and those who don't take such possibilities into account, for example, if they're artists or thinkers concerned with preserving their own talent, with creating the conditions for their own development, even at the worst moments. It must be admitted that, in one sense, only this first group profoundly affects the works of their age. They're charged with a distinctive eroticism; their readiness for sacrifice proves that they're in love with the world. They don't suspect, they can't imagine, that the world is in love with them, too. They may die young or at an advanced age, it makes no difference. Great memory will embrace them, take care of them.

Only one thing can be said in defense of the artists and all those cautious and cunning intellectuals who "preserve their talent" by making risky compromises and who do not, as a result, stir their contemporaries' admiration: a certain part of their work

is or may be addressed to subsequent generations. Some artists—
not all—touch the moment in which they live with only one
foot, their dreams exceed the calendar's reach. Hence they have
serious reasons for not seeing themselves as full-time inhabitants
of their age. They know, or perhaps just suspect, that if they die
too soon, they'll be completely erased from the earth's surface.
Great memory won't give them a second thought.

I don't know if that's enough to justify their maneuvering,
their opportunism, sometimes even their cowardice. There are
no general rules here, fortunately. (Let's just hope that the people
busy "preserving their talent" actually possess it . . .). And whatever rules there are may sometimes fade over time. It's usually
far easier to excuse the conformists who lived in antiquity or the
early Middle Ages than those we've actually known or might
have known . . .

•

A moment of happiness, inexplicable, while strolling along the
Vistula. It was a warm afternoon and it began to rain. I had an
umbrella with me, but I took refuge nonetheless in the gate of a
house on Smocza Street, not far from Wawel Castle, near the
Church on the Rock, in whose crypt Czeslaw Milosz now rests,
and I stood there for some time, looking at the poplars and sniffing
their branches' bitter scent, which I like so much and remember
from my childhood in Gliwice. I wasn't in a hurry, I waited for
the rain to stop and felt a joy whose only source, so it seems, was
that the world existed, it was May, and a new generation of swifts,
looking like their precursors' twins, were whistling shrilly.

•

In Gliwice, when I was around seventeen, I studied Bergson's
Creative Evolution in a prewar edition—a translation, of course;
I still didn't know French. I opened that book in a local library

and inhaled its inspiring contents with cheeks flushed, in some reading room where you couldn't check out the books. I couldn't have known then that I was belatedly repeating the gesture of many older brothers and sisters who'd found in Bergson, several decades back, a confederate in their resistance to the prevalent, dry spirit of positivism. I still didn't know anything, I knew almost nothing of twentieth-century intellectual history, I lived in a half-Sovietized country, but some mysterious powers had propelled me to this reading nonetheless. It's strange, how does it happen, how is it possible that an unlicked cub, as I was then, a student at a mediocre Silesian high school, could track down Bergson; as if an organism instinctively (intuitively) had sensed the vitamins that book contained. I found out only much later how important Bergson had been for artists and intellectuals of an earlier generation, for persons desperately seeking to escape the sterile landscape of the so-called *scientific worldview*, a worldview smelling of cheap glue and wobbly school scissors. I remember reading in Raïssa Maritain's memoirs how she and her future husband, Jacques, had met early on as young students at the Sorbonne; both suffered from the spirit of narrow empiricism that prevailed back then, they suffocated at the lectures of professors who acknowledged only science, disciples of August Comte. And after long thought, both decided to risk crossing over to the other side of rue Saint-Jacques, to the Collège de France, where they satisfied their yearning for *something different* at the lectures of Henri Bergson. Only the lectures had by now become a social event, *le tout Paris* was in attendance. But this is a different story, decidedly different. And yet another story, Bergson's death in January 1941, in a France under German occupation. He was Jewish, and suddenly the great writer and thinker had been transformed into someone who might in principle be deported to Auschwitz at any minute. The immediate cause of death is thought to have been the pneumonia he contracted while waiting in a long line to register as a Jew. And then

Paul Valéry's courageous speech, bidding Bergson farewell in the Académie française, which didn't lack for enthusiastic proponents of collaboration. And then still later, after the war that had changed so much, it could happen that someone might find support in his works even though Bergson had gradually lost his popularity, historians of philosophy treated him with increasing criticism.

•

On another occasion, Brodsky—not in an essay this time, rather an energetic conversation with creative-writing students in Houston, in 1988—attacked the repetition of motifs in art and life alike, he advocated for originality, novelty (not in poetic form, though, since formal repetition became all the more crucial in unifying poetry beyond time). Someone asked Brodsky whether in the Soviet Union, where some image of Lenin, a painting or a sculpture, was apt to turn up at every step, he was bothered more by the endless Lenins or by the simple fact of "repetition," the senseless replication of a single motif. Joseph thought for a moment and replied, the latter.

•

A few days ago I spent a couple of minutes in St. Mary's Basilica— it was a weekday—where perhaps a dozen people were kneeling in prayer. Every now and then someone's cell phone rang. Horizontal communication refused to surrender, it kept on battling its vertical counterpart.

•

Why do we boldly maintain that biographies tower above treatises and dissertations from a formal viewpoint? Because treatises and dissertations are constructed with an eye to the final conclusion, while biographies end peacefully, quietly, unexpectedly, they end in December or April, without proving a thesis, making a point—they end only because the hero dies. And this answers to our own helplessness vis-à-vis the fundamental questions we face better than the ambitious intentions of scholars, who always insist on the last word.

•

A little book by Seferis—I know it in English translation—ranks among my favorite prose works written by poets. The title: *A Poet's Journal: Days of 1945–1951*. Seferis begins this diary while the war was still dragging on, although his country had been liberated from the German forces. In December 1945 internal struggles erupted in Greece, the Communists clashed with anti-Communist forces, causing great destruction. Seferis was exhausted by war and emigration—as a diplomat, a civil servant, he accompanied the Greek government in exile to Crete, Egypt, and South Africa. The years of emigration were a nightmare for him; he wasn't threatened by immediate danger like those who'd remained in Greece, but constant worry over his homeland's fate (it sounds rather bathetic, but the brutal occupation truly tormented him) and the petty, minor intrigues typical of any emigration combined to poison his life. Ibis Editions also put out another small volume, excerpts from the diaries of his wartime wanderings, sad, barren, as if heat scorched, short of oxygen. He couldn't work in exile; when this period finally drew to a close, Seferis viewed these years as wasted. But now the return to Athens finally comes, though he's greeted, true enough, by fresh ruins, consequences of the civil war. Still the wounds are slowly healing, a normal existence of sorts begins, meetings with friends, and half friends—such as Sikelianos, another Greek poet, whom, so it seems, Seferis both admires and *doesn't understand* (in the deepest sense of that word). The category of half friend would come in handy; since we have in fact so few true friends . . . One might also speak of half enemies . . . Features of typical literary life reemerge after the war's disruptions. For example, the visit of Paul Éluard, celebrated then, who was traveling throughout Europe, Athens received him with great pomp (five banquets in one day), though Seferis himself treated Éluard's poetry rather skeptically; or Seferis's meeting with the far more congenial Henri Michaux, also in Athens at the time. A return to his ministry job follows—which our poet, who doesn't possess the makings of a true bureaucrat, greets without enthusiasm. What's most interesting, though, are the notes that signal his gradual recuperation, his gradual release from the catastrophe of war, from silence, from the wasteland. The poet's rediscovery of the Greek landscape, its islands, its sun, its May days and evenings, plays a key role here, as does the physical experience of swimming in the Mediterranean, that gleaming sea so hospitable to swimmers. In the fall of 1946 Seferis spends many weeks on the island of Poros, he swims regularly, jots down observations, notes the days' taste, the sea's tint, he describes the light. And he returns to health.

•

The first warm days after a harsh winter. Only the last prisms of snow, black with soot, are melting on street corners, but in the Planty Gardens you can already smell and hear new life; a great mass of birds who somehow survived this bad winter—I don't know how and where they hid from the worst frosts—are now beginning their most intensive months, the months of love and singing.

Spring has returned, Krakow's Planty Gardens have once more become a splendid tropical park, and the blackbirds and thrushes, who'd sequestered themselves through late fall and winter, triumphantly possess the city.

•

A spring of great events. The presidential airplane crash near Smolensk on April 10. I first heard about it on Saturday morning from the clerk in the shop where I was buying tea and macaroni. She had the radio on and told me that something had gone wrong with the plane. The city was plunged in sudden grief. The streets grew somber. In the afternoon we went to Wawel Cathedral, where a mass was being held for the victims—an enormous crowd stood there, all completely absorbed, calm, grieving, thoughtful, faces inspiring trust. The crowd was so enormous that only a small fraction could actually fit inside the cathedral walls, people stood beneath the bare sky, in a courtyard where two enormous magnolias had just begun to bloom. The moment was beautiful, beautiful in its tragic terror. As in Yeats: "A terrible beauty is born." But shortly thereafter, a few days later, the birth of hysteria, the return of politics, an end to mourning in the sense of pure, disinterested grief, the shift to self-seeking, partisan feelings. The first moments didn't divide people, just the opposite, they brought them together in shared sorrow. It doesn't last, unhappily.

•

And then the threat of flooding in Krakow; after a few days of intense rain, the mountain rivers, the Vistula's tributaries, swelled ominously until finally the Vistula herself, the mother river, the mother superior to all the brooks and streams, also rose to dangerous heights. Squeezed between its embankments, a gigantic Vistula heaved through Krakow's center like a violent criminal, a yellow river bearing branches and beams . . . The Debnicki Bridge was closed, the water rose almost to the asphalt, it looked as if it were just about to flood the bridge. Hundreds of city dwellers watched the river with holy terror, the lazy country cousin had become a monster. Finally the embankments were breached at two points. The local radio rose to the challenge and spent days on end warning listeners of threats; it became the city's central contact point, directing volunteers to places in need. Yesterday one of the main radio announcements dealt with an animal shelter threatened by floodwaters; the radio repeatedly passed on requests for help in rescuing dogs and cats from the shelter. We went over in the afternoon. The cats were already taken, we left empty-handed. But the sight was unforgettable: dozens of people, all in warm jackets, some in knee-high rubber boots, with cat cages brought from home, others carrying muzzles, all waiting in a long but rapidly moving line, and every moment someone would leave the little building with a nervous dog on an improvised plastic leash, either a mutt or what might have been a purebred. This all took place almost without bureaucracy: in her square-ruled notebook, the shelter worker simply took down the names and numbers of those picking up the animals. Some dogs seemed gleeful, glad to be sprung from camp, from juvenile detention, while others were clearly scared, they resisted, pulling back to the cages where they felt safe, they wanted to go home to jail.

•

A few days ago, I went back to the movie theater Kijow for the first time in a long while; it reminded me of something that happened a number of years ago, it must have been in 2002. It was the premiere of Andrzej Wajda's film *Revenge*. Several people were onstage, including Wajda and his wife, Krystyna Zachwatowicz. The theater was packed. Krystyna Zachwatowicz whispered something to her husband, who then went to the microphone and said, It seems that Czeslaw Milosz is here with us. The old poet rose from his chair. At which the huge audience rose to its feet and gave him an ovation.

•

Sunday; from my balcony I see my neighbor Malgosia, who lives on the ground floor of the next building, a lover of animals and plants, grooming her ginger cat in the courtyard. The sun is shining. An idyllic scene. The ginger cat is clearly delighted by her treatment, she rubs coquettishly against her owner's knees, her tail grows large and fluffy.

•

For many months, years even, my father was oblivious, he existed in a purely vegetative state, cut off from other people. He slept a lot, it seemed that he'd gone to the world of dreams for good. He died near the end of September—the immediate cause of death was a high fever, probably meningitis. It was over in just a few hours. I flew from Chicago to the funeral. It took place on a cold but sunny day in the cemetery that had over time become the city's largest gathering point for the displaced. In the small crowd that had assembled to pay their regards, resettled inhabitants mixed with both locals and the young people who no longer heeded previous categories. Two months later my aunt Ania died. Her brother's death seems to have unsettled her mind. His death didn't affect her immediately, but after a while, after the funeral, she began to fret that she'd be late for the funeral, and it never stopped worrying her. She started leaving her house at the strangest times, day and night, as old people do in the advanced stages of dementia. She got lost in the city that she'd never accepted, she couldn't find her way home, she couldn't find her own place, her apartment. She kept setting out for her brother's funeral. Finally she was taken to the hospital with pneumonia and passed on there. "Passed on"—we no longer say it, but we may be permitted an outworn phrase from time to time.

•

Half a day in Dresden—a reading. The invitation came from the Dresden Literaturforum, but the reading itself took place, your attention please, in the Hygiene Museum (which was in fact, so I was informed, an anthropological museum). Earlier I'd managed to get a look at the famed Zwinger Palace, at the gal-

lery of old masters, where I spent a couple of hours. I stood helpless before the paintings for some time, nothing was reaching me,
I wondered if I shouldn't just go back to the hotel (I'd headed to
the gallery right after reaching Dresden, after a five-hour drive
from Krakow). Even Vermeer said nothing to me this time. The
Zwinger has two Vermeers, one of them, depicting a merry tav-
ern scene (and a beautiful carpet), was on loan to an exhibit in
Holland. The second remained, *Girl Reading a Letter*—a plain
girl turned toward a window, studying a missive whose contents
we will never know, but that painting didn't want to open for
me either. The Dresden gallery was partly destroyed during the
great bombardments of February 1945, then painstakingly rebuilt and damaged once more, only slightly this time, by a flood
in 2002. Still, it preserves its earlier arrangement of paintings, an
arrangement typical of old-fashioned museums, that is, a vast
quantity of canvases crowd the walls, competing for the viewer's
attention. It's not easy dealing with this crush of works, works of
uneven quality, near the explosion of a few second-rate baroque
paintings resembling, from a distance, the fantasies of a drunken
butcher. Viewers often grant them a friendly glance, sometimes
without removing the camera from their eyes even for an instant, as if they were compiling a gigantic catalog of artworks,
electronic loot they planned to examine at their leisure upon returning home. Of course this leisure time never materializes.

This was my second visit to the Zwinger; once, some ten
years ago, I went to Dresden from Leipzig for a few hours. That
time I spent some time looking at the famous *Sleeping Venus.*
This is one of a few masterpieces signed by not one but two great
artists: Giorgione and Titian. Giorgione died young, killed
probably by the plague, and after his death the painting was
completed by his friend Titian, who had a long life and many
paintings before him. We stand before a canvas once touched by
the fingers of both Giorgione and Titian. I know that restorers'

fingers may long since have erased all traces of the two masters' palms, still it's difficult not to be moved.

This time, though, I was drawn to a portrait by Rembrandt. The painting is dark, as always with Rembrandt, but dark, too, with a thick patina of time, it has most likely long gone unrestored. It shows a man in a hat embroidered with pearls. The man is old and tired. He doesn't look at us, he looks off somewhere to the side. He's probably seated, but we don't see a chair's back behind him. His expression is rather indifferent, as if he's not particularly enthralled by this posing. Indifferent, but also cautious. His face seems to say, I'll be leaving any moment now. The painting likely dates to 1667, so it was painted scarcely two years before the artist's death. It's not a self-portrait, but it *could* be. The model's weariness seems to mirror the artist's. I've spoken too soon, though: even if this was a difficult period for him, as we know, Rembrandt may not have been wearied by painting this splendid portrait. He may have felt sorrow, but this sorrow no doubt expanded with joy as the canvas filled. The man, the model, is slightly hunched. I'll confess, he reminds me a bit of my exhausted professor of philosophy, Leszczynski, Witkacy's friend, who, so I supposed, despised the world that emerged in the wake of the Second World War. And it would be an image of despair, a record of resignation, indifference, age, if not for the pearls on the broad, soft velvet hat, almost a beret. I realized at one point that the pearls weren't simply a typical decorative element (there's also a brooch on the subject's breast). The pearls shine with a delicate radiance. Pearls can't be the main source of light in the painting; the light (so we guess) comes somewhere from the left. But the pearls also shine. Over time—when you stand before the picture for a while—the pearls take on ever-greater meaning. In this landscape of sorrow and exhaustion, the pearls are different. The pearls shine. The face is matte. Everything in this old man that had been light, a soul, is preserved in the pearls, has passed into the pearls. When I realized this, the painting came to life and lived on for some time. And what of it, that the soul survived for an instant in the pearls, that it left this man's face, his heart? What's important is that it didn't abandon him completely. Perhaps it will return in time to its former home.

PERMISSIONS ACKNOWLEDGMENTS

Grateful acknowledgment is made for permission to reprint the following material:

Excerpts from "La Jolie Rousse" by Guillaume Apollinaire, translated by Roger Shattuck, from *Selected Writings*, copyright © 1971 by Roger Shattuck. Reprinted by permission of New Directions Publishing Corp.

George Seferis, "The King of Asini," from *Collected Poems (George Seferis)*. Translated, edited, and introduced by Edmund Keeley and Philip Sherrard. Copyright © 1995 by George Seferis. Reprinted by permission of Princeton University Press.

"Rovigo" from *Rovigo* by Zbigniew Herbert, translated by Alissa Valles. Copyright © 2013 by Zbigniew Herbert. Reprinted by permission of Harper-Collins Publishers Inc.

Printed in the USA
CPSIA information can be obtained
at www.ICGtesting.com
LVHW091139150724
785511LV00005B/422

9 780374 537517